Man Swarm

Man Swarm

And the Killing of Wildlife

Dave Foreman

First in the *For the Wild Things* series by
The Rewilding Institute and Raven's Eye Press

Raven's Eye Press
Durango, Colorado

Raven's Eye Press
Durango, Colorado
www.ravenseyepress.com

Foreman, Dave.
Man Swarm and the Killing of Wildlife/Dave Foreman
p. cm.

1. Population
2. Conservation
3. Extinction
4. Wildlife
I. Title

ISBN: 978-0-9816584-7-6
LCCN: 2011925353

Cover & interior design by Lindsay J. Nyquist, *elle jay design*

Printed in the United States of America
1 3 5 7 9 10 8 6 4 2

Dedication

To

Hugh Iltis

Whose stout heart and sharp mind has always seen that
the population explosion leads to the death of
wild things and the loss of wilderness

Other Books by Dave Foreman

Ecodefense: A Field Guide to Monkeywrenching
(editor with Bill Haywood)

The Big Outside
(with Howie Wolke)

Confessions of an Eco-Warrior

Defending the Earth
(with Murray Bookchin, edited by Steve Chase)

The Lobo Outback Funeral Home
(a novel)

The Sky Islands Wildlands Network Conservation Plan
(lead author and editor)

New Mexico Highlands Wildlands Network Vision
(lead author and editor)

Rewilding North America:
A Vision for Conservation in the 21st Century

Table of Contents

Annotated Chapter List

Foreword: A View from 1848, by John Stuart Mill xv

Introduction – The Swarm of Man, the Killing of Wildlife xvii

What this little book hopes to do.

One – Man's Population Explosion 1

Mass extinction and human overpopulation. A historical and numerical look at the population explosion and what it means to Earth.

Two – What's It Truly All About? 17

Eileen Crist shows how the population-stabilization and limits-to-growth campaign has stumbled because it has not targeted how overpopulation kills other Earthlings.

Three – Carrying Capacity and the Upright Ape......... 27

The biology of carrying capacity and how it holds true for Man, too. William Catton on how we've overshot carrying capacity.

Four – How the Man Swarm Eats Earth 41

A beginning survey of how our growth is behind the Seven Ecological Wounds, and a call for more, targeted research.

Five – Cornucopia Dreaming.............................. 69

A look at cornucopianism and the Idea of Progress. The madness of Julian Simon deconstructed by thinking scientists.

Six – Birth Dearth Follies 85

What is wrong with the thinking of those who fear a "birth dearth" and who call for population growth in those countries that have stabilized their populations.

Seven – Was Ehrlich Wrong?.............................. 93

Weighing the claims of those who say that Paul Ehrlich and other population "doomsayers" of the 1960s and 1970s have been disproved.

Eight – A History of Thinking about Man's Limits......103

Five ways of seeing the Impact of overpopulation. A survey of thinking since Herodotus about overshooting carrying capacity.

Nine – The Great Backtrack..............................119

The sundry historical, political, and sociological grounds for why conservationists and environmentalists have backtracked on overpopulation worldwide and in the United States after 1975.

Ten – Population or Affluence—Or Technology? 139

How technology plays in I=PAT. Recent studies showing that we cannot lighten our ecological footprints by checking affluence alone; freezing population growth is essential.

Eleven – The Bugbear of Immigration 157

The overwhelming role of immigration behind population growth in the United States and why it is such a thorny devil with which to deal.

Twelve – How to Cap Immigration to the United States.....................................183

Bold, kind, and thoughtful steps to cap immigration, lawful and unlawful, to the United States.

Thirteen – What Do We Do?..............................201

Straightforward, bold steps we can take to freeze and then lower population through conservation action, personal choices, and political decisions.

Epilogue – Whither Life?.................................233

The two key steps to take.

Glossary 237

Illustrations List

Figure 1.1	Mankind Population Growth 50kya to 2050 C.E. Graph	3
Box 1.1	Net Primary Productivity (NPP)	4
Box 1.2	I=PAT	5
Figure 1.2	Man and Tiger Populations India 1900 to 2025 C.E. Graph	8
Figure 1.3a	Growth 0 to 2050 C.E. Graph	10
Figure 1.3b	Growth 1804 to 2050 C.E. Graph	11
Figure 1.4	Ethiopia Population Growth 1950 to 2050 C.E. Graph	15
Box 3.1	Malthus	29
Box 3.2	Overshoot	37
Box 3.3	Biomass and NPP	39
Table 4.1	The Seven Ecological Wounds	46
Table 4.2	Population Growth of Biodiverse Countries	67
Table 11.1	Footprints of Countries Sending U.S. Immigrants	161
Table 11.2	Endorsers of 1998 Sierra Club Immigration Initiative	166
Box 11.1	U.S. in 2100	172
Table 12.1	Steps to Cap Immigration to U.S.	186
Box 13.1	Family Planning Successes	202
Table 13.1	Apply the Brakes Leaders	209
Box 13.2	Apply the Brakes	210
Table 13.2	What to Do to Stabilize World Population	212
Box 13.3	Conservationists' Population Pledge	216
Box 13.4	How to Help International Family Planning	226

Acknowledgements

I've dedicated *Man Swarm* to Professor Hugh Iltis, world-class botanist, co-discover of the wild ancestor of corn (teosinte), and longtime director of the world-known University of Wisconsin-Madison herbarium. I first met Dr. Iltis some years ago when I spoke at UW-Madison. He was the first to raise his hand after my talk and he bearded me for not targeting more how overpopulation was the key driver behind the extinction crisis and other wounds to wildlife and their neighborhoods. Though we haven't spent nearly enough time together, since our first meeting I've thought of him as my mentor on overpopulation. Unlike others who have written and spoken out on the population explosion, Hugh has always underlined how it harms other Earthlings and the wild Earth, while others go on about famine, resource depletion, and the like. In a talk at the first Earth Day in 1970 at the University of Michigan, he dealt with how our thoughtless overbreeding was—and is—the mainspring of the mass extinction now slaying wild things right and left. More than anyone else, he has shaped my path for taking on our plight. He also stands for me as a truly great man or woman who is mostly overlooked and not given their due. Thank you, Hugh Iltis, for giving your long life to making Earth a better home for all Earthlings and for your bold and fearless truth telling.

A handful of others I have been lucky to know have been for me outstanding in the field of warning about overpopulation. Among them are Paul and Anne Ehrlich, Dave Brower, Peggy and Ed Wayburn, Al Bartlett, Martin Litton, Katie Lee, Alan Weeden, Don Weeden, Brock Evans, Eileen Crist, Alan Kuper, William Catton, Captain Paul Watson, Stephanie Mills, and Ed Abbey. As for those whose writings on overpopulation have taught me, I name them and quote them throughout *Man Swarm.* I like to say upon whose shoulders I stand, and name those who see things as I do (at least in some things).

Over the years of my wilderness and wildlife work, I have had many backers, both with big and with little checkbooks. Among those who have generously backed my work on overpopulation are Fred Stanback, Alan Weeden, Don Weeden and the Weeden Family Foundation, Allan and Marilyn Brown, Brad and Shelli Stanback, Harry and 'Becca Dalton, Eileen Crist, and Richard Grossman. I've had other trusted funders, but the above, I think, are the ones who have been most tied to dealing with overpopulation.

I also must thank my fellows who started the Conservation Leaders' Forum and our Apply the Brakes website: Bill Elder, David Johns, Don Weeden, John Davis, Roy Beck, John Rohe, Andy Kerr, and Kelpie Wilson. Others have come on board with the Apply the Brakes website since we started. Among my friends there are Susan Morgan, Ronni Egan, George Wuerthner, and Katie Lee.

Then there are those who have answered my questions and found hard facts for *Man Swarm.* Outstanding are Leon Kolankiewicz, Roy Beck, and Bill Elder. Don Weeden, David Johns, Bill Elder, and Leon Kolankiewicz read and commented on some draft chapters of the book. Two of my fellows stand out for their hard work helping me with *Man Swarm*. Eileen Crist, environmental studies professor at Virginia Tech, has not only been a top inspiration, teacher, and muse for me, she read the whole manuscript at two late stages and offered highly worthwhile guidance. Phil Cafaro, a philosophy professor at Colorado State and a founder of Progressives for Immigration Reform, read the next-to-final manuscript and commented in amazing depth. He gave me extra work, it is true, but he made *Man Swarm* a better book. I am likely overlooking some who looked at early, early drafts of the scribbles that at last made their way into *Man Swarm*. I'm sorry if I have indeed overlooked anyone I should be thanking. If you are one of these unnamed ones, I'll be happy to buy you a beer next time we run into each other.

At the top of my thank-you list are two of my longest friends and my most loyal coworkers, Susan Morgan and John Davis. Among other things, Susan and John are professional editors, and they worked with me at every step on *Man Swarm* from start to end. The two of them, a continent apart (North Cascades and Adirondacks) are the editors not only for *Man Swarm* but also for the whole *For the Wild Things* series. On *Man Swarm* they are nearly coauthors as much as my editors. We are a cottage industry even though we live thousands of miles away from one another. They know I appreciate them, but probably not how much I appreciate them. No matter how we weigh friendship, both John and Susan are as true as true friends can be.

The Rewilding Institute was able to hire Christianne Hinks, a strong New Mexico conservationist and river-running pal of ours, as half-time associate director at the beginning of 2011. Though she came late into this project, she has jumped into it with both feet. She's such a good proofreader, among other things, that I'm calling her "Hawkeye."

I thank Monkeywrench Dad, Ken Wright of Raven's Eye Press in Durango, Colorado, for publishing and promoting *Man Swarm*. Raven's Eye is the partner of The Rewilding Institute in the *For the Wild Things* series. One of the good things from working with Raven's Eye is getting Lindsay Nyquist of *elle jay design* to do the layout and design of *Man Swarm*. Having done the printer-ready layout and design for a few books such as *The Big Outside* back when I had Ned Ludd Books, I know how much work it is. I am darned happy to have Lindsay putting *Man Swarm* into book form. She is good at what she does (much better than I am at book design) and she is good to work with. I'm looking forward to having her help with the rest of the books in the *For the Wild Things* series.

My wife, Nancy Morton, is my holdfast. She also expects me to be the best Dave Foreman I can be. I likely fall short, quite short at times, but I am better because of her. Now, if it works the other way, too, I don't know.

Finally, though she died in the middle of my writing *Man Swarm,* I thank my cat friend, Chama, for keeping me alive and for her thoughtful love and encouragement for fourteen years. I've never known anyone wiser, or anyone who understood me so well. Nor have I ever had a truer soul-mate. If I worked to make myself better, it was in many ways to be worthy of her friendship, which was not given carelessly, but had to be earned.

—Dave Foreman

Sandia Mountain Foothills

February 2011

Foreword

A View From 1848 by John Stuart Mill

There is room in the world, no doubt, and even in old countries, for a great increase in population, supposing the arts of life to go on improving, and capital to increase. But even if innocuous, I confess I see very little reason for desiring it. The density of population necessary to enable mankind to obtain, in the greatest degree, all the advantages both of cooperation and of social intercourse, has, in all the most populous countries, been attained.

A population may be too crowded, though all be amply provided with food and raiment. It is not good for man to be kept perforce at all times in the presence of his species. A world from which solitude is extirpated, is a very poor ideal. Solitude, in the sense of being often alone, is essential to any depth of meditation or of character; and solitude in the presence of natural beauty and grandeur, is the cradle of thoughts and aspirations which are not only good for the individual, but which society could do ill without. Nor is there much satisfaction in contemplating the world with nothing left to the spontaneous activity of nature; with every rood of land brought into cultivation, which is capable of growing food for human beings; every flowery waste or natural pasture plowed up, all quadrupeds or birds which are not domesticated for man's use exterminated as his rivals for food, every hedgerow or superfluous tree rooted out, and scarcely a place left where a wild shrub or flower could grow without being eradicated as a weed in the name of improved agriculture.

If the earth must lose that great portion of its pleasantness which it owes to things that the unlimited increase of wealth and population would extirpate from it, for the mere purpose of enabling it to support a larger, but not a better or happier population, I sincerely hope, for the sake of posterity, that they will be content to be stationary, long before necessity compels them to it.

It is scarcely necessary to remark that a stationary condition of capital and population implies no stationary state of human improvement. There would be as much scope as ever for all kinds of mental culture, and moral and social progress; as much room for improving the Art of Living, and much more likelihood of its being improved, when minds ceased to be engrossed by the art of getting on. Even the industrial arts might be as earnestly and as successfully cultivated, with the sole difference, that instead of serving no purpose but the increase of wealth, industrial improvements would produce their legitimate effect, that of abridging labor.

From the 1848 version of Principles of Political Economy, *Book IV, Chapter VI, Section II by John Stuart Mill.*

John Stuart Mill (1806-1873) was a leading British philosopher and economist, who championed liberty.

Introduction

The Swarm of Man, The Killing of Wildlife

If true ecological balance exists, then human populations should be stable. They would not grow rapidly for long, nor would they crash.[1]

—Steven LeBlanc

Unlooked-for but swift, we have come on like a swarm of locusts: a wide, thick, darkling cloud settling down like living snowflakes, smothering every stalk, every leaf, eating away every scrap of green down to raw, bare, wasting earth.

It's painfully straightforward. There are too many Men for Earth to harbor.[2] At nearly seven billion of us, we have overshot Earth's

1 Steven A. LeBlanc with Katherine Register, *Constant Battles: The Myth Of The Peaceful, Noble Savage* (St. Martin's Press, New York, 2003), 30.

2 I use *Man* or *Men* capitalized for the species *Homo sapiens, woman* for the female of the species, and *man* uncapitalized for the male. This is more in keeping with earlier English, which had another word for male *Homo sapiens*: wer, which lives on today as werewolf. Today's English is odd for a modern tongue not to have a straightforward word for our kind that is also not the gendered word for the male. To have to call ourselves by a Latin word, human, is cumbersome and abstract. I do not write Man in a sexist way but for the goodness of the English tongue.

carrying capacity. The Man swarm yet swells like the black, living, withering mouth-clouds that have ransacked fields since the first digging stick scratched a line in dirt. The crippling of Earth's life support system by such a flood of upright apes is bad news for us.

But it is much worse news for the other Earthlings—animals and plants, wildeors and worts—who are taking a far worse beating than are we for our devil-may-care childishness and greed.[3] Long ago we overshot Earth's carrying capacity for keeping wild things hale and hearty. For many years it has been the booming and spreading overflow of naked apes—us—that has been the greatest threat to brimming, many-fold (manifold) life on Earth.

For anything beyond a few years ahead, the bedrock work of conservation—shielding wildlands and keeping all kinds of wildlife alive—is up in the air without freezing and then lowering the population of Man.

Soon after I was born, Aldo Leopold, in my mind the top conservation thinker of the twentieth century, wrote in the beginning of his wonderful book, *A Sand County Almanac,* "[T]here are those who can live without wild things, and there are those who cannot." For as long as I can recall, I've been one of those cannots. I have no wish to live in a world without wild things.

In this short book, I hope to show others of you who have no wish to live without wild things that unless we can freeze and then make Man's footprint on Earth smaller we will have an Earth with fewer and fewer wild things. I hope to give you the understanding and the

3 A key insight of Charles Darwin's is that all lifekinds can track their beginnings back to a shared forebear. Biologists today call this forebear the Last Common Ancestor or LCA. We—plants, animals, fungi, and microorganisms—are kin. Thus we all should share the name "Earthling." Some think "wildlife" means only mammals, but all untamed living things, plants and fungi, too, should be called wildlife. *Wildeor* is an earlier English word for wild animal. I'll write wildlife with a broad brush for all untamed life and wildeor only for wild animals. I'll also use the lovely old word for plants—*wort*. Such words make me feel as though my fingernails are full of damp dirt and my nose is down in the duff. To my ears, plants sound potted and animals brushed.

background to talk to others about why population stabilization should be a bedrock conservation and environmental care—once again.

More of our kind means fewer wild things. A stabilized human population means hope for wild things. A shrinking human population means a better world for wild things. And for men and women and children.

It's that straightforward.

My goals in *Man Swarm* are to help wilderness and wildlife lovers:

1. Understand that the population explosion is ongoing both worldwide and in the United States;
2. Understand that the overpopulation of Man is the main driver of the extinction of sundry kinds of wildlife, the wrecking and taming of wildlands and wildwaters, and greenhouse gas pollution, which leads to global weirdness and ocean acidification;[4]
3. Understand the beliefs of cornucopians and others who do not see a population threat;
4. Know how wise men and women over the last 2,500 years have seen the harm done by overpopulation;
5. And learn that there are many ways we can work to freeze and then lower population.

The world now has nearly seven billion of us; we will grow to nine or twelve billion in the next hundred years unless we do something—or unless something awful happens to us, which is likely unless we wake up.

The United States, the wealthiest, most wasteful empire in history, has about 310 million. Unless we do something, the population of the United States will double in the next hundred years to above 600 million or even to more than 800 million.

4 Pollution by carbon dioxide and other "greenhouse gases" is leading to much more than overall warming. The upshot is tangled beyond anyone's ken, hence the need to say "global weirding" instead of "global warming."

Is this what you want?

Are we going to do anything about it?

At the first Earth Day in 1970, Hugh Iltis, the great botanist at the University of Wisconsin-Madison (where Leopold also taught), warned that we had begun a mass extinction of other Earthlings. Hugh is one of my mentors and has always taught that our overpopulation drives this mass extinction. This book comes from his trailblazing.

Note:

Man Swarm is a book about how too many Men threaten all other lifekinds on Earth. Population growth worldwide comes from more births than deaths. However, population growth in a nation or shire can also come from more folks moving in than moving out—immigration. In the United States, immigration is by far the greatest driver of population growth, as it is in the United Kingdom, Canada, Australia, and some other countries that would have already gained stabilized or slightly shrinking populations otherwise. Unlawful immigration over the U.S.-Mexico border is one of the hottest political fires in the United States and overwhelms thought and talk about growth here. Therefore, I have gone out of my way not to let unlawful immigration from Mexico take over this book and the deep threat of world overpopulation with which it deals. My doing so is not chicken—as you'll see, what I write about unlawful sneaking over the southern border of the United States is tough—but not mean. But in writing *Man Swarm,* I came to see that the weight of unlawful immigration to the United States from Mexico could overwhelm the much greater threat of worldwide overshoot and the ransacking of wildlife. The thrust of *Man Swarm* is that crowds of *Homo sapiens* lead to the death of other Earthlings and to the shrinkage of the tangled and manifold life that brightens our winsome, wonderful, blue-green and white-clouded world in the lifeless darkness of space.

* * * *

In the Great American Tea Party, which has been going on for no less than thirteen score years, some stir their tea to the right and some stir to the left. Whichever way they stir, though, they share underlying ways of seeing the world. In the swirls of their teacups, great conspiracies take shape out of the muddle and become sharp. From their ragged brains, they take fuzzy or frayed or even dreamed-up threads and weave them into thick, sturdy, wide-cast but hidden nets of great evil.

So, unhappily, here, I must take a quick look at the mostly left-wing gang of the uber-politically correct that calls any conservationist/environmentalist/animal-welfarist/resourcist who worries about immigration part of a "Green Hate" racist conspiracy. Believe me, they'll burn this book and would gladly burn me, too. Once again, they'll yell that I am anti-immigrant and therefore an anti-Mexican racist. The lynch-mob mindset and unswerving self-belief of Tea Partiers is no less hotheaded on the left than it is on the right.

I loathe giving this rotten untruthfulness any kind of standing by acknowledging it in writing. In the open, I am deaf to silly brickbats, but alone I follow Ed Abbey and bask with earnest merriment in fiendship from others. But when it comes to being damned for looking down on folks with Spanish last names or on Mexicans, I have not yet gained Abbey-Zen aloofness.

Why? First and foremost, all of my nieces, nephews, grandnieces, grandnephews, and many in-laws and cousins have Spanish last names: Pacheco, Serna, Santillanes, Chavez .... My family is a mingling of New Mexico Anglo homesteaders here over one hundred years and Nuevo Mexicano settlers here three to four hundred years. It likely has a hearty sprinkle of Native American DNA on all sides: my wife Nancy has enough Cherokee to clean the bar for tribehood, and I tease my niece Monica that she looks just like the Aztec princess in the calendars you find in restaurants all over Mexico.

I was born in New Mexico by happenstance but I live here today by choice—mostly because I feel at home in New Mexico's blended lifeways. Other states seem odd. You see, unlike in other southwestern states—Texas, California, and Arizona—the offspring of early Spanish settlers in New Mexico have kept a strong political, cultural, and economic hold after U.S. takeover in 1849. Moreover, the sundry Pueblos have kept a cultural, spiritual, and economic wholeness and freedom unmatched by Native tribes elsewhere in the U.S.[5]

Now, let's go farther south. Since 1970, I've wandered the back-of-beyond in Mexico—mountains, *barrancas,* sand dunes and thorn-deserts, *playas,* coral reefs, jungles—looking for jaguars, macaws, grizzlies, wolves, crocodiles, sharks, big fig trees, and empty, far-away, lonely wilderness. I've found much of what I was looking for and glimmers and spoor of the rest. I've also found friends: conservationists, birders, field biologists, river runners, and others. We've worked together to shield prairie dogs and thick-billed parrots. I've helped bring back black-footed ferrets to prairie dog towns in Mexico. My Mexican friends are as a true as any friends I've had, and care about wild things as much as anyone I know. Whether in meeting room or wilderness, there is no gap between them and my fellows from the U.S., Canada, Australia, and elsewhere.

I know it does little if any good to show politically correct Tea Party folks how they are wrong. So, I don't hope to get those slinging "Green Hate" lies to truly understand me or to back off. I do hope, though, that good folks, however they think about immigration, will at least acknowledge that I am anything but an anti-immigrant racist.

—Dave Foreman

Sandia Mountains Foothills

February 2011

5 I'm not downplaying the hardship of U.S. (or Spanish) takeover in New Mexico, only that it was worse elsewhere, and that this led to an outcome of stronger and less-fettered homegrown lifeways that give New Mexico a folkhood like nowhere else in America.

CHAPTER 1

Man's Population Explosion

The massive growth in the human population through the 20th century has had more impact on biodiversity than any other single factor.

—Sir David King,
science advisor to the British government

In those few words, Sir David King wraps up the last hundred years better than anyone else has. It is the blunt truth.

It is why those of us who cannot live without wild things must once again work to freeze and then lower the population of Man worldwide.

Complex animal life evolved sometime before 500 million years ago. Plants came a little later. Since then, the tree of life has grown up and out into all kinds of odd and far-flung boughs, limbs, twigs, and leaves. Now, though, is a stand-alone hour in this awesomely long tale of life. Never before has there been a being such as us—one with the might to swiftly and thoroughly remake the world. Only those who are blind to the wildworld can look about and not feel dread as swelling thousands of other kinds of Earthlings are shoved off into the dawnless night-pit of extinction. Please recall: all living things on Earth from bacteria to ravens are Earthlings no less than are we.

In the half-a-billion years of shelled and backboned wights and sundry green worts, five breathtakingly big extinctions show themselves as we peel away geological layers.[1] Each of these five big die-offs was brought on by blazing iceballs zipping through the solar system to hit Earth or by the brawny shoulders of geology shoving continents hither and yon. Biologists and conservationists call today's extinction the Sixth Mass Extinction, owing to its sweep and heft. This extinction stands alone, however, since cosmic or geological might does not bring it on as they have with the other big extinctions. Instead, it is brought willfully and even thoughtfully by one kind of life, warring against all others.[2]

Today's Great Extinction has a living scythe with which to mow down life.

One species.

Homo sapiens.

Us.

Man.

Given its seed, and heeding our lodestone of goodness, truth, and fairness, maybe we should not call today's ecological crash the "Sixth Mass Extinction." Perhaps instead we should call it the *First Mass Murder of Life.*

---

1 *Wight* is an earlier English word for creature or being. I use it both for an animal and for a fellow or individual Man.

2 Dave Foreman, *Rewilding North America: A Vision for Conservation in the Twenty-first Century* (Island Press, Washington, DC, 2004). In Part A of *Rewilding North America* I look in depth at extinction.

How out of kilter is today? Never before has one kind of being broken out of its neighborhood (home ecosystem(s)) to become a mighty throng sweeping over Earth to almost everywhere, and then scalping and remaking those other wild neighborhoods, too. Never before has one kind of life gobbled up so much of all other life and of what that life needs to live.

Never before have so few become so many and in a flash spread over the whole world—with billions now standing where thousands once stood. For every *Homo sapiens* alive 50,000 years ago, there are one million alive today. In other words, our kind has grown a million-fold

Figure 1.1. Population Growth Man 50kya to 2050 CE

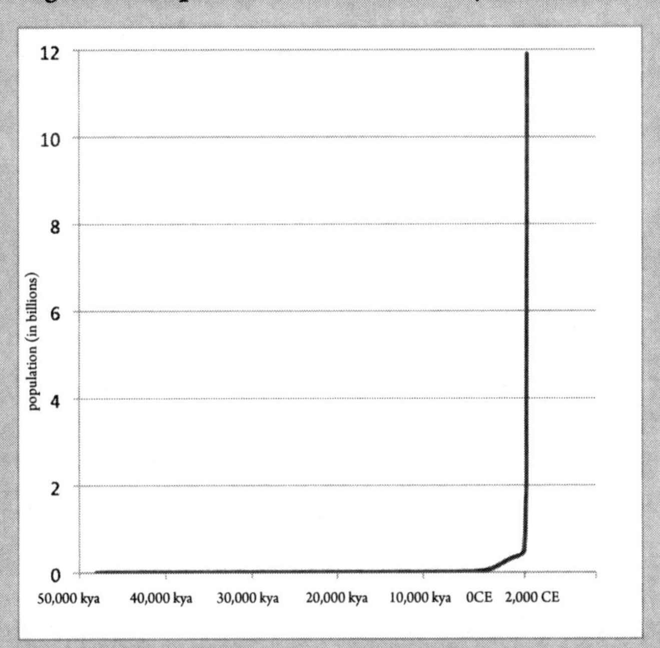

See text for sources, which include United Nations Population Division and the Bixby Center, University of California San Francisco. The baseline for "years ago" is 2000 C.E. Therefore, 10kya is 8,000 B.C.E. The beginning of the Current Era (C.E.) is 2kya (two thousand years ago).

in 50,000 years. It's something like the scene in Walt Disney's movie *Fantasia* where Mickey Mouse, playing the "Sorcerer's Apprentice," fecklessly waves the sorcerer's wand and clones an unstoppable gang of exponentially multiplying brooms toting buckets of water and flooding the wizard's workshop. So do we flood Earth with ourselves. (See Figure 1.1.)

When we were a little fewer than six billion, ecologists reckoned that we were already taking more than 40 percent of Earth's Net Primary Productivity (NPP). NPP is the yearly sunlight striking Earth that photosynthesis in plants makes into energy that other life can then take to make biomass (see Box 1.1). We are now almost seven billion. Demographers foresee we will soon zoom to nine or twelve billion or more. When we are that many, how much of NPP will we take? Sixty percent? More? What will be left for everything else? We are doing more than hogging the interest; we are using up life's capital—taking

Box1.1. NPP: Net Primary Productivity

Man thoroughly lords over Earth. How much we hold sway is shown by the key ecological yardstick of Net Primary Productivity (NPP): "All the solar energy annually captured worldwide by photosynthesizers and not used by them to run their own lives...." In 1986 Man was using or redirecting some 40 percent of the terrestrial NPP of our world, or 25 percent when ocean NPP was brought in. Ecologist Stuart Pimm uses 105 pages in his worthy 2001 book, *The World According to Pimm,* to carefully recalculate the data to find that Man is using 42 percent of terrestrial NPP. He then reckons that we are also taking "a quarter to a third of the oceans' production."

Paul R. Ehrlich and Anne H. Ehrlich, *The Population Explosion* (Simon & Schuster, NY, 1990), 36-37.
Stuart L. Pimm, *The World According to Pimm* (McGraw-Hill, NY, 2001), 10.

away what is needed by deep-diving squid and by the geese that fly over the Himalayas, by pond duckweed and by rock-gripping bristlecone pines up where the air is thin. We are wiping out the building blocks evolution needs to play out its unfathomable, uncanny yet-to-be. And what if we go to twelve billion? Or beyond?

In 1974, physicist John P. Holdren and biologist Paul Ehrlich, then both at Stanford University, set down in *Science* the key scientific formula of our time: *I=PAT.*[3] Paul and Anne Ehrlich later spelled out what it means, "The impact of any human group on the environment can be usefully viewed as the product of three different factors. The first is the number of people. The second is some measure of the average person's consumption of resources...Finally, the product of those two factors ... is multiplied by an index of the environmental disruptiveness of the technologies that provide the goods consumed.... In short,

3 John P. Holdren and Paul R. Ehrlich, "Impact of Population Growth," *Science* vol. 171 (1974), 1212-17.

Box 1.2. I=PAT

In 1974, physicist John P. Holdren and biologist Paul Ehrlich, then both at Stanford, laid out in *Science* one of the foremost scientific formulas: I=PAT. Paul and Anne Ehrlich later wrote, "The impact of any human group on the environment can be usefully viewed as the product of three different factors. The first is the number of people. The second is some measure of the average person's consumption of resources....Finally, the product of those two factors...is multiplied by an index of the environmental disruptiveness of the technologies that provide the goods consumed....In short, Impact = Population x Affluence x Technology, or I=PAT."

Paul R. Ehrlich and Anne H. Ehrlich, *The Population Explosion* (Simon & Schuster, NY, 1990), 58.

Impact = Population x Affluence x Technology, or I=PAT."[4] (See Box 1.2.) For the long-term health of the tangled web of life, I=PAT is more meaningful than $E=MC^2$. I'll hearken back to I=PAT often in the pages to come. When I use them as bits of I=PAT, I'll capitalize Impact, Population, Affluence, and Technology. I see Impact (I) as the harm we do to other Earthlings, or as ecological wounds. Others may see Impact more as harm to the life support system Earth gives Man.

THE WORST WOUND OF OVERPOPULATION

In this short book, I hope to show lovers of wild things that Man's population ka-boom shrivels and shatters the dazzle of wild things that dwells on Earth. Unlike most books that have warned of overpopulation, I will spend little time on tales about coming starvation, breakdown of civilizations, running out of oil, and wars and anarchy over dwindling raw goods. It's not because I pooh-pooh these likelihoods, but because the most dreadful and unforgivable outcome of Man's population explosion is what we are doing to other Earthlings. And it isn't something that might happen in years to come; it is happening right now. Professor Eileen Crist of Virginia Tech warns that "it is not our survival and well-being that are primarily on the line, but *everybody else's*."[5] She is right. Nonetheless, most who have written about overpopulation have underplayed and overlooked the way our growth drives the end of the wild ones. Owing somewhat to that wrong step, conservationists have mostly stopped working on overpopulation. Many who ward wildernesses and shield endangered species don't seem to think about why population stabilization should be a conservation chore, although only forty to thirty years ago most conservationists knew it was. On the other hand, wherever I give talks today, I find some in the crowd who ask how can we hope to keep or rebuild wilderness

4 Paul R. Ehrlich and Anne H. Ehrlich, *The Population Explosion* (Simon and Schuster, New York, 1990), 58.

5 Eileen Crist, "Limits-to-Growth and the Biodiversity Crisis," *Wild Earth*, Spring 2003, 65.

and wildlife if we don't halt growth.[6] They are right. Without freezing human numbers, we can't keep our National Parks, we can't stop the loss of polar bears and elephants and whales, and we can't hope to put the brakes on greenhouse gases and halt climatic Ragnarok.

THE POPULATION EXPLOSION IN A NUTSHELL

Sixty-five thousand years seems like forever, yet it is a finger-snap in geological time. Maybe our handicap comes from having a lifespan of only seventy or so years. But walk with me as I slog back 65,000 years. Then there were more than ten kinds (species[7]) of great apes: in east and southeast Asia, two kinds of orangutans, two or more kinds of *Homo erectus* offspring, and tiny little folks (Hobbits) on Flores and other islands; in Africa, two gorillas, chimpanzees, bonobos, and likely two hominin kinds, one of which was becoming us—*Homo sapiens;* and, in Europe and western Asia, Neandertals. Also, in central Asia, another kind of *Homo,* not us and not Neandertal.[8] Of the species in this great ape clade, who do you think was fewest?

It was likely our forebears. Genetic and other scientific work shows that there were fewer than 10,000 of the elder *Homo sapiens* living 65,000 years ago—maybe only 5,000.[9] Fifty thousand years later, we had spread out of Africa to Asia, Australia, Europe, and the Americas. Only Antarctica and a few out-of-the-way islands were yet without us.[10] In a few more thousand years we were building yearlong settlements and starting to grow wheat and lentils. We had already brought some wolves into our packs and would soon tame goats and sheep. Some little

6 Instead of writing *population growth* over and over, I will mostly write *growth* only. If I'm talking about some other kind of growth, I'll say so.

7 *Kind* has long been used in English, even by Darwin, to mean *species.*

8 *Hominin* is a rather new term human paleontologists use for species in the kinship group of Man, not that of other apes.

9 Nicholas Wade, *Before the Dawn: Recovering the Lost History of Our Ancestors* (The Penguin Press, New York, 2006), 52.

10 Man found Iceland, New Zealand, Madagascar, and Hawaii only in the last two thousand years or less.

desert cats would tame us. Our tally had climbed to a million or so by then, about ten thousand years ago. By that time, our nearest kin—the three to six other *Homos*—were gone, and we likely had much to do with their going. The Sixth Mass Extinction was going full tilt with the killing of big wildeors wherever we newly showed up.[11]

Another way to look at it is that 50,000 years ago, there were more tigers than *Homo sapiens.* More gorillas, more chimpanzees, more orangutans, more blue whales, more jaguars, more white rhinos.... Today, for every wild tiger on Earth, there are *two million* human

11 Foreman, *Rewilding North America.* Paul S. Martin and Richard G. Klein, eds., *Quaternary Extinctions: A Prehistoric Revolution* (University of Arizona Press, Tucson, 1984).

Figure 1.2. Man and Tiger Population in India, 1900-2025 C.E.

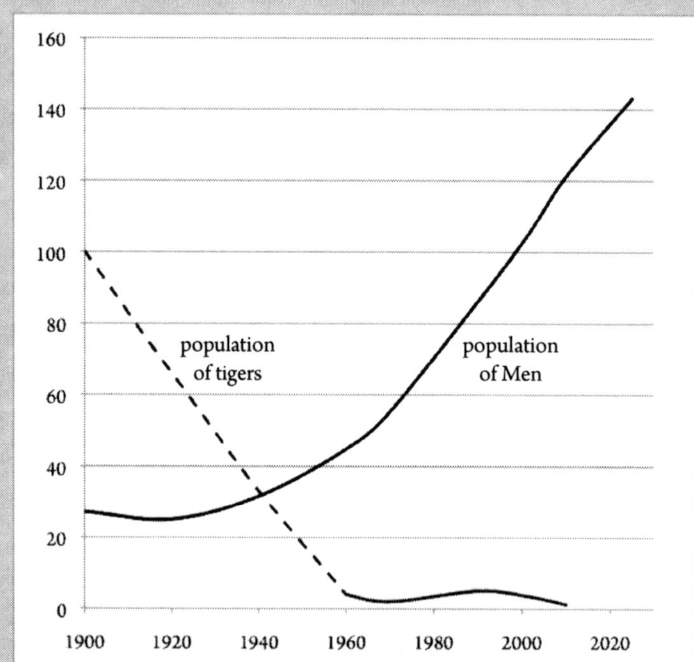

The source for Man is United Nations Population Division. The vertical axis shows the population of tigers in thousands, while it shows the population of Man in tens of millions. Thus, 100,000 tigers correspond to 1 billion Men.

beings. Sit quietly with your eyes closed and hold that flip in your head for a minute or two. (See Figure 1.2.) In India alone, there were some 100,000 tigers in the wild one hundred years ago. As the population of Man shot through the roof in India, the population of tigers fell through the floor. I'll look at this more in Chapter 4.

Then tackle this one: In 2002, about 350,000 Man-babies were being born every day. This was more than the total population of all of the other great apes (gorillas, chimpanzees, bonobos, and orangutans) put together.[12]

Father-son historians William and J. R. McNeill write, "By the time the first metropolitan web was forming around Sumer some 5,000 years ago, the earth hosted perhaps 10 to 30 million people."[13] The widely acknowledged world population of us for 1 C.E. is 250 million.[14] By 1700 C.E., about the time Benjamin Franklin was born, we had grown to 610 million. Throughout this time of preindustrial civilization, heavy childhood deaths and the "occasional demographic crisis" (epidemics) slowed the dash of growth.[15] As did our bloody swords and spears.[16]

So. Sixty-five thousand years ago: we were less than 10,000. Ten thousand years ago: 1,000,000. Five thousand years ago: 10,000,000 to 30,000,000. Two thousand years ago: 250,000,000. Three hundred years ago: 610,000,000. Our population grew sturdily, but pretty slowly and over many, many years. For every Man 65,000 years ago, there were

---

12 Richard Cincotta, ecologist and senior researcher, Population Action International, 2002.

13 J. R. McNeill and William McNeill, *The Human Web: A Bird's Eye View of World History* (W. W. Norton & Company, New York, 2003), 221. Sumer, between the Tigris and Euphrates rivers, is the first known city.

14 J. R. Weeks, *Population*, 29. *C.E.*, by the way, means *Current Era*, and is written instead of *A.D.*

15 McNeill and McNeill, *The Human Web*, 221.

16 Steven A. LeBlanc with Katherine E. Register, *Constant Battles: The Myth Of The Peaceful, Noble Savage* (St. Martin's Press, New York, 2003).

100,000 in 1700 C.E. (See Figures 1.3a and 1.3b.) Soon, however, our population growth was to *explode.*

Physician and University of Colorado anthropology professor Warren Hern wrote in 1999 that

> *[T]he human population doubled 4 times from A.D. 0 to 1976, with the doubling times dropping from 1650 years (est. 500 million at 1650 A.D.) to 46 years (from 2 billion in 1930 to 4.29 billion in 1976). People who are 40 years old or more in 1998 are among the first people in history to have lived through a doubling*

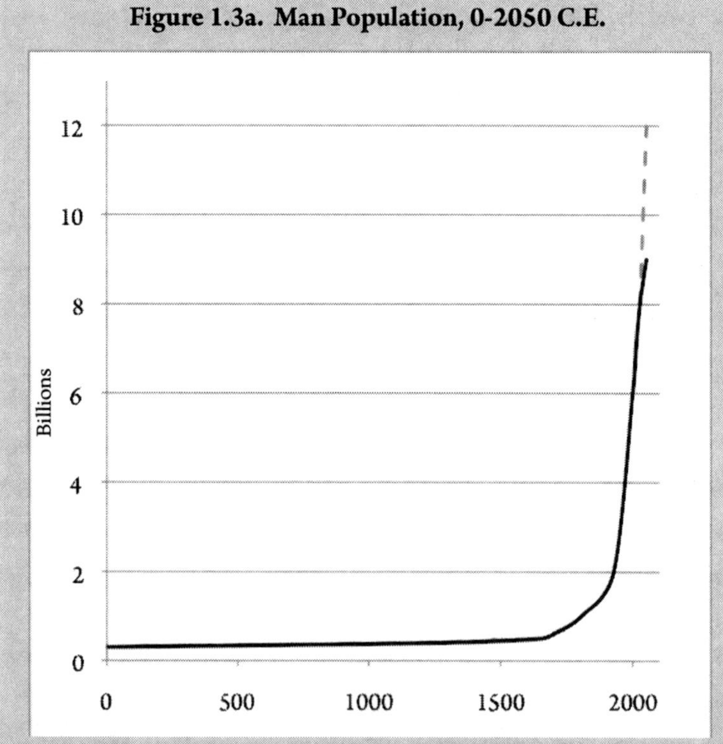

Figure 1.3a. Man Population, 0-2050 C.E.

Source: United Nations Population Division and other sources, including the Bixby Center University of California San Francisco. Forecasts for 2050 population range from 9 billion to 12 billion. See text.

Figure 1.3b. Man Population by Billions, 1804-2050 C.E.

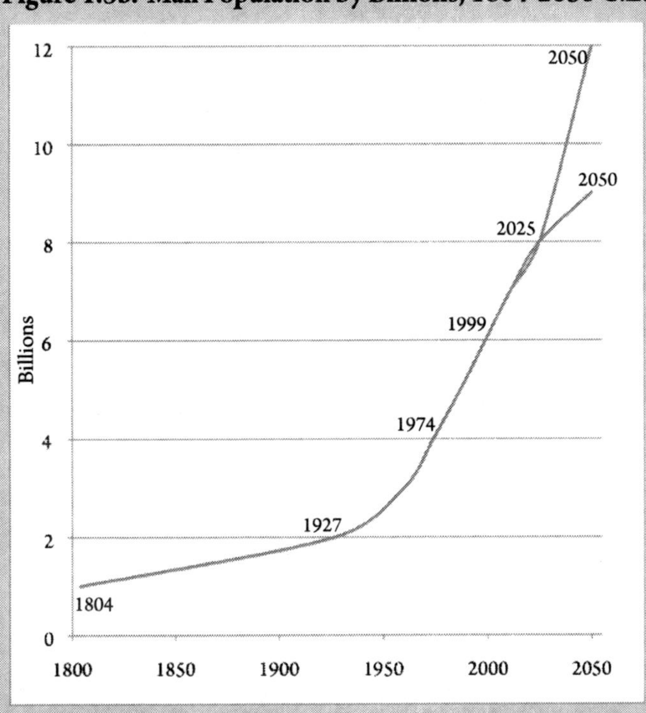

This graph uses the same sources as 1.3a, but shows Man's growth by billions, from 1 billion in 1804 on.

of world population; people who are 75 years old have seen the human population triple.[17]

As I write this in February 2011, it is thirteen years since 1998. I was born in 1946 and have now seen world population triple in my lifetime from about 2.2 billion to nearly seven billion. My father-in-law, Robert Morton, born in 1912 and still alive at ninety-eight has seen world population more than quadruple.

17 Warren M. Hern, "How Many Times Has the Human Population Doubled? Comparisons with Cancer," *Population and Environment: A Journal of Interdisciplinary Studies,* Vol. 21, Number 1, September 1999, 59-80. (Population doubling time is the number of years it takes a population to double.)

Earlier Hern wrote:

As of 1993, we have added more humans to the total human population of the world in the past 40 years than we added in the previous three million years. The human population has quadrupled in the last century. Between seven and 8% of all human beings ever born are alive today. Until recently, the rate of growth of the human population has been increasing, which means that it exceeds even exponential growth.[18]

Please stop reading for a bit. Sit back and let Hern's words sink in. They ought to jar your mind.

Man's population grew more in the last forty years than in the previous three million.

This is why we talk about the human population *explosion.*

The population bomb has blown up—but the shrapnel hasn't yet hit us hard. What it has hit hard are wild things.

HOW HIGH WILL HUMAN NUMBERS GO?

No one gainsays that our population has grown since 1700. Nor is anyone believable at odds with the exponential growth curve of human population. Where the clash comes is with forecasts, with cornucopians saying that population growth is slowing, even as they

18 Warren M. Hern, "Has The Human Species Become A Cancer On The Planet?: A Theoretical View Of Population Growth As A Sign Of Pathology," *Current World Leaders: Biography & News/Speeches & Reports Issue,* Vol. 36, No. 6, December 1993. Hern references N. Keyfitz, "The Growing Human Population," *Scientific American,* 261(3), 1989, 119-126; United Nations, "The 1992 Revision of World Population Prospects," *Population Newsletter,* no. 54 (Population Division, Department of Economic and Social Development, United Nations Secretariat, New York, 1992); J. R. Weeks, *Population: An Introduction to Concepts and Issues,* fifth edition (Wadsworth Publishing Company, Belmont, CA, 1992); P. Demeny, "The World Demographic Situation," in J. Menken, ed., *World Population & U.S. Policy* (Norton, New York, 1986); A. A. Bartlett, "Forgotten Fundamentals of the Energy Crisis," *American Journal of Physics* 46(9), 1978, 876-888.

say such growth is not a worry. (A wise one knows to raise an eyebrow when tossed this kind of two-sided dodge.) Some of the wrangle comes from the handful of ways to reckon population growth: rate of growth, whether the rate of growth itself is going up or down (and by what speed), how many hungry mouths are added each year, number of women coming into their baby-making years, population doubling time, and so on.

Biologist Garret Hardin laid out why we need to look at all these kinds of population growth. Say that the *percentage rate* of growth slows from 2.1 percent to 1.7 percent a year over a few years while the *absolute rate* of yearly growth goes from 64 million to 79 million to 93 million in that time. How can this be? *Because there are more women giving birth at the lower rate.* Hardin wrote in 1993, "The absolute rate of increase has increased every year since the end of World War II. It is the absolute increase, rather than the relative rate, that stresses the environment."[19] In 2009, about "75 million more mouths" than in 2008 were pleading for food.[20] It was much the same in 2010, with another 75 million more hungry ones than in 2009. And so it goes.

Conservationists need to understand this. Thinking that a drop in the population growth rate means that population is not growing is a warning that our schools are no longer teaching arithmetic.[21] Maybe one can forgive journalists and the public for being mathematical dolts, but economists should be deft in numbers. Yet, amazingly, some economists and other social engineers now fear that population is falling and this will lead to all kinds of lousy things—socially and economically. I'll deal with these "birth dearth" collywobbles later.

19 Garrett Hardin, *Living Within Limits: Ecology, Economics, And Population Taboos* (Oxford University Press, New York, 1993), 11-12.

20 John Cairns, Jr., "Silence That Kills," July 21, 2009, www.johncairns.net.

21 We see this same woodenheadedness when people think that were we to lower the tons of greenhouse gases being pumped into the atmosphere every year it would mean that the percentage of greenhouse gases in the atmosphere was going down.

Another way to look at population is by population age structure. Even if there is a drop in the growth rate, national population still rises for many years. Why? As big "age cohorts" go through their childbearing years, they have many, many children. One-third of Earth's population in 1995 (2 billion) was under fifteen years of age, while only about five percent of it (300 million people) was over sixty-five. The youngsters are making far more babies now than how many oldsters are dying; therefore population is growing.[22] Lopsided percentages are still under fifteen years old. With such a landslide of youngsters coming into their breeding years, even if they right away go to having only the replacement rate of 2.1 children per woman, it will take two or three generations or fifty to seventy-five years before population stabilizes.[23] In many African countries today, between 40 and 50 percent of the population is under fifteen years of age. With that lopsidedness, forecasts for growth in these sorrow-lands are unbearable.

This is yet another twist. Population does not grow evenly over the world. While Italy, Japan, and Russia may have ended their growth, elsewhere—Africa foremost—growth is unbelievably high. Take forlorn Ethiopia, where hunger stalks the land like a marrow-sucking wraith; Ethiopia had fewer than nineteen million souls in 1950, had forty million or so when it had its Earth-shaking famine in 1984, has eighty-five million today, and is slated to have about 174 million in another forty years. (See Figure 1.4.) This is why I write *unbelievably high.* Indeed, I find it hard to believe that Ethiopia can grow to 174 million folks by 2040. How on Earth can this happen? I don't mean how can we let it happen, I mean how is it biologically, physically possible for it to happen? There is more than a whiff of madness in the growth forecasts we take for granted.

22 Anne Ehrlich, "Implications of Population Pressure on Agriculture and Ecosystems," *Advances in Botanical Research,* Vol. 21, 1995, 84.

23 J. Kenneth Smail, "Confronting A Surfeit Of People: Reducing Global Human Numbers To Sustainable Levels," *Environment, Development and Sustainability* 4, July 2002, Kluwer Academic Publishers, the Netherlands, 24.

Figure 1.4. Ethiopia Population Growth, 1950-2050 C.E.

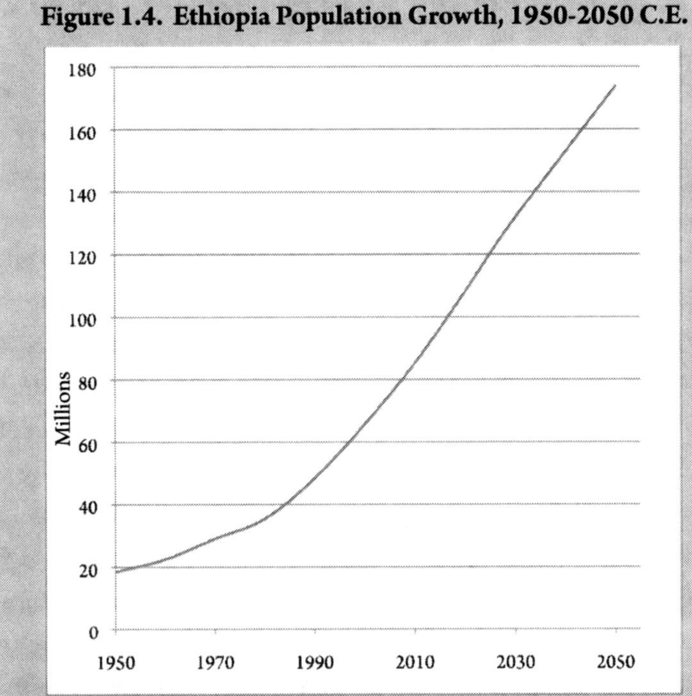

Source: United Nations Population Division: World Population prospects: 2008 Revision, Medium variant as of Feb. 18, 2011.

Later, in Chapter 4, Table 4.1 will show population growth for some countries of high biological diversity, high extinction threats, and high growth. After cobbling it together, I had to make myself a stiff drink.

Another piece of the puzzle mostly overlooked is "that ongoing global gains in human longevity will continue to make a major contribution to world population expansion over the next half-century, *regardless of whatever progress might be made in reducing fertility."*[24] (My emphasis.) This is a big deal, but few think about how longevity grows population.

24 Smail, "Confronting A Surfeit Of People," 24.

Thirty and forty years ago, so-called "doomsayers" such as Paul Ehrlich and Garret Hardin woke up governments and workaday folks alike with their warnings. Birth control of all kinds became widespread in the 1970s. Good work was done—at least for a while. But in no way has the population bomb been defused. As we've seen, we add some 75 million more Man-mouths every year. That is 750 million every ten years. Go back a few pages. Three hundred years ago, the whole world of Man was 610 million. We are adding more than that every ten years. Don't believe those foisting tales that the population bomb has fizzled.

So. What is the answer to this section's heading? How high will world population go? Uber-Pollyannas talk about leveling off at 8 billion by 2050 without enlightening us how this will happen (we're already at 7 billion). Establishment projections seem to hover about 9.2 billion. But Dr. Joseph Speidel of the University of California's Bixby Center for Reproductive Health Research & Policy warns, "If birth rates remain unchanged, world population will grow to 11.9 billion" by 2050.[25] The "official" projections of 9.2 billion by 2050 are grounded, then, in the belief that birth rates will somehow go down. But will they without hard work? Or something awful?

Human population, then, has exploded gruesomely in the last two hundred or so years. It will keep shooting up for some time. So what?

In the next chapter we'll look more sharply at what is truly at stake.

25 J. Joseph Speidel, MD, Cover Letter for "Family Planning and Reproductive Health: The Link to Environmental Preservation," January 18, 2008.

Chapter 2

What's It Truly All About?

It is critical to focus on what is presently dead certain: that overproduction and overpopulation have been driving the dismantling of complex ecosystems and native life, and leaving in their widening wake constructed environments, simplified ecologies, and lost life forms.

—Eileen Crist

A WASTREL who pisses away the family fortune slops about in a puddle of carelessness. A madcap, yowling toddler never bridled by mommy and daddy is a rotten little brat. Wastrels and brats are blind to limits. An acknowledgment of limits underlies both maturity and responsibility. Living within the carrying capacity of the land has been one of the main props of resourcism, conservation, and environmentalism—at least until a little while ago; now the pilings of each are splintering without it.[1] Why do I say this? Snipping the wires on the population bomb was high on the to-do lists of conservationists, environmentalists, and resourcists in the 1960s and 1970s. Forty years and over two *billion* more mouths later, however, all three shy away from hard talk on population growth. Roy Beck and Leon Kolankiewicz, who have thoughtfully prodded and poked at this puzzle, write, "As [the modern environmental] movement enters its fourth decade, perhaps the most striking change is the virtual abandonment by national environmental groups of U.S. population stabilization as an actively pursued goal."[2]

This step back is all the more upsetting given the long history of worry about limits to growth.

I first read Paul Ehrlich's *The Population Bomb* in 1969 or 1970. Soon thereafter I read the foremost book about our flaying of the land—*Deserts on the March* by Paul Sears. In the spring semester of 1972, I took a few biology courses at the University of New Mexico. One was called "Conservation." Our textbook was *Population Resources Environment* by Paul and Anne Ehrlich—which went into academic depth on everything from erosion and pollution to birth control techniques.[3] With this schooling, I learned that Man's population growth was at the

1 As I use the terms here, resourcism is the expert-run exploitation and "wise" management of natural resources for "sustainable" use by humans. Conservation is the protection of wildlands and wildlife. Environmentalism is the prevention and control of pollution for human health. However, Beck and Kolankiewicz and most others see all three of these movements as the "Environmental Movement." Indeed, this is the common way of seeing it. In my forthcoming book *Take Back Conservation* I argue that they are different movements.

2 Roy Beck and Leon Kolankiewicz, "The Environmental Movement's Retreat from Advocating U.S. Population Stabilization (1970-1998): A First Draft of History," *Journal Of Policy History,* Vol. 12, No. 1, 2000, 123. An abridgement was reprinted in *Wild Earth,* Summer 2001, 66-67.

3 Paul R. Ehrlich and Anne H. Ehrlich, *Population Resources Environment: Issues In Human Ecology* (W. H. Freeman and Company, San Francisco, 1970).

root of nearly every wildland woe—such as coal strip-mines, dams on wild rivers, and new roads in the National Forest backcountry, all of which I was fighting at the time. California's booming crowds needed more electricity, which led to coal-fired power plants and coal strip-mines in New Mexico and Arizona. The Baby Boom after World War Two and into the 1970s led to the need for more houses, which led to more timber cutting and logging roads on the National Forests. The need for more electricity and the need for flood protection, water-based recreation, and water for growing Western cities led to the need for more dams on wild rivers. In truth, then, we conservationists were fighting against these believed "needs" brought by growth in the western United States.

As we will see later, consumption (or affluence) and technology both come into play, too, for driving these "needs" and thereby how much Man harms wild things. We can talk until we're all blue in the face about which does most to overshoot carrying capacity. I think how many we are is the key, but how richly we live and how wasteful we are also have to be dealt with.

Conservationists, environmentalists, scientists, and resourcists in the early seventies all saw the population bomb as the big threat. The Ehrlichs' book was ballyhooed in *Saturday Review, The New York Review of Books,* and other highbrow publications. Pete Seeger, the great folk singer of the left, touted it on its back cover: "I have just finished reading it from cover to cover and am now busy recommending it to all my friends." Forest rangers brought it up in their public talks.

Now talk of overpopulation is slighted. Even the Sierra Club—which published *The Population Bomb*—has become wittingly weak-kneed about it. So long as former Senator Gaylord Nelson—"the Father of Earth Day"—was alive, The Wilderness Society—for which he worked after his Senate career—was steadfast on population, but with his passing they seem to have dropped it like a hot potato, too. I know of no mainstream national conservation group that is straightforward and forthright on overpopulation, since *Wild Earth* magazine and The Wildlands Project in the 1990s and early 2000s.[4] The same goes for local and regional outfits. However, as I write this, the tough little wolverine of U.S. conservation groups, the Center for Biological Diversity, has started a population program—whether it will have sharp teeth, I don't yet know.

We can weigh the strength of conservation groups on overpopulation by the steps they take: One is to acknowledge the threat; two is to teach it; and three is to do something. How forthright and tough are they on the plight? Do they acknowledge overpopulation as the driver of extinction and other ecological wounds? Do they call for freezing population or, better yet, lowering it? And do they stand behind the kind of steps needed? I wish you well in your search. My little nonprofit, The Rewilding Institute, is strong, as is the Conservation Leaders Forum. The Rewilding Website (www.rewilding.org) will carry an up-to-date tally with click-on links to whatever groups we find that are tough on overpopulation.[5]

Caring about worldwide overpopulation is also shunned outside the conservation clan; indeed, it seems that both those who write about and those who are harmed by the outcomes of overpopulation are blind to what is behind their many plights. A *New York Times* article about hunger and lack of wild food for a tribe in the Amazon shows off Chief Kotok of the Kamayura. The reporter writes about the once-many fish no longer being there and how Kotok's "once-idyllic existence had turned into a kind of bad dream." He is "stressed and anxious" about how to care for his "24 children."[6] Did you catch that? It seems that

4 When Wildlands pulled the plug on *Wild Earth* over costs, it also dropped population as a care. Since Wildlands gave me the boot at the same time, anyone who truly backed work on overpopulation was gone.

5 I had planned to have such a list in an appendix in this book, but the landscape shifts so fast, it would soon be out of date.

6 Elisabeth Rosenthal, "An Amazon Culture Withers as Food Dries Up," *New York Times*, July 25, 2009.

neither Chief Kotok nor the *Times* reporter did. Might having twenty-four children have anything to do with there being fewer fish in the river and less game in the jungle? Another article in the *Times* tells about a wailing farmer in Syria who has been wiped out by not being able to feed his family. He has two wives and—wait for it—*fifteen* children.[7] I could keep on with such tales until you were bored stiff. So it goes in today's world as we are beset with woes right and left, most of which come from or are made worse by growth, but where it seems taboo to even whisper that growth of the Man swarm might have something to do with them.

The big question for lovers of wild things is the one that Garrett Hardin threw at us in 1972: "[H]ow do we get the general body politic to accept the truth?"[8] Today, though, we must first ask, "How do we get conservationists and environmentalists to accept the truth?" In my worst nightmares, I never thought we'd come to this sad day when my own gang wimped out on the underlying threat: The unending rampage of topsy-turvy growth.

Over the last two hundred years, some of the world's most farsighted thinkers have warned about human overpopulation. If we look at the warp and woof of their writings, we can tease out five threads of population-growth outcomes: (1) hunger and starvation because we can't grow enough to feed ourselves; (2) squandering natural resources (raw goods) until we run out; (3) landscalping and the loss of land fertility; (4) cultural, economic, and political upheaval; and (5) harm to wild things. Most limits-to-growth seers have worried most about the first four—after all, they are about us. Far fewer have given heed to how our growth gobbles up wild neighborhoods and pulls the

7 Reuters, "Water Crisis Uproots Syrian Farmers," *New York Times,* July 26, 2009.

8 Garrett Hardin, "We Live on a Spaceship," *Bulletin of the Atomic Scientists,* XXIII (1972), 23-25, reprinted in Roderick Frazier Nash, ed., *American Environmentalism: Readings In Conservation History* Third Edition (McGraw-Hill, New York, 1990), 238.

extinction-trigger at a swelling stream of species each year—soon to be an overwhelming flood.[9] As a lover of wild things, my worry has always been about how our growth bashes all the other Earthlings.

THE BIG STUMBLE OF THE LIMITS-TO-GROWTH GANG

In 1995, crusty philosophy professor and High Sierra climber George Sessions wrote, "One's position on the human overpopulation issue serves as a litmus test for the extent of one's ecological understanding and commitment to protecting biodiversity and the integrity of the Earth's ecosystems."[10] He does not say anything about running out of food or oil; he speaks for wild things. Maybe ol' George's litmus should be everyday fare for weighing would-be staff and board members for wilderness and wildlife outfits.

Like Sessions, Professor Eileen Crist at Virginia Tech is an amazingly unclouded thinker. She has been a lodestar for me on population. Her 2003 essay in *Wild Earth,* "Limits-to-Growth and the Biodiversity Crisis," is a landmark in population stabilization strategy. As we've seen, most who warn about population growth talk about how booming numbers will lead to two things: not being able to feed ourselves, and running out of oil, water, and other must-needs. Crist sees two weaknesses with this path: (1) "Limits-to-growth proponents cannot predict exactly when, or how, industrial civilization" will overshoot natural limits and crash; and (2) "In crucial ways, the debate between the limits-to-growth proponents and the cornucopians is extraneous to the ecological crisis, especially to the plight of nonhumans; and it constitutes a digression."[11] I've more or less

9 Aldo Leopold often wrote "land community" or "community" to mean the scientific word "ecosystem." I like that since ecosystem and other scientific words can often seem cold and abstract whereas something like community seems lived in. However, I like the word "neighborhood" even more (it sounds cozier than community), so I'll call ecosystems "wild neighborhoods."

10 George Sessions, "Political Correctness, Ecological Realities and the Future of the Ecology Movement," *The Trumpeter,* Fall 1995, 191.

11 Eileen Crist, "Limits-to-Growth and the Biodiversity Crisis," *Wild Earth,* Spring 2003, 63.

understood this for a long while, but it wasn't until I read Crist's article that the heft of it smacked me over the head with a two-by-four. After reading her article, I shifted how I talk and write about population. This book is the upshot.

Crist writes:

> *The core issue is not the quandary of real-world limits but* what kind *of real world we desire to live in. I submit two points: (1) the biodiversity crisis is essentially sidestepped by the limits-to-growth framework; and (2) what is invidious about the cornucopian view is not that it is (necessarily) wrong-headed, but the dismal reality it envisions and would make of Earth.... It is critical to focus on what is presently dead certain: that overproduction and overpopulation have been driving the dismantling of complex ecosystems and native life, and leaving in their widening wake constructed environments, simplified ecologies, and lost life forms.*[12]

She asks something hard: "Does the framework of 'breaching limits' address the momentous event of the biodiversity crisis? Arguably, it does not. It is perfectly possible that a mass extinction of 50%, 60%, or more of the Earth's species would not be pragmatically catastrophic for human beings."[13]

One needs only to look at some of the most heavily settled and domesticated lands, such as the British Isles and northwestern Europe, to see how life can be fat and full for Man with few wildeors and little or no land with its native vegetation. Some such lands may be productive for Man even after many years.

The dread is that the addled androids following the sci-fi utopianism of pro-growth seer Julian Simon and other cornucopians could hatch a fully Manmade Earth affording life to billions of Men or Man-computer monsters. A nightmare world of deafening mechanical hum where no bird sings and where every wild thing has withered by the petrochemical lake.

12 Crist, "Limits-to-Growth," 63.

13 Crist, "Limits-to-Growth," 64.

Conservation biologist Michael Soulé warned of a like dystopia in 1996 when he wrote, "In summary, it is technically possible to maintain ecological processes, including a high level of economically beneficial productivity, by replacing the hundreds of native plants, invertebrates and vertebrates with about 15 or 20 introduced, weedy species." He ended with, "WARNING! Be suspicious of 'ecologists' who are pitching ecological services (for people) and who speak of 'redundant' species or 'hyperdiversity.'"[14]

Another trap of making overmuch of our struggle to feed ourselves or keep the cheap oil flowing is that it will lend oomph to those who want more dams for irrigation and more oil wells wherever a drop can be slurped from Earth. Over the winter of 2005-2006, polls showed a frightening shift in public opinion for drilling in the Arctic National Wildlife Refuge. It seems that whenever energy prices go up, public backing for keeping land wild goes down. Upheaval over shortages plays right into the hands of those who want no hindrances on where they can go to grub out whatever is worth a buck, no laws calling for careful and trustworthy work, every kind of handout to help them rake in bucks from the commonwealth, and more. We might even ask if it behooves conservationists to talk about "peak oil" and like shortages. Too much talk about resource shortages might make it harder to set aside new Wilderness Areas.

Leaders of mainstream conservation and environmental groups have been shortsighted in not acknowledging that whenever the needs of Man come up against the needs of wildlife, it is wildlife that loses. In the world or a nation with a growing population, then, wildlife will lose over the long haul.

Even environmentalists who tout "ecosystem services," and how alternative energy and organic farming can power and feed our teeming throng may be at worst milder kinds of the Simonized mad

14 Michael E. Soulé, "Are Ecosystem Processes Enough?" *Wild Earth*, Spring 1996, 60.

technologists.[15] Crist writes, "To contend that we need to sustain 'natural capital' for human well-being and survival is not an ecological argument, and bears no necessary connection to the conservation mission." She slaps lovers of wild things awake, I hope, with, "The crucial question, then, is not whether a colonized world is viable but rather: Who (besides Simon and company) wants to live in such a world?" She holds that we need "to be as clear and precise as possible about the consequences of the humanized order under construction: in this emerging reality it is not our survival and well-being that are primarily on the line, but *everybody else's*."[16]

The outcomes of Man's growth yesterday, today, and tomorrow are scalped wildlands, endangered and extinct wildlife, and sweeping climatic upset. These awful upshots are what lovers of wild things should bring up when we talk about growth. Let the resourcists talk about ecosystem services; we lovers of wild things need to talk about the inborn worth of wild things and how it is a sin for Man to shove them off into the pit of extinction.

Our mad dash to grow more food and to suck out oil and gas in faraway spots is what has led to the landscalping that drives the landslide of extinction. At the 2005 meeting of the American Geophysical Union in San Francisco, researchers from the University of Wisconsin-Madison showed that since 1700, "the amount of cultivated land on the planet has increased from 7 to 40 percent."[17] In the last 300 years, then, one-third of Earth's wildlands have been tamed and chopped up into crop fields. One-third of Earth's land has had wild trees, shrubs, grasses, and other worts torn out and crops planted in their stead.

15 I am strongly behind organic farming and also back nonindustrial "alternative energy" when it is not harmful to wild things. I'm an advisor to the Wild Farm Alliance, grow my own organic tomatoes and fruit, and buy organic greens and other worts from a "community supported farm." I own and live in a passive solar house. But we shouldn't fog our heads with dreams that there are Earth-friendly ways to get seven billion and more of us what we want or even truly need.

16 Crist, "Limits-to-Growth," 65.

17 *The Guardian*, San Francisco, December 7, 2005.

Conservation biologist Reed Noss has carefully and thoroughly tallied the loss of sundry ecosystems in the United States. There are once-sprawling wild neighborhoods such as Tallgrass Prairie, Southeastern Canebrakes, and Longleaf Pine Forests that hardly exist anymore.[18] All this has happened since Benjamin Franklin was born. Most of it has happened since Abraham Lincoln was born (1809). Throughout the earlier 10,000 years of farming, only seven percent, or one out of every fourteen acres, of landed Earth was tamed by our crops. Now 40 percent or two out of every five acres is. No wonder thousands of species have been lost and the end looms for many thousands more. Lester Brown, in his wakeup! book on the hunger ahead, *Outgrowing The Earth,* says that there is only one country that can make greatly more farmland by ripping up wilderness. And what country is that?

Brazil.

Goodbye Amazon. Goodbye Cerrado. Goodbye to most of the biggest tropical wilderness left on Earth. Goodbye to one of the most species-rich tangled banks on Earth.

Hello miles and miles and miles of new soybean fields.[19] It is the hungry billions spurted out by the baby flood that will eat the wild things of Brazil.

In Chapter 4, I'll show how the Man swarm and further growth drives many of the ways we murder other Earthlings. First, let's look at the overall question of carrying capacity.

---

18 Reed F. Noss, Edward T. LaRoe III, and J. Michael Scott, *Endangered Ecosystems of the United States: A Preliminary Assessment of Loss and Degradation,* Biological Report 28 (National Biological Service, U.S. Department of the Interior, Washington, D.C., February 1995); Reed F. Noss and Robert L. Peters, *Endangered Ecosystems: A Status Report on America's Vanishing Habitat and Wildlife* (Defenders of Wildlife, Washington, D.C., December 1995).

19 Lester R. Brown, *Outgrowing The Earth* (W.W. Norton & Co., New York, 2004), 156-176.

Chapter 3

Carrying Capacity—and the Upright Ape

The cumulative biotic potential of the human species exceeds the carrying capacity of its habitat.

—William R. Catton, Jr.

In 1944, a handful of reindeer were set loose on St. Matthew Island in the Bering Sea off Alaska. Although this 128-square-mile island had good habitat, neither reindeer nor their kin caribou had been there earlier.[1] Also missing were hunters of the reindeer—gray wolves. From the first twenty-nine animals, the population boomed to six thousand in nineteen years. The herd crashed to only forty-two reindeer three years later.[2]

Most of us can listen to this tale and nod our heads. Of course. The reindeer overpopulated their home and ate up their island. Nonetheless, most folks shy away from shifting this tale to Man, thanks to the widespread myth of *human exceptionalism*: Man is a kind alone.

1 At least not for thousands of years since it had been a high spot on the Bering Land Bridge during the Ice Age.

2 William R. Catton Jr., *Overshoot: The Ecological Basis of Revolutionary Change* (University of Illinois Press, Urbana, 1982), 216-217.

A nonesuch. We are not thralls to biology, like wildeors (animals). At heart, this belief bolsters all cornucopians, witless though it is.

There is, however, an even more unsettling saga of a mammal overshooting carrying capacity on an island. This time the wight walked on two legs. Henderson Island is one of the most out-of-the-way dots in the South Pacific. A European ship first stumbled upon it in 1606. No one lived there then. It seemed that no one had ever lived there. Henderson's lack of Man settlement had to be rethought in the 1980s when bird paleontologists Storrs Olson and David Steadman found the bones of three extinct species of pigeons and three extinct species of seabirds on the island. Only after they dug up the bones did they find Polynesian archaeological sites. Men *had lived* on Henderson, hunted native birds to extinction, and then died out themselves or left. Jared Diamond writes, "Given the widespread evidence for overexploitation of wild animals by early Polynesians, not only Henderson but the other mystery islands as well may represent the graveyards of human populations that ruined their own resource base."[3] I find it sadder by far, however, that the Henderson Island folks scuttled the island's ecosystem and brought about the extinction of at least six kinds of birds.

The nightmare we are up against today is whether we can keep from flipping Earth into Henderson Island. Unless we can cut back our own breeding, Henderson may be our tomorrow. And we will do to the wildlife of Earth what the Polynesians did to the wildlife of Henderson.

Before I go on, let me throw out a warning about "carrying capacity." Biologists know what it means for other Earthlings. But what about carrying capacity for Man? The wisest of the Olympians was "gray-eyed" Athena. I don't know if Eileen Crist has gray eyes, but she makes me think of Athena when she writes, "I find the very idea of 'human carrying capacity' pernicious. In most of the literature I've

3 Jared Diamond, *The Third Chimpanzee: The Evolution and Future of the Human Animal* (HarperCollins, New York, 1992), 324-325.

read raising the question of 'what human carrying capacity is' seems to be a veiled way of asking: How many people can sustainably use, exploit, degrade, or destroy (portions of) the biosphere without risking collapse for human beings or human civilization?"[4] So, beware when you otherwise read of carrying capacity for Mankind. In this chapter (and book), however, carrying capacity cares for all Earthlings.

Dreary Parson Malthus

Two hundred years ago, an early English economist named Thomas Malthus wrote, "Population, when unchecked, increases in a geometrical ratio. Subsistence increases only in an arithmetical ratio."

4 Eileen Crist, letter to author, 2010.

Box 3.1. Malthus

Two hundred years ago, Parson Robert Thomas Malthus wrote, "Population, when unchecked, increases in a geometrical ratio. Subsistence increases only in an arithmetical ratio." In his essential book, *Overshoot*, population expert William Catton crafted an ecological explanation of what Malthus meant:

> *Throughout the essay Malthus was referring to human population, and by subsistence he meant food.... these conceptions were unduly narrow. But the really basic Malthusian principle is so important that it needs to be restated in the more accurate vocabulary of modern ecology. It states a relationship of inequality between two variables:* ***The cumulative biotic potential of the human species exceeds the carrying capacity of its habitat.***

Simple. There are limits. We can overshoot them. This is a basic biological fact.

William R. Catton Jr., *Overshoot: The Ecological Basis of Revolutionary Change* (University of Illinois Press, Urbana, 1982), 126.

But what does this mean ecologically? William Catton, Jr., author of *Overshoot*, which I think is the best book on population, writes:

> *Throughout the essay Malthus was referring to* human *population, and by subsistence he meant food.... these conceptions were unduly narrow. But the really basic Malthusian principle is so important that it needs to be restated in the more accurate vocabulary of modern ecology. It states a relationship of inequality between two variables:* ***The cumulative biotic potential of the human species exceeds the carrying capacity of its habitat.***

So. There are limits. We can overshoot them. This is a bedrock biological truth.

It is the way things are—like gravity.

Catton tells us that this breakthrough from Malthus led Charles Darwin to see natural selection as a key tool in evolution. Restated in the ecological language of today, what Darwin spun out of Malthus was:

> *The cumulative biotic potential of* any *species exceeds the carrying capacity of its habitat.*

So, within a lifekind, each will struggle with each for short goods. Some will be better than others in that scrap. The more fit ones will more often live to breed and hand on their winning genes; the less fit ones will often die before they breed, or will rear fewer offspring.[5] One hundred and fifty years ago, two English naturalists half a world away from each other—Charles Darwin in England and Alfred Russel Wallace in the Dutch East Indies—grasped that this was the main way one kind of being evolved into another or into many: *natural selection.*

Archaeologist Stephen LeBlanc brings this core biological thought to bear for understanding the prehistory and history of Man

5 Catton, *Overshoot,* 126-7. In his sweeping review of evolution, the great biologist Ernst Mayr also showed how Darwin drew on Malthus. Ernst Mayr, *What Evolution Is* (Basic Books, New York, 2001), 116. I think *What Evolution Is* is the best book on evolution.

in his myth-smashing book *Constant Battles*. Whether in bands or empires we have fought with our neighbors as far back as our kind goes. The saga plays out like this: population grows; carrying capacity is overshot; hunger and starvation step in; you fight your neighbors for what they have; such fighting most of the time cuts population; and the game begins anew. Overpopulation, then, has always been a Grendel in nearby shadows. I'll look at this unending tussle more in Chapter 10.

Age of Exuberance

William Catton writes,

> *The past four centuries of magnificent progress were made possible by two non-repeatable achievements: (a) discovery of a second hemisphere, and (b) development of ways to exploit the planet's energy savings deposits, the fossil fuels. The resulting opportunities for economic and demographic exuberance convinced people that it was natural for the future to be better than the past.*[6]

Carl Sauer, America's leading geographer at the time, had seen much the same during the Dust Bowl years when he wrote in 1938, "Our ideology is that of an indefinitely expanding universe, for we are the children of frontiersmen....We have not yet learned the difference between yield and loot."[7]

We opened an *Age of Exuberance* five hundred years ago with Columbus's westward sailings. Before that, Europe was crowded and raw goods were short. There were only twenty-four acres of land for each European. With the finding and exploitation of the New World, however, there were now 120 acres of land per person "available in the expanded European habitat." This overthrew the way Europeans had seen the world. As Catton says, "The new premise of limitlessness

6 Catton, *Overshoot,* 5-6.

7 Carl O. Sauer, "Theme of Plant and Animal Destruction in Economic History," *Journal of Farm Economics 20* (1938), 765-775, reprinted in Shepard and McKinley, editors, *Environ/Mental: Essays on the Planet as Home* (Houghton Mifflin, Boston, 1971), 59-60.

spawned new beliefs, new human relationships, and new behavior."[8] English settlers in North America in the 1600s were so overawed by the wealth of the new land that they hatched the Myth of Superabundance—the mainspring for the westward movement and the careless, carefree, uncaring scalping of the land for the next three hundred-some years.[9]

However, the New World was not empty of Men when Europeans "discovered" it. Nor were Australia and New Zealand. Sundry bands, tribes, chiefdoms, and kingdoms already dwelt in these unfathomably big landscapes, though most often not thickly. Europe took over these lands and brought down or killed the folks already there (with great help from illnesses brought by Europeans, for which earlier folk of the Americas, Oceania, Australia, and New Zealand had no immunity[10]). *Takeover* did not begin in 1500, though. As I wrote in *Rewilding North America*, we *Homo sapiens* have been taking over lands for at least 40,000 years from other species of hominins.[11] Furthermore, in that same 40,000 years, bands of *Homo sapiens* have been taking over lands from other bands of *Homo sapiens*, first in Africa and Eurasia, and then in Australia, the Americas, Oceania, and New Zealand. For the last 10,000 years, farmers have been taking over land ever more fully from hunter-gatherers and other farmers. But never before had a literate civilization taken over a whole new world as Europeans did with the Americas.[12]

8 Catton, *Overshoot*, 24.

9 I write about this further in my upcoming book *Conservation vs. Conservation.*

10 William H. McNeill, *Plagues and Peoples* (Anchor Press/Doubleday, New York, 1976). In this book, McNeill upends world history to show how greatly diseases have driven the saga of world civilization. It is a book that must be read if one is to be historically literate.

11 Foreman, *Rewilding North America* (Island Press, Washington, D.C., 2004). These other hominin species were *Homo neanderthalensis, Homo erectus, and Homo floresiensis*, and maybe others.

12 Catton, *Overshoot*, 26-28.

About two hundred years ago, writes Catton, "Carrying capacity was tremendously (but temporarily) augmented by a quite different method; takeover gave way to drawdown." An agrarian economy became an industrial economy through the exploitation of fossil fuels—the buried leavings of photosynthesis from hundreds of millions of years ago. Coal, oil, and natural gas made agricultural yield boom, through fertilizers and pesticides made from them and machinery fueled by them (which also freed up one-quarter to one-third of all cropland from growing feed for draft horses and oxen).

On the heels of the fossil-fuel breakthrough came another—death control. Scientific medicine, with the germ theory leading to curbing infection, public health work, and then to antibiotics and vaccinations, deeply cut baby and childbirth deaths, and the human population grew even faster.[13] More folks began to live longer thanks to scientific medicine. Longer lives boost how many folks are alive at one time, though this is not often acknowledged as one of the things goosing growth. Moreover, the Earth's disease webs linked up, leaving few clusters new to the big killers—thus the old ills were not as deadly as they once had been.

GHOST ACREAGE

Cornucopians love to hold up tiny Holland as a crowded land that is healthy and wealthy. If Holland can do it, then it can be done anywhere—even in the neediest, hungriest lands. But such Pollyannas are overlooking takeover and drawdown. Georg Borgstrom, Michigan State University food scientist and author of the 1965 *The Hungry Planet,* saw through this make-believe with his insight of *Ghost Acreage.* Drawing from Borgstrom, Catton writes, "The food required by such a nation's population comes only partly from the harvest of 'visible acreage'—farm and pasture land within the nation's borders. A very

13 Catton, *Overshoot,* 28-30. See also J. R. McNeill and William McNeill, *The Human Web: A Bird's-Eye View Of World History* (W.W. Norton & Company, New York, 2003).

substantial fraction comes from net imports of food. Not all the imports come from other countries; some are obtained from the sea. Borgstrom therefore subdivided 'ghost acreage' into two components, 'trade acreage' and 'fish acreage.'" In 1965 Great Britain was drawing 48 percent of its food from trade acreage and 6.5 percent of its food from fish acreage.[14] Great Britain's ghost acreage is even more today.

Besides ghost acreage, today's agriculture banks on *Fossil Acreage*—"the number of additional acres of farmland that would have been needed to grow organic fuels with equivalent energy content."[15] Since the steam engine began to swap muscles for coal two hundred years ago, "per capita energy use in the United States reached a level equivalent to eighty or so ghost slaves for each citizen." The world average is "about ten ghost slaves per person."[16] When fossil fuels run out, dare we ask how many ghost slaves per person we'll have to give up?

Also bear in mind that Holland is a thoroughly tamed landscape. There is no wilderness, no wildwood, no wolves, bears, or lynx. It is humanized to the utmost.

Catton warns,

> *The human species, through technological progress, had made itself more than 90 percent dependent on phantom carrying capacity.... Phantom carrying capacity means either the illusory or the extremely precarious capacity of an environment to support a given life form or a given way of living. It can be quantitatively expressed as that portion of a population that cannot be permanently supported when temporarily available resources become unavailable.*[17]

Catton wrote the above when there were five billion humans; 90 percent of the population fed thanks to phantom carrying capacity then would have been 4.5 billion, leaving only 500 million that can be fed over time.

14 Catton, *Overshoot,* 38-39.

15 Catton, *Overshoot,* 41.

16 Catton, *Overshoot,* 43.

17 Catton, *Overshoot,* 44-45.

The McNeills write, "The rice, wheat, and potatoes that feed the world's population stem from oil as much as from soil, water, and photosynthesis."[18] We are also drawing down as farmers on the North American Great Plains and elsewhere mine fossil water from Ice Age groundwater and erode away soils built over tens of thousands of years (soil mining). Such water and soil will not come again until after another Ice Age.[19]

Our befuddlement over the grounds for our good times is shown by our use of the word "production" for the drawing down of ghost acreage. Pumping up oil or strip-mining coal is not production at all; it is taking or extraction.[20] You cannot "produce" a nonrenewable resource. You can only extract it and use it; then it is gone. Poof! Except for its waste. And by extracting and using fossil fuels, we do produce a heck of a lot of waste, waste that is nasty and deadly to a wide sweep of Earthlings, even us, waste that is so great that it is shifting the makeup of the atmosphere throwing the climate out of kilter and making the oceans acidic.

Catton writes, "*Homo sapiens* mistook the rate of withdrawal of savings deposits for a rise in income."[21] However, this high-flying life built on drawdown instead of true production looses a heady optimism. Catton writes, "Ecologically speaking, the American dream expressed in human terms an exuberance that *characteristically* follows invasion of a new habitat by *any* species that happens to have the traits required for prompt and effective adaptation to it."[22]

Fleeting overbliss can be healthy and is likely natural after winning in love, war, or the hunt, but endless bliss is madness. Call it irrational exuberance.

18 McNeill and McNeill, *The Human Web,* 285.

19 This would be after another hundred thousand years but for how we are upsetting "normal" climate cycles. Goodness only knows how long it will be before another Ice Age comes and goes now.

20 Catton, *Overshoot,* 49-51.

21 Catton, *Overshoot,* 167.

22 Catton, *Overshoot,* 80.

What sets the carrying capacity of a landscape? The resource that will run out the soonest sets carrying capacity (this is known as Liebig's "law of the minimum"). If iron, timber, clean air, land, and oil are overflowing but a country runs out of water, it has overshot carrying capacity.[23] The resource that seems to have run out first for industrial Man is the wherewithal of the atmosphere and the oceans to hold harmlessly our wastes of carbon dioxide, methane, and other greenhouse gases. We haven't thought of such waste "sequestration" and other "ecosystem services" as resources or raw goods like coal and timber before. We are about to learn quickly.

This way of looking at carrying capacity thinks only of Man, as Eileen Crist warns. The true yardstick of our carrying capacity should be what we do to wild things, and by this I do not mean only ecosystem services, but the health and soundness of other Earthlings and their self-willed neighborhoods. A landscape without big wilderness and without room for native wildlife, big flesh-eaters foremost, is one in which humans have overshot carrying capacity. By this yardstick, humans overshot carrying capacity in much of the world long ago. Likewise, the faddish whim of *sustainability* looks only at Man's needs. A society is not truly sustainable if it brings on extinction of other Earthlings or if it tames all its lands and waters, leaving nothing with its own will. It is unlikely that any Man-bunch has been sustainable for long even for its own needs alone. Truthfully defining "sustainability" and then reckoning what we must do to gain it is the great challenge of all time for Man. Thus far, we have not even been willing to truthfully think about how wide it sweeps. The newer yardstick of ecological footprints bears the same weakness as do carrying capacity and sustainability. A key chore for conservation is to craft new ways of reckoning such yardsticks that also weigh the self-willed needs of other Earthlings and their wild neighborhoods along with free-flowing evolution.

23 Catton, *Overshoot,* 158-159.

Detritovores and NPP

In an ecosystem, there are many ways to make a living. A balsam fir photosynthesizes energy from sunlight and carbon dioxide (*photosynthesizer*). A moose eats the fir (*herbivore*). Wolves eat the moose (*carnivore*). Another path is that of a *detritovore*. Look at fall leaves washing into a shallow pond. When warm weather comes back, algae bloom lustily with the not-for-long wealth of the leafy food. However, the leaf-brought nutrients then drop and a "massive die-off of these innocently incautious and exuberant organisms" happens, writes Catton. Detritovore ecosystems often "bloom" and "crash." What we don't want to acknowledge is that today's civilization has become a detritovore ecosystem with our drawdown of fossil energy.[24]

Box 3.2. Overshoot

carrying capacity: maximum permanently supportable load

corucopian myth: euphoric belief in limitless resources

drawdown: stealing resources from the future

cargoism: delusion that technology with always save us from

overshoot: growth beyond an area's capacity, leading to

crash: die-off

From William R. Catton, Jr., *Overshoot* (University of Illinois Press, Urbana, 1982), cover

We Men lord over Earth. How much we hold sway is shown by the ecological yardstick of net primary production (NPP), which is, "All the solar energy annually captured worldwide by photosynthesizers and not used by them to run their own lives," Paul and Anne Ehrlich write. NPP is what makes biomass. Ecologist Stuart Pimm, who knows and understands as much about extinction as does anyone, writes,

24 Catton, *Overshoot,* 168-171.

"Biomass is how much living stuff the planet has. Production is how much new stuff grows each year—the products of photosynthesis."[25] In 1986, Man was taking in one way or another some 40 percent of the terrestrial NPP of our world, or 25 percent when ocean NPP was brought in.[26] Pimm takes 105 pages in his sweeping 2001 book, *The World According to Pimm,* to carefully re-reckon that we are gobbling up 42 percent of terrestrial NPP. He then shows that we are also taking "a quarter to a third of the oceans' production."[27] Catton warns, "Such total exploitation of an ecosystem by one dominant species has seldom happened, except among species which bloom and crash.... Having become a species of superdetritovores, mankind [is] destined not merely for succession, but for crash."[28] We are what Reg Morrison, author of *The Spirit in the Gene,* calls a plague species.[29] The lot of a plague species is our lot—unless we can do what we have never done before and hold ourselves back.

Too bad for Man, though. As we'll find in Chapter 5, cornucopians who hold sway in nearly all beliefs and lands today have a deep dislike for holding back in any way. It would be hard enough to turn away from our childish greed if we all acknowledged that carrying capacity holds for our kind, too. But with the lords of all lands unwilling to even brook the thought of carrying capacity for Man, it is nigh on to hopeless that we will ever bridle ourselves.

I hope you get two things out of this chapter. One is that by overshooting carrying capacity, we are setting ourselves up for crash. This is the message of Catton's book *Overshoot.* It is not an airy-fairy

---

25 Stuart L. Pimm, *The World According to Pimm: a scientist audits the Earth* (McGraw-Hill, New York, 2001), 10.

26 Paul R. Ehrlich and Anne H. Ehrlich, *The Population Explosion* (Simon and Schuster, New York, 1990), 36-37. (163).

27 Pimm, *The World According to Pimm.* See also Foreman, *Rewilding North America,* 56-59.

28 Catton, *Overshoot,* 172-173.

29 Reg Morrison, *The Spirit In The Gene: Humanity's Proud Illusion and the Laws of Nature* (Cornell University Press, Ithaca, New York, 1999).

Box 3.3. Biomass and NPP According to Pimm

To better understand Net Primary Production (NPP), also called *production* by ecologists, we need to understand *Biomass*. Stuart Pimm, whose book *The World According to Pimm* is the foremost guide to our overall impact on Earth, writes, "*Biomass* is how much living stuff the planet has. *Production* is how much new stuff grows each year—the products of photosynthesis." Pimm further writes "They have the same relation to one another as the amount of money in the bank and the annual interest it generates."

Earth's land varies greatly in how productive it is. An acre of Tropical Rainforest or Tallgrass Prairie produces more biomass than does an acre of desert. Botanists have carefully worked out the many kinds of plant communities on Earth and calculated the average yearly production from each. By mapping the whole acreage of each kind of plant community and then multiplying that by its yearly production per hectare and then adding the totals for all plant communities together, ecologists find that the whole of Earth's land produces "about 130 billion tons of biomass per year (give or take a few tens of billions)." So, when we talk about Man using or taking 42 percent of terrestrial NPP, it is 42 percent of about 130 billion tons of biomass—or about 60 billion tons: "two-fifths of the land's production." Pimm goes into detail, but readable and understandable detail, to get to this figure. Then he does the same for ocean NPP and freshwater.

Stuart L. Pimm, *The World According to Pimm: a scientist audits the Earth* (McGraw-Hill, NY, 2001), 10, 23, 105.

fantasy. It has happened to a sweep of cultures throughout the last ten thousand years. Two is that we must redefine carrying capacity, ecological footprints, and sustainability to include all Earthlings in their full health and heartiness. Any sustainability that does not do so is a wicked, selfish, deadly, false sustainability.

Chapter 4

How the Man Swarm Eats Earth

One of the penalties of an ecological education is that one lives alone in a world of wounds.[1]

—Aldo Leopold

Except for giant meteorite strikes or other such catastrophes, Earth has never experienced anything like the contemporary human juggernaut. We are in a bottleneck of overpopulation and wasteful consumption that could push half of Earth's species to extinction in this century.[2]

—E. O. Wilson

For fifty thousand years, we have been romping and stomping over the wildworld for need, greed, and feckless glee. As we grow, spread, and boost our might with technology, our romping and stomping slices

1 Luna B. Leopold, ed., *Round River: From the Journals of Aldo Leopold* (Oxford University Press, New York, 1953), 165.

2 E. O. Wilson, "Acting now to save life on Earth," *Seattle Post-Intelligencer,* April 22, 2007. Adapted from his book, *The Creation.*

deeper, deadlier, and with more wounds everywhere on land, sea, and in the air.

There are many ways in which we wound wild Earth and kill wild things. But behind them all is Man swarm—our population boom. Even in the short run, we cannot keep wilderness and wildlife without stopping Man's growth. Furthermore, it is nothing less than a lie we tell ourselves that we can stop climatic weirdness without capping and then lowering how many we are on Earth. The Center for Biological Diversity says flatly, "Today, overpopulation is at the root of virtually all threats to species around the globe."[3]

As I wrote in Chapter 2, we can sort into five stacks the kinds of woe the Man swarm or PAT (Population x Affluence x Technology) brings:

1. Landscalping
2. Resource depletion
3. Starvation
4. Social, political upheaval
5. Ecological/Evolutionary wounds

Think of me as a French pig snuffling for truffles. My woods for this week have been a stash of books and anthologies dealing in some way or other with overpopulation. The truffles for which I snuffle are words about the harm too many people do to wild things. I am an unhappy pig. I've found darn few truffles. I am hungry.

I have shoved up a bunch of papers out of the duff with my snout. In the 1950s and 1960s, much ink was spread as the threat of human population growth was prodded, weighed, and twirled this way and that. Many writers were biologists. But even they were looking at how Men would be harmed by too many of their fellows, not at what an Earth overflowing with Men would do to wilderness and wildeors.

3 "Owning Up to Overpopulation," *Endangered Earth,* Fall 2009, Center for Biological Diversity.

(Even biologists Ehrlich and Hardin seldom looked at the plight of worts and deors.) Overall, those who get drawn into the headache of dealing with population growth have looked at the first four stacks. We lovers of wild things, however, worry more about how the flood of Man drowns other Earthlings. As I wrote in Chapter 2, I follow Eileen Crist, who writes that population-freeze and resource-depletion workers have made a key mistake by mostly looking at the first four. She shows that we cannot say when we will run out of things such as oil or when killing hunger will strike hundreds of millions of *Homo sapiens* at once. We cannot say when the outcomes of greenhouse gases become unbearable. Indeed, undertaking such soothsaying has hurt our believability. On the other hand, we can rightly and strikingly show how the spread and growth of Man has harmed wild things and wild Earth as a whole. We can show how it is doing so right now. One who early on saw the threat of overpopulation to wild things was psychologist John Calhoun, writing in 1966, "If this process of fragmentation continues while the human population increases to three or four times its present numbers all surviving forms of nondomesticated life will be restricted to small completely isolated cells. With the exception of bats, and birds and a very few very mobile insects... evolution will have come to a halt for most terrestrial organisms."[4]

The five stacks of woe

To be sure, the other four outcomes of growth also hurt wild things. Landscalping, the everyday hammer of civilization crash, wipes out the wild homes and neighborhoods of wildeors, wrecks watersheds and thereby fouls streams and rivers, silts in lakes and ocean estuaries, and often "flips" ecosystems into a withered and shriveled being.

4 John B. Calhoun, "Psycho-Ecological Aspects of Population," Unit for Research on Behavioral Systems National Institute of Mental Health, URBSDOC No. 62, rev. (1966), reprinted in *Environ/Mental,* 129.

Draining raw goods until there is little left leads to scrambles to grub out whatever is left in still-wild places and then to rip it out in hasty, careless ways. When gasoline prices shot up in the United States in 2008, polls showed growing backing for drilling offshore and in the Arctic National Wildlife Refuge. Chants of "Drill, baby, drill," in the 2008 presidential campaign were hotheaded marks of feared resource scantiness. Wild things then pay with the blowout of BP's deep-ocean well in the Gulf of Mexico.

Food shortages are the worst dearth for Man. Deep, lasting hunger leads folks to eat anything they can find—even each other.[5] Hungry women, children, and men become refugees crowding into wherever they think they might find food and thereby trample and ransack healthier lands. In a world of tabloid-television news, heartbreaking tales of starving mothers and children lead to calls to jump up food-growing elsewhere, which then leads to the stripping and withering of wildlands not good for long-time cropping. More irrigation dams throughout the world will be another upshot of starvation brought on not by too little food but by too many mouths.

Lester Brown sees water shortages as one of the worst things over the hill. Some 70 percent of the world's freshwater now goes into irrigating crops. Ground water is being sucked out by irrigation wells and is dropping ever lower, so wells have to be bored deeper.[6] When this happens, springs dry up. Rivers and streams run to cracked mud and blowing dust. Without trusty old watering holes, wildlife of all kinds are shoved to the edge, have to leave, or die. Withered, flyblown carcasses of great wildeors are the upshot of our overuse of water. The freshwater upheaval rooted in the Man swarm is not only a threat to Man, it is even more of a threat to thousands of kinds of other Earthlings. Lester

5 Christy G. Turner II and Jacqueline A. Turner, *Man Corn: Cannibalism and Violence in the Prehistoric American Southwest* (University of Utah Press, Salt Lake City, 1999).

6 Lester Brown, "Could Food Shortages Bring Down Civilization?" *Scientific American,* April 22, 2009.

Brown brings up a spooky statistic: "175 million Indians consume grain produced with water from irrigation wells that will soon be exhausted."[7] What will those 175 million (or, perhaps, 275 million, given India's ongoing growth) do when the water and the grain run out? What will they do to the land and to wildlife living nearby? Where will they go? How much weight will there be on the Indian government to "open" land now in National Parks and other tiger havens?

Where millions on the edge have overshot carrying capacity and now are starving, and food aid is thoughtlessly rushed in, we can be sure of one thing. When deadly hunger hits that land again in twenty years, there will be twice as many moaning, empty bellies as before, making more wretchedness and hunger down the trail, unless that aid comes with hardnosed, unyielding birth-control goals. Moreover, without an end to population growth in that weeping land, the homes of what wildeors are left will have been ransacked.

Besides starvation, social breakdown brought on by too many hopeless young men and boys could lead to hordes doing their utmost to take over lands that are wealthier but not so crowded. Food/energy/hope-starved countries will make war on one another; wild things are often the great losers in war. Some Hutus in Rwanda truthfully acknowledged that overcrowding was behind their slaughter of Tutsis; they wanted their land, for themselves and their children. Look for much more of this tribal killing within "nations" as everything gets tighter thanks to growth.

So, most of the unhappy outcomes from overpopulation and overshooting carrying capacity that harm our kind also wound wildeors and wildlands of all kinds. Now let's target the way wild Earth is straightaway wounded by too many Men.

---

7 Brown, "Food Shortages." See also Lester R. Brown, *Plan B 3.0: Mobilizing to Save Civilization* (W.W. Norton & Co., New York, 2008); available from www.earthpolicy.org/Books/PB3/index.htm.

Overpopulation and Ecological Wounds

In *Rewilding North America,* I dealt out the ways we harm the wildworld into Seven Ecological Wounds: direct killing, habitat wrecking and upheaval, habitat fragmentation, exotic species invasion, crushing and upsetting ecological and evolutionary processes, biocide pollution, and greenhouse gas pollution. These wounds pile up and work together. (See Table 4.1.)

Table 4.1. The Seven Ecological Wounds

Wound 1: Overkill

For at least 40,000 years, since *Homo sapiens* spread out of Africa, Man has been killing all kinds of wildlife—foremost big wildeors, keystone rodents, birds, tortoises—driving some over the edge of extinction and many others to the brink by means of overhunting, subsistence hunting, fur trapping, fishing, sea birding, whaling, market hunting, trophy hunting, hunting for "medicinal" bones and organs, hunting for feathers and other adornments, collecting, trapping, predator and "pest" control, domestication, and so on.

Wound 2: Scalping and Taming Wilderness

For thousands of years, Man has scalped and tamed wilderness all over the world on land and sea by means of agricultural clearing, logging, grazing by domestic livestock, burning, killing keystone species, wetlands draining, mining, urbanization, suburban and exurban sprawl, sea-bottom trawling, dams, water diversions, groundwater pumping, channelization, oil and gas development, and many other ways.

Wound 3: Fragmentation of Wildlife Neighborhoods

Mostly since the rise of the first empires, Man has broken up wildlife habitat and blocked migration paths by means of all the ways listed for wilderness wrecking above, and by road and highway building, canal digging, pipelines, power lines, off-road vehicle play, and so on.

Wound 4: Upsetting and Weakening Ecological and Evolutionary Processes

For at least 40,000 years, Man has upset and weakened essential ecological and evolutionary processes—foremost wildfire, predation, ecosystem "engineering" by keystone herbivores, hydrological cycles of flooding and low flow, and pollination—by means of burning, wildfire control, hunting of keystone species, irrigation and dam building, and in many other ways.

Wound 5: Spread of Exotic Species and Diseases

Since the beginning of long-distance trading, and likely before, Man has both willfully and unwittingly carried many kinds of vertebrate and invertebrate animals, plants, wildlife and plant diseases, and disease vectors out of where they had evolved into new habitats. There, some grow readily in disturbed spots cleared of native vegetation and are without natural controls and thus can outcompete native species.

Wound 6: Biocide Poisoning of Land, Air, Water, and Wildlife

Farms, feedlots, sewers, outhouses, mines, oil and gas drilling on land and sea, smelters, factories, foundries, metal shops, dumps, recycling shops, oil refineries, power plants, automobiles, airplanes, pipelines, oil tankers, cities, broadcasting of agricultural and public-health biocides, and other works of Man have poisoned Earth and all living things with heavy metals, toxic wastes, petroleum waste, chemicals, biological wastes, radioactivity, and other banes.

Wound 7: Global "Weirding" or Climate Change and Ocean Acidification

Since the beginning of the industrial era, air pollution from cars, power plants, smelters, and domestic livestock; wrecking of natural carbon dioxide sinks by logging and other landscalping; and other works of Man have led to a rise of greenhouse gases (carbon dioxide, methane, soot, etc.) in the atmosphere that play hob with climate, and in the oceans that lead to acidification, which is deadly to corals and other kinds of life.

Adapted from *Rewilding North America*. See Dave Foreman, *Rewilding North America* (Island Press, Washington, DC, 2004) for a much fuller rundown on each of these wounds. What is in the text of this chapter is a shallow brush, hued with how Man's population growth drives the wounding.

We've been looking at I=PAT where Impact comes from Population times Affluence (consumption) times Technology. Taken shallowly, I=PAT lumps together the deeds of all kinds of folks. This is how we get tales such as one American doing thirty-five times the harm of one Bangladeshi. What happens on the ground is more tangled than this quick, shallow lineup. Some folks, such as middle-class Americans, draw raw goods from the whole Earth. Others, such as third-world peasants draw rather little from elsewhere in the world, but may hack deadly wounds in their neighborhoods. Overall, though, most men, women, and children harm wild things worldwide *and* in their own neighborhoods. So, to better understand ecological wounds, we need to look at the whole sweep. On one hand, a run-of-the-mill American cranks out much more greenhouse gas, but on the other a Bangladeshi peasant may be much more of a threat to the life of a tiger. Likewise, someone with a million-dollar starter castle in Aspen gobbles up more things than someone living in an old shack on a National Forest inholding. But the backwoods bumpkin might kill one of the highly endangered Mexican wolves in the wild. So, we need to look at both World Impact (I_W) and Neighborhood Impact (I_N), or I_W=PAT and I_N=PAT. World Impact and Neighborhood Impact are not the same. Weighing one kind against the other is juggling apples and durians. And woe betides whosoever drops a durian on their head.

More than seventy years ago, Aldo Leopold saw keeping rare species hale in their own neighborhoods as *the* work for conservationists.[8] Since the mid-1970s, naturalists, conservationists, and biologists have known that wholesale extinction wreaked by Man is the biggest threat to the world. Besides wiping out many of our fellow Earthlings, widespread extinction shatters the building slabs natural selection needs and thus upsets evolution. Break off the rhinoceros

8 Aldo Leopold, "Threatened Species," *American Forests,* March 1936; reprinted in David E. Brown and Neil B. Carmony, editors, *Aldo Leopold's Southwest* (University of New Mexico Press, Albuquerque, 1995), 193-98.

limb on the tree of life and evolution has nothing with which to cobble new rhinos. Man's snowballing growth is breaking off many such tree-of-life limbs much as a wicked ice storm in Kentucky snaps pine-tree limbs. So, our population explosion will be felt not just in the short run but in the long, long run as well. The tombstone for our kind will be the ghastly wrack of a world once brimming with life of unfathomable and manifold kinds. Unless we choose to take another path.

Showing how the growing Man swarm is the main driver behind the extinction landslide is the key to get conservationists and wild-thing lovers to work once again to freeze and then lower human population. We must show how the growing footprint of Man hastens and deepens the Seven Ecological Wounds. For the rest of this chapter, I'll sketch a few examples of how population growth worldwide and in neighborhoods here and there drives each ecological wound. This is just a beginning; we need to stack up many more examples of how population growth is behind the loss of biodiversity. Furthermore, whenever conservationists spotlight threatened landscapes or wildlife, we need to bring in the ways high population and ongoing growth are behind the threat.

Right now this is not being done. When horror stories pop up about the dreadful loss of wildlife somewhere in the world, population growth is rarely mentioned, much less blamed for it. A glaring example comes from a 2009 news story about the crash in wildlife numbers in the big game haven of Kenya. Nowhere in the article is Kenya's skyrocketing population mentioned. Of the fabled "Big Five" animals, only the buffalo is not now endangered, while Kenya could lose the others—lion, elephant, rhino, and leopard. In all cases wildlife are threatened because swarming new populations of Men are pouring into former wildlife habitat. When conflicts arise, the wildeors are killed. In 1963, 20,000 lions lived in Kenya—in 2008 there were only 1,970. A ninety percent loss. Elephants went from 167,000 in 1963 to 16,000 in 1989. They are back to 32,000, which is still piddling. Black rhinos were poached down from 20,000 in 1970 to 391 in 1997. Now they are at 603 only with tough protection. Other big, wide-ranging wildlife are at all-time lows.[9] Conservationists need to take such figures and show how exploding human populations are to blame and that, without serious birth reduction, wildlife will go.

Another painful example comes from one of the world's two leading science journals—*Science*, published by the American Association for the Advancement of Science (AAAS). I wish I could say that shallowness is not something found in *Science* even in its news section. When it comes to acknowledging how population growth adds to the woes before the world, shallowness stands tall, though. In a 2010 article on alternative energy, nothing is said about population growth being behind energy demand. To wit: "One of the most daunting aspects of the coming energy transition is its sheer size. It will have to be huge. Since 1800—when wood and animal feed provided more than 95% of U.S. energy—world energy use has increased by a factor of more than 20."[10] But the article leaves it at that, as if each Man in the world today is using twenty times as much energy as did each alive in 1800. No mention is made of how population growth plays into this equation. Since 1800, however, world population has grown seven-fold and the population of the United States, home to the world's fattest energy gluttons, has shot up sixty-fold. Whereas world population has grown one-third as much as world energy consumption, *U.S. population has grown three times as much as world energy consumption.* Might any of this population growth have contributed to growth in energy use? Might stopping population growth make the shift to non-fossil-fuel energy easier? The article in *Science* doesn't even think to ask these questions.

9 Joe Kiare, "Kenya on the brink of recording big five extinction," *The Standard Online*, 6/12/09.

10 Richard A. Kerr, "Do We Have the Energy For the Next Transition?" *Science* Vol. 329, 13 August 2010, 780-781.

These glaring journalistic examples—forthcoming extinction of big wildeors in Kenya and weighing the rise in energy use in the last 200 years and the need to shift to renewable sources—fairly howl for why we must bring in population growth for all kinds of analysis. In no way are the two articles—one from popular media and the other from a scientific journal—standalones. I can truthfully say, from my wide reading, I have found that acknowledging overpopulation as a player in the biodiversity crisis is overwhelmingly either given no heed whatsoever or is given short shrift. Hence my plea in this chapter for research showing and journalism reporting how our population growth drives ecological wounds to Earth and the woes with which Mankind must grapple.

There have been some hopeful starts on such analysis, but not an ongoing trend. In 1995, *Wild Earth* published a highly promising article by Professor Charles Hall and three of his students in the State University of New York College of Environmental Science and Forestry in Syracuse. Their study, "The Environmental Consequences of Having a Baby in the United States," carefully weighed sundry factors behind key human impacts on the wildworld. In their conclusion, Hall and his students bluntly write, "We would like all potential parents to be aware that, of all the decisions they will ever make, their decision on whether or not to create a child will have the largest impact on our global environment. The most effective way an individual can protect the global environment, and hence protect the well-being of all living people, is to abstain from creating another human."[11] I'm sorry to say that I don't know if any further work was done along this line. It begs for further work.

11 Charles A.S. Hall, R. Gil Pontius Jr., Lisa Coleman, and Jae-Young Ko, "The Environmental Consequences of Having a Baby in the United States," *Wild Earth,* Summer 1995, 78-87. I hope to soon have pdfs of all population articles from *Wild Earth* on The Rewilding Website www.rewilding.org. If someone with the right skills would like to help, please let me know!

Now, let's look at how growth is behind the Seven Ecological Wounds.

Wound 1: Overkill

When I was in grade school I read the *Weekly Reader* telling us how more thorough "harvesting" of the seven seas would feed more and more mouths. Well, we did that. The upshot is crashing fisheries throughout the world, die-off of coral reefs, and the *functional extinction* of once-teeming *highly interactive species* such as cod, sharks, and tuna. When highly interactive species are killed off, their neighborhoods crumble and wither.[12]

As hungry little settlements swell and spread out, they gobble up the bigger wildlife from rainforests and other wildlands. Even a little knot of huts with near-Stone-Age tools can clean out the bigger wildlife in a nearby protected area. As more babies become more mommies and daddies, hunters go ever farther afield with snares, nets, and old guns. There are tropical National Parks still full of tall, never-cut trees and heavy lianas that are empty of big wildeors thanks to this belly-driven hunting.

Historically, hunting has caused the extinction, local extirpation, or near-extinction of wildlife, including once-highly abundant bison, passenger pigeons, shorebirds, whales, cod, elephants, sea turtles, and many more. Such hunting has been driven by the "need" for meat and for new settlements and cropland by growing populations of Men worldwide and locally.

12 *Highly interactive species* or *keystone* species are those most needed for the health of a wild neighborhood. Beavers are one kind in the way they build ponds and thereby shape the landscape. Jaguars are another in how their hunting of other wildlife is *top-down regulation* of their prey's behavior and crowding. *Rewilding North America* gives much more depth on this.

Wound 2: Scalping and Taming Wilderness

Although direct killing is still fulsome in much of the world, it has become less of a threat in the United States. Here, ransacking and taming wildlands may do even more harm than the other wounds. The growing Man swarm in the U.S. is the lead driver for scalping neighborhoods lived in by wild things and remaking them into new neighborhoods for men, women, and children. Philip Cafaro and Winthrop Staples write, "Between 1982 and 2001, the United States converted 34 million acres of forest, cropland, and pasture to developed uses, an area the size of Illinois." Moreover, the acreage cleared, paved, built-on, and otherwise remade for Man has been going up since 1982 from 1.4 million acres to 2.2 million acres every year. The bulldozers' hunger yet grows and they eat more acres every year.[13]

Crop fields and heavily grazed pastures are no better and sometimes even worse for wildlife than are towns. But when farms and ranches are pimpled with homes, streets, and strip malls, their food-growing acreage has to be made up for elsewhere by plowing wildland or by more irrigation, fertilizers, and pesticides on less giving land. Some of the richest cropland in California and elsewhere in the U.S. has been lost to sprawl.

The building of bigger homes and the shift from the Rustbelt to the Sunbelt speeds the cancerous sprawl of suburban and exurban bedroom neighborhoods in the United States. But the growing population in the U.S. is an even bigger driver of sprawl. Like it or not, in the United States and other wealthy countries, immigration is the main thrust for swelling populations. Even if folks come here only with what is on their backs, their goal is to rise on the ladder of the good life—which they do, thereby taking more from Earth than had they not left home. Without downplaying waste and highlife, if the U.S.

13 Philip Cafaro and Winthrop Staples III, "The Environmental Argument for Reducing Immigration to the United States," *Backgrounder,* Center for Immigration Studies, June 2009, 3.

had fifty or sixty million fewer folks, there would be fewer ranchettes, subdivisions, and such in the California coastal chaparral, the Sonoran Desert outside of Phoenix, woods next to Atlanta, and so on. I'll look more at how population growth drives sprawl in Chapter 10.

More mouths lead to more acres of wildland scalped for cropland, too. As we earlier saw, since 1700 and keeping pace with the population explosion has been the widespread, worldwide wiping out of wild neighborhoods for wildlife and plowing them into croplands. Recall that University of Wisconsin researchers say "the amount of cultivated land on the planet has increased from 7 to 40 percent" since 1700.[14] In 300 years, then, the acres needed to feed Man have gone from less than 10 percent to nearly half of Earth's land acres—more than a fivefold rise. Spin a globe. One third of what you see that is not water or ice has gone from neighborhoods for wildlife to food lands for Man in just 300 years—which is only three percent of the time since full-on agriculture began and less than one percent of the time since *Homo sapiens* crossed the Red Sea out of Africa. This mind-numbing, heart-breaking wreckage of the wild is the main driver for the extinction of the Carolina parakeet in the U.S. and heaps of other beings worldwide, and for the nosedive in how many tigers and elephants, butterflies, and other wild ones are left.[15]

In India, leapfrogging growth of tribal folk today is nibbling away at tiger reserves. New laws are afoot to let tribals settle in once-well-shielded wildlands that have been the last havens for tigers and other wildeors. Indian conservationists worry that tigers will not last long where this happens. Coomi Kapoor warns that the decline of tigers in

14 *The Guardian,* San Francisco, December 7, 2005.

15 A worthwhile job would be to do a timeline of maps showing the spread of cropland in the United States from the 1700s to today. Likewise enlightening would be maps for other continents. Such timeline maps would be a strong, eye-catching way to show how much wildland has been plowed to cropland for Man in the two or three hundred years since our population boomed.

India comes from the "pressure of human population, especially tribal groups."[16] In India, Bangladesh, Sumatra, and elsewhere in Asia, when booming crowds overrun wildlands, clashes with tigers and elephants grow and big cats and tuskers die. Likewise, when Americans shove new houses, yards, and streets into wildlands, we hear more and more bleats to "control" cougars, coyotes, and other wildlife that were living there long before exurban apes thronged in. Fish and Game Departments seem only too happy to squeeze their trigger fingers to rid a new suburb of threatening wildeors, even though the wild things were there first.

Norman Myers, the British biologist who may have been the first to warn that we were in a mass extinction, has looked at biodiversity "hotspots" and population growth. Hotspots, as reckoned by some international conservation groups, are twenty-five areas covering only 1.4 percent of the world's land but home to a whopping 40 percent of all known species. Many millions of dollars are going into hotspot conservation. But, in 2002 Myers warned, "Most of the hotspots are in developing countries, where they are subject to population pressures among other problems. Within the 840,000 square miles of all the hotspots (one quarter as big again as Alaska), plus their hinterlands totaling another 10% of Earth's land surface, there are more than 1.2 billion people, approximately one fifth of humankind, with an average population density almost twice that of the world and with an average annual growth rate almost two fifths higher than that of the world."[17] It's worse today. Yet Myers stands pretty much alone in warning about growth in hotspots.

Besides growth itself, immigration from poor, high-growth countries to wealthier ones can tear up wilderness homes for endangered wildlife. In a case close to home, unlawful immigrants wound the

16 Coomi Kapoor, "Indian tigers' days numbered," India Diary, *The Star,* March 3, 2008.

17 Norman Myers, "Biodiversity: What's At Stake," *Pop!ulation Press,* Population Coalition, Redlands, CA, September/October 2002, 7.

world-class wilderness of the Mexico-United States border. Here, I'll touch on only one plight from that dryland. The Sonoran pronghorn (wrongly called "antelope") is one of the most endangered beings in the world. It lives in the Sonora-Arizona borderlands and finds its best refuge in the Cabeza Prieta National Wildlife Refuge and Wilderness Area. Or did. According to the *Tucson Citizen* newspaper, much of the unlawful immigration through the Arizona desert "funnels" through a narrow valley in the refuge where the pronghorn have their best habitat. Sometimes 200 unlawful crossers a night stride through, trampling the rare wildflowers and the plants pronghorn eat and draining or fouling the even rarer waterholes the pronghorn must have. It has long been nip and tuck whether the Sonoran subspecies of pronghorn can be saved, but the horde of immigrants tearing through the pronghorn's wilderness home may be the last straw.[18]

Wound 3: Fragmentation of Wildlife Neighborhoods

Whether it is starter-castle "estates" strung along wide freeways farther away from cities and workplaces in the United States or new slash-and-burn crop patches (*milpas*) and logging roads in third-world countries, we throw up barriers and *fracture zones* that box wildeors into smaller and smaller lots; this cleaves migration north (south below the equator) or to higher elevations as home ranges shift because of climate breakdown. Population growth spreads us into once empty (of Man) lands where wildeors had been free to roam widely before our takeover. The shape or siting of the new settlement web is often more deadly than how many acres are cleared. A few settlers or "estates" with a handful of roads can stomp down a footprint that breaks up a big wildland. Nonetheless, the sprawl first comes from more men, women, and children. More off-road vehicles tearing up wildlife pathways between summer and winter range come from more people. More

18 Claudine LoMonaco, "Migrants intrude; scarce pronghorn die," *Tucson Citizen*, July 1, 2005.

people here and there means more blacktop roads in between with curves straightened out for faster driving and thereby more deadly for the lynx or elk used to wandering over a once-slow dirt road.

One way to tell what kinds of wildeors are about is to look at roadkill. The hopeful spread of wolves, lynx, and cougars in the United States is shown but also stopped by deaths along interstate highways and other main roads. More Coloradoans, say, means more cars and pickups and SUVs means more upgraded roads means death traps for wildlife.

Wound 4: Upsetting and Weakening Ecological and Evolutionary Processes

Our crowding on the land and further spreading into lands once empty of Men plays hob with ecological and evolutionary processes, such as wildfire, river flooding and drying, predation, and pollination. More and more of us squeeze into lush, rank river bottoms and thereby make a "need" for upstream flood-control dams, which then stop healthy hydrological processes. More of us need more water for irrigating crops and making more electricity, both of which call for Brobdingnagian dams on rivers. In the United States and Canada, the spread of homes into forests leads to putting down natural wildfires; stopping such lightning-sparked fires harms forest health and sets up the woods for bigger, unhealthy, unquenchable blazes later.

Men, whether Denver suburbanites or Kenyan herders, are unfriendly to big cats, wolves or wild dogs, and other wild hunters; and, so, as Denverites or Kenyans spread afield, they kill wildeors and the ecosystem loses top-down regulation of prey species.[19] Likewise, people in new settlements of whatever kind don't want beavers or elephants upsetting their high-dollar landscaping or their slash-and-burn cornfields.

19 See *Rewilding North America* for the whys and wherefores of this much-needed job by flesh-eating wildeors.

When we take over wildlands, we often also make the land unfriendly to native pollinators. Biologists who study pollination, whether by native kinds of bees or moths, hummingbirds, or bats, have warned that many such pollinators are fewer and fewer every year.

Wound 5: Spread of Exotic Species and Diseases

The spread of Man spreads non-native species. Pumped-up trade between growing (in population and wealth) countries also spreads invasive species. Ballast water in freighters brings swarms of harmful exotics, such as zebra and quagga mussels, green crabs, and the spiny water-flea. When folks go into new lands they hack out welcome ground for invasive, exotic, weedy life that pushes out native species. Plant diseases, such as Dutch elm disease and chestnut blight, are among the most deadly things spread by trade and shifting settlements. Such ills lead to upheavals in native-plant communities.

More Indians, more Brazilians, more Americans mean more ships hauling more crap back and forth—and hauling more exotic species back and forth.

Wound 6: Biocide Poisoning of Land, Air, Water, and Wildlife

Way back in 1971, biologist Daniel McKinley warned, "All animals create waste, but only man makes products that nature cannot reclaim, and at such a rate that he can spoil the world before it purifies itself."[20] This Man-waste not only sickens and kills children, women, and men, but also even more so harms and kills other Earthlings. People spray and spill biocides and befoul Earth with all kinds of banes. Worldwide, it may seem that wealthy lands pollute more than do those of the third world. But down on the ground or in the water,

20 Daniel McKinley, "Preface Two," in Paul Shepard and Daniel McKinley, editors, *Environ/Mental: Essays on the Planet as Home* (Houghton Mifflin Co., Boston, 1971), ix.

peasants can spread and spill more banes than do most Europeans or Americans. Likewise, Americans in the hinterlands have their hands on more banes and are more lackadaisical in handling them than are even suburban yard lords. The lower on the ladder of income and schooling one goes, whether in Essex County, New York, or the slums of Lagos, the lower the understanding of how awful some chemical brews can be. Thickening settlements lead to even more smoke and filth, many kinds of which are biocides to wild things. The spread of *Homo sapiens*, whether as suburbanites, city dwellers, or peasants, onto new lands brings with it careless spilling of pesticides, motor oil, antifreeze, and other nasty crud.

Leaping industrialization in China, India, and other booming third-world countries is much sloppier and dirtier than in wealthy lands. Indeed, the most poisoned, polluted, and dirty land, air, and water is in China and other newly industrializing lands; and the most toxic settings are in workshops and dumps of the most wretched lands and "failed states," where there is little or no oversight. In the latter countries, the evil banes aren't all homemade, though; some are rich nations' exports of junked computers and other electronic gadgets for recycling—a witch's brew of world and local pollution. In wealthy lands, laws, regulations, and enforcement are better and watchdogging is better. In the third world, there is little oversight of how folks mess around with pesticides, oil, and other crap. Wherever, though, more of us means more spreading of death.

Much as we would like to get rid of these banes, we must acknowledge that more of us brings more pollutants and poisons, that the chemical industry works to fill a need brought by the gusher of babies. It's hard to clean up a mess when those making the mess are more every year, sometimes twice as many every score of years.

Wound 7: Global "Weirding" or Climate Change and Ocean Acidification

As early as 1969 Paul Ehrlich and John Holdren saw one of the upshots of overpopulation as a rise in "the atmospheric percentage of CO_2," leading to a "greenhouse effect" (though they didn't use those words yet).[21] Unlike other species, Man lives worldwide. The whole Earth is our home—and our dump. For the Earth-wide flock of Men, the needed resource that has run out first is not food, water, oil, or rare minerals, but the wherewithal of the atmosphere, seas, and woods to soak up our industrial, transportation, and agricultural belches and farts of carbon dioxide, methane, and other greenhouse gases. Yes, the wealthy pump out more greenhouse gases per capita, but third-worlders add much by setting fires in forests, grasslands, and shrublands.

Here Affluence (A) and Technology (T) are big players in how much Impact (I) one may have. However, enough small players can outweigh a few big players. What drives the logging and burning of the Amazon rainforest to make new cattle paddocks and soybean fields? Too many mommies and daddies and bouncing babies in Brazil, plus the swelling throngs of hungry mouths in the rest of the world who crave the food cornucopians hope the "last agricultural frontier" can grow. This will lead to more of a jump in Brazil's greenhouse-gas load and to the loss of tropical forests that if kept would go on putting to bed carbon from the atmosphere—and forests that may be the dearest pool of tangled and manifold life left on Earth.

China has now shot by the United States as the worst greenhouse-gas belcher in the world, thanks to its whopping population racing after greater wealth. But if China had only half a billion mouths instead of nearly a billion and a half, it would not have done so. Moreover, if China's growth had not been braked by the much-cursed one-child

---

21 Paul R. Ehrlich and John P. Holdren, "Population and Panaceas A Technological Perspective," *BioScience* 19 (December, 1969), 1065-1071, reprinted in *Environ/Mental,* 265.

policy, China would be blowing out much more greenhouse pollution and may have by now already tipped the world over the edge into a god-awful tomorrow. The one-child policy in China may be giving the world a few more years to try to handle the staggering greenhouse gas load. Indeed, the Chinese themselves acknowledge that there would be 400 million more Chinese today without the one-child rule.

Family planning experts, weighing the threat of greenhouse-gas pollution, write in *The Lancet,* "In a world of 12 billion inhabitants, much more severe measures would be needed to stabilise the planet's environment than in a world of 8 billion people. Prevention of unwanted births today by family planning might be one of the most cost-effective ways to preserve the planet's environment for the future."[22] It could also be one of the best ways to keep some freedom.

Then-British Prime Minister Tony Blair in 2006 acknowledged that it was "now plain that the emission of greenhouse gases, associated with industrialization and economic growth from a world population that has increased six-fold in 200 years, is causing global warming at a rate that is unsustainable." Alas, Blair is one of the few leaders to acknowledge how the population explosion is behind global warming. The United Kingdom's Optimum Population Trust says, "Policies to tackle climate change, by contrast, almost universally ignore population: it is seen as too sensitive and controversial." The upshot is that the solutions for greenhouse gas pollution are all technical and economic.[23] Overlooking population as the main driver and population freezing and lowering as the main solution holds not only for greenhouse gas pollution but also for all of the Seven Ecological Wounds.

22 John Cleland, Stan Bernstein, Alex Ezeh, Anibal Faundes, Anna Glasier, and Jolene Innis, "Family planning: the unfinished agenda," *The Lancet,* November 18, 2006.

23 A Population-Based Climate Strategy—*An Optimum Population Trust Briefing,* May 2007. www.optimumpopulation.org

In a 2007 study, the Optimum Population Trust found that forgoing children was the best way to reduce the UK's greenhouse gas load. "Each new UK citizen less means a lifetime carbon dioxide saving of nearly 750 tonnes, a climate impact equivalent to 620 return flights between London and New York." The press release from the Trust goes on to say, "Based on a 'social cost' of carbon dioxide of $85 a tonne, the report estimates the climate cost of each new Briton over their lifetime at roughly £30,000 ($63,240). The lifetime emission costs of the extra 10 million people projected for the UK by 2074 would therefore be over £300 billion."

"A 35-pence condom, which could avert that £30,000 cost from a single use, thus represents a 'spectacular' potential return on investment—around nine million per cent."

The Trust cuts through the fog of climate weirdness with, "The most effective *personal* climate change strategy is limiting the number of children one has. The most effective *national* and *global* climate change strategy is limiting the size of the population."

"Population limitation should therefore be seen as the most cost-effective *carbon offsetting strategy* available to individuals and nations—a strategy that applies with even more force to developed nations such as the UK because of the higher consumption levels."

The Trust makes a sharp warning that must be heeded by all working to back off on greenhouse gas emissions. "Even if by 2050 the world had managed to achieve a 60 per cent cut in its 1990 emission levels, in line with the Intergovernmental Panel on Climate Change's recommendations and UK government's target, almost all of it would be cancelled out by population growth."[24] In a companion briefing, OPT writes, "Put another way, even if the world managed to achieve a 52 per cent cut in its 1990 emission levels (21.4 billion tonnes) by

24 News Release "Combat Climate Change With Fewer Babies—OPT Report," Optimum Population Trust, May 7, 2007. www.optimumpopulation.org

2050—not far off the IPCC's 60 per cent target—it would be cancelled out by population growth."[25] How so? Over the years the added folks from overbreeding will drive emissions back up.

So, as dreadfully hard as it will be to cut our greenhouse gas emissions, it will be pissin' in the wind without stopping population growth. Like it or hate it, that is reality. Again, what the Trust says for greenhouse gas pollution holds true for the other wounds as well.

It is widely known that carbon dioxide is the leading greenhouse pollutant (though pound for pound methane is more harmful). Much less widely known is that black carbon, or soot, is next, although it only has been known in the last two or three years. Soot was not even named as "a warming agent in the 2007 summary report by the Intergovernmental Panel on Climate Change." Most of the black carbon now comes from cooking fires of twigs and dried dung in crummy little stoves in the third world. Sadly, it's the only way now that the crammed-together and yet fast-growing crowds of peasants in India and elsewhere have to cook their scanty meals. The crude technology has much to do with this woe, but it is greatly made worse by the swarm of such stoves and by how many more of these poorest of the poor come every year. *The New York Times* reports, "While carbon dioxide may be the No. 1 contributor to rising global temperatures, scientists say, black carbon has emerged as an important No. 2, with recent studies estimating that it is responsible for 18 percent of the planet's warming, compared with 40 percent for carbon dioxide." Soot owns an even greater share of the blame for melting glaciers in the Himalayas and other high mountains, and "might account for as much as half of Arctic warming." When it settles out of the atmosphere, soot makes ice and snow dark, thereby they reflect less of the sun's energy back into space and they melt faster, too.

25 A Population-Based Climate Strategy—*An Optimum Population Trust Briefing*, May 2007. www.optimumpopulation.org

Work is being done to get low-soot cookstoves to folks in need, though getting tradition-bound women to cook on them instead of their old, homey stoves will not be a snap. The write-up in the *Times* rightly nudges along quick spread of better stoves, but nowhere is a word about the most-needed thing to do on third-world soot, which is to freeze population growth.[26]

I'm not trying to let the U.S. off the hook here. What we've done or haven't done on greenhouse gas pollution has been worse than shameful. Overall, each one of us in the U.S. burps more CO_2 and other greenhouse gases than do folks in any other country in the world, and we are each burping more every day. In the years 1990 to 2003 our "*per capita* CO_2 emissions increased 3.2 percent," write Phil Cafaro and Win Staples. That doesn't tell the whole tale, though. Over that same time, overall U.S. emissions went up much more—by 20.2 percent! How so? Well, our population rose 16.1 percent.[27] In other words, the growing Man swarm of the United States was about five times more to blame for our greater greenhouse pollution than was the rise from each of us.

As we mull over what leads to each of these seven wounds both worldwide and nearby, we must acknowledge that Affluence and Technology play big. Nonetheless, we cannot let that overshadow the way overpopulation and high growth drive ecological wounds, whether straightforward killing of threatened Earthlings or cranking out carbon dioxide, methane, and other heat-trapping gases.

We who love wild things need to gather more facts and figures of how our growing swarm drives each of the Seven Ecological Wounds. One good, though rather technical, stab at doing so was published in the *Proceedings of the Royal Society* in 2003. Two fisheries biologists, Charles Fowler and Larry Hobbs, asked whether humans are sustainable

26 Elisabeth Rosenthal, "Third-World Stove Soot Is Target in Climate Fight," *The New York Times,* April 16, 2009.

27 Cafaro and Staples, "Environmental Arguments," 5.

by comparing us with thirty-one other species on "measures of biomass consumption, global energy consumption, population size and extent of unoccupied areas," among others. They found, "All but nine out of the 31 tests showed humans to be outside the 99% confidence limits for variation among the other species. In only one case was the measure of humans not significantly different from the mean of other species at the 90% level of confidence."[28] What this means is that we are wildly out of whack in comparison with other species on sustainability. More of this kind of work is needed and it needs to be put into a form that is understandable to nonscientists.

See Chapter 13 for what you can do to help stem the bleeding from these wounds, through ending population growth.

For much of Asia, Latin America, and Africa, the time since the end of World War Two has been an onslaught against wilderness and wildlife that is mind-numbing. It has also been the time of head-spinning population growth in the same lands. This is not happenstance. Population growth has been the main axe hacking at the tree of life. This same time, by happenstance, is my lifetime, as I was born in 1946. From 1948 to 1950, I lived with my father and mother at Clark Air Force Base in the Philippines. What I recall from my earliest memories is a wonderful, wet, green wilderness full of bright wild things. In the sixty years since I said good-bye to that thick tangle of life, though, the Philippines have been scalped and wrecked. In my life the same has happened to other wild, healthy lands around the middle of Earth.

Table 4.2 shows population growth in some countries of outstanding worth in wildlife; these are also the countries that have had the population bomb go off and that have gobbled up much of their wild web. Instead of me telling you what you will find in this table, I

28 Charles W. Fowler and Larry Hobbs, "Is humanity sustainable?" *Proceedings of the Royal Society Lond.* B (2003) 270, 17 November 2003, 2579-2583.

think it best to let you graze through it to see how much the Man swarm has grown since World War Two and how much the United Nations and others forecast that the Man swarm will keep growing until 2050. This quick look at one hundred years has much to teach. For each of these countries, I've also listed a few of the wild ones threatened by growth.

In no way do I wish to downplay the might of globalization and the way the United States, China, Japan, Europe, and a few others ransack the rest of the world for raw goods. Nonetheless, leapfrogging growth in even the most technologically backward lands puts an unbearable squeeze on wild things and wildlands. The kind of growth we see in Table 4.2 is the growth of a plague species or of a metastasizing cancer. Unless stopped, it will be the death of wild things in these lands as well as a hammer driving the children, women, and men of these lands deeper into hunger, woe, hopelessness, and sorrow.

Table 4.2. Population Growth in Countries of High Biodiversity

COUNTRY	POP 1940-50	POP 2010	POP 2050	2010 % <15	Threatened and Endangered Species
Afghanistan	12 m	29.1 m	53.4 m	42.9%	Snow Leopard
Belize	65,000	314,522	543,690	37.3%	Jaguar, Coral Reefs, Tapir
Bolivia	3.8 m	9.9 m	16 m	35.1%	Spectacled Bear, Vicuna
Botswana	285,000	2 m	2.9 m	34.3%	Lion, Elephant, Wild Dog
Brazil	47.2 m	201.1 m	260.7 m	26.5%	Jaguar, Maned Wolf, Giant Otter
China	430 m	1,330 m	1,304 m	17.9%	Panda, Amur Leopard, Hainan Gibbon, Tiger
Congo (Zaire)	10.7 m	70.9 m	189.3 m	46.7%	Mt. and Lowland Gorillas, Bonobo, Okapi
Costa Rica	772,000	4.5 m	6.1 m	25%	Jaguar, Quetzal
Ethiopia	6.8 m	88 m	278.3 m	46.2%	Ethiopian Wolf, Grevy's Zebra
Honduras	1.2 m	8 m	12.9 m	37.4%	Jaguar, Tigrillo
India	314 m	1,173.1 m	1,656.6 m	30.1%	Tiger, Rhino, Elephant, Lion, Lion-tailed Macaque
Indonesia	72 m	243 m	313 m	27.7%	Tiger, Elephant, Rhino, Bay Cat
Iran	13.9 m	76.9 m	100 m	21.3%	Cheetah, Sturgeon
Iraq	4.1 m	29.7 m	56.3 m	38.4%	Leopard, Wolf
Kenya	4.2 m	40 m	65.2 m	42.3%	Lion, White & Black Rhinos, Wild Dog
Liberia	1.6 m	3.7 m	8.2 m	44.3%	Pygmy Hippo, Chimpanzee
Madagascar	4.4 m	21.3 m	56.5 m	43.3%	Lemur species, Fossa
Mexico	19.6 m	112.5 m	147.9 m	28.7%	Jaguar, Scarlet Macaw, Thick-bill Parrot, Vaquita
Mozambique	5.5 m	22.1 m	41.8 m	44.1%	Elephant, Lion
Myanmar (Burma)	16.9 m	53.4 m	70.7 m	27.9%	Tiger, Lesser Muntjac, Malayan Tapir
Nepal	6.5 m	29 m	46 m	35.6%	Tiger, Rhino, Snow Leopard, Musk Deer
Nigeria	23 m	152.2 m	264.3 m	41.2%	Gorilla, Chimpanzee
Peru	7.9 m	29.9 m	38.6 m	28.5%	Andean Mt. Cat, Huemul, Spectacled Bear
Philippines	18.5 m	99.9 m	172 m	34.9%	Monkey-eating Eagle, Tamarau
Sudan	7.5 m	43.9 m	97.2 m	40.2%	Elephant, Lion, Addax
Thailand	20 m	67.1 m	71.1 m	20.3%	Tiger, Elephant, Fea's Muntjac
Turkey	20 m	77.8 m	101 m	26.9%	Leopard, Brown Bear
Uganda	3.9 m	33.4 m	128 m	50%	Chimpanzee, Mt. Gorilla
Venezuela	4.3 m	27.2 m	40.3 m	30%	Jaguar, Harpy Eagle

Vietnam[1]	25.5 m	89.6 m	111.2 m	25.6%	Tiger, Saola
Laos		6.4 m	10.1 m	40.5%	Tiger, Giant Muntjac
Cambodia		14.5 m	22.3 m	32.2%	Tiger, Clouded Leopard
TOTAL	25.5 m	110.5 m	143.6 m		
Zambia	1.7 m	13.5 m	38.4 m	44.8%	Lion, Elephant, Rhino
Zimbabwe	1.8 m	11.7 m	25.2 m	43.1%	Elephant, W & B Rhino

This table shows population for selected countries in 1940-1950, today, and projected for 2050. It also shows the percentage of the 2010 population under 15 years of age and a sampling of the species endangered by population growth. Sources: population 1940-1950: The International Standard Atlas of the World *(Book Production Industries, Chicago, 1949) from "most authoritative estimates available"; population 2010 and 2050:* The World Almanac 2011 *(World Almanac Books, New York, 2010) from Population Division, U.S. Census Bureau; and* The World Factbook, *Central Intelligence Agency. Wildlife presence is drawn from various sources, including Dr. David Macdonald, ed.,* The Encyclopedia of Mammals *(Facts on File, New York, 1985). Note: The first version of this table was based on* The World Almanac 2008, *which drew on the same sources, but three years earlier. Population figures for 2010 and especially forecasts for 2050 had to be broadly revised, some higher and some lower. This shows that population figures for third-world countries are far from exact. For example the 2050 forecast for Ethiopia here is 278.3 million; the 2008 forecast was 144.7 million, an outlandish difference of 130 million. On the other hand, the 2050 forecast here for Nigeria is 264.3 million; the 2008 forecast was 356.5 million, about a 90 million difference. Nonetheless, the point of this table is unchanged: countries with some of the most highly endangered species in the world are still undergoing a massive population explosion, and population forecasts for 2050 in these countries paint a most dire picture for the future of wild things.*

1 Before 1950, Vietnam, Laos, and Cambodia were French Indochina.

CHAPTER 5

Cornucopia Dreaming

We now have in our hands—in our libraries, really—the technology to feed, clothe, and supply energy to an ever-growing population for the next 7 billion years.[1]

—Julian Simon

It is a totally spurious idea to claim that rising population anywhere in the world is responsible for the deteriorating environment.[2]

—Barry Commoner

THE LATE JULIAN SIMON, professor of direct mail at the University of Maryland, was the darling of free marketers who truly believe that even the sky is not the limit. Barry Commoner, a socialist and early pollution fighter, was a bitter foe of Paul Ehrlich and others who saw Man's population growth as a threat. Simon and Commoner show how right and left are often of the same mind that growth is nothing to worry about.

1 Norman Myers and Julian Simon, *Scarcity or Abundance: A Debate on the Environment* (W. W. Norton, New York, 1994), 65.

2 Sandy Irvine, "The Great Denial: Puncturing Pro-natalist Myths," *Wild Earth*, Winter 1997/98, 8.

The cornucopia, from Greek mythology, is a goat's horn overflowing with fruit, vegetables, and grain that is always refilled with whatever one wishes. It stands for everlasting fullness and wealth. Therefore, those who pooh-pooh worries about overpopulation or limits to growth are named *cornucopians*. Maybe of all the Greek myths, the cornucopia has the most meaning today.

Right and Left marching together

In mood and ideology, cornucopians shut out any thought of limits. Even some who back many conservation and environmental steps cannot bring themselves to believe the truth that Earth and its "resources" are not endless. Let me keep on my path with Simon and Commoner and take the two political bookends—Marxists and free-market boosters—to show how today's society believes in ever-growing wealth. Those in between—the whole political bookshelf—also share such cornucopian dreams. This widespread belief in endless progress is why the worldwide establishment will not work to stop growth, why it cannot fathom the end of growth, why ongoing growth is a "given" in all reckoning.

In the shallow unecological way most of us seem to look at everything, economic libertarianism and Marxism seem far away from each other. If we look deeper, however, we find that Marxism and libertarianism share an underlying Weltanschauung of humans foremost as economic beings. They both see Earth as an overflowing warehouse for industrial civilization, a warehouse that is never empty.[3] Unclouded British conservationist Sandy Irvine writes that "the right-wing economist Julian Simon has revived [Marx's Labor Theory of value] as the theory of People as the Ultimate Resource."[4]

3 See Garrett Hardin, *Living Within Limits: Ecology, Economics, and Population Taboos* (Oxford University Press, New York, 1993), 5.

4 Irvine, "The Great Denial," 14.

Both Marxism and free-marketism have swapped God for Man. They see eye-to-eye that:

Man is rational

Man is a blank slate

Man is an economic being

Progress is perfecting individual humans

The world is a warehouse

Growth is good

Progress is foretold

There are no limits, or any limits can be overcome by technology

They also share a godless yet supernatural belief of how things work: historical determinism. Each thinks its economic-political-social order is not just the best, but is somehow foreordained by history as its end. True believers of both cults see the workers' state or the free market as some abstract ideal or Platonic essence that has been waiting in the wings for the right time to be birthed into being by history. Key for either being seen as the "end of history" is that the resources on which each is grounded are endless.

In 1977, during the Cold War, cultural anthropologist Marvin Harris wrote, "Thanks to science and engineering, the average standard of living in the industrial nations is higher than at any time in the past. This fact, more than any other, bolsters our faith that progress is inevitable—a faith, incidentally, shared as much by the Comintern as by the U.S. Chamber of Commerce."[5]

In *The Arrogance of Humanism,* Rutgers biologist David Ehrenfeld warns that this faith, which he calls *humanism,* sits on a stack of assumptions, which "cut across political lines":

All problems are soluble by people.

5 Marvin Harris, *Cannibals and Kings* (Vintage Books, New York, 1991), 271. The Comintern, or Communist International, was a board of directors of sorts for the international Communist movement.

> *Many problems are soluble by technology.*
>
> *Those problems that are not soluble by technology, or by technology alone, have solutions in the social world (of politics, economics, etc.).*
>
> *When the chips are down, we will apply ourselves and work together for a solution before it is too late.*
>
> *Some resources are infinite; all finite or limited resources have substitutes.*
>
> *Human civilization will survive.*[6]

This faith scraps even the thought of limits.

(I've long thought that for anyone to be hired by a conservation or environmental group, they should have first read *The Arrogance of Humanism.*)

THE IDEA OF PROGRESS

Anthropocentric arrogance is wrapped up with The Idea of Progress, a rather new whimsy in Western Civilization holding that civilization is a steady march of betterment with no end in sight. As one reads cornucopian forecasts, one can see how The Idea of Progress bucks up the faith. And The Idea of Progress has a breathtakingly wide sweep, which is why even many conservation and environmental leaders cling to it. Keep in mind, though, that the founders of the wilderness movement—Aldo Leopold, Benton MacKaye, Robert Sterling Yard, Bob Marshall, and others—were strongly driven by antimodernist fears. Conservationists should read Paul Sutter's *Driven Wild* to learn how early wilderness conservationists stood against go-go-boosterism. They did not believe that we could have both wilderness and a bandwagon of gadgets, that we could have both wildlife and never-slowing growth.[7] We conservationists need to go back to the wisdom of our elders.

6 David Ehrenfeld, *The Arrogance of Humanism* (Oxford University Press, New York, 1981), 16-17.

7 Paul S. Sutter, *Driven Wild: How the Fight Against Automobiles Launched the Modern Wilderness Movement* (University of Washington Press, Seattle, 2002).

But if today's conservation leaders are mostly still in the grip of the progress Weltanschauung, some security experts now raise their eyebrows at the beliefs of Progress and Growth. Indeed, I believe that some thinkers outside "The Environmental Movement" are more willing to look at the pitfalls of population growth now than are the leaders of our team. Former *Wall Street Journal* reporter Robert Merry weighs The Idea of Progress in his thought-sparking, forthright book, *Sands of Empire.* He warns, "It's one thing to talk about man's seemingly inexorable advances in scientific knowledge.... It is something else entirely to suggest... that these advances actually are altering and improving the nature of man...."[8] Longtime science journalist Eugene Linden writes, "Any vision of the future that either expects or demands a new human, a higher consciousness, or some other transformation of human nature should be automatically suspect."[9] The Idea of Progress, whatever the political or ethnic getup it wears (and it wears many), loudly calls for such a vision.

When English settlers from crowded, picked-over Europe clambered ashore in the New World in the 1600s they found what seemed to them an endless wealth of game, fish, furs, timber, firewood, fat land, and elbowroom. They waxed about such *Superabundance* and believed that it could never end.[10] We are truly their children. Today's wrangles about human population growth, dwindling ocean fish stocks, stripping of forests, suburban sprawl, climate weirdness, and so on are a death match between the holy Myth of Superabundance and new scientific understandings of ecological carrying capacity on a finite Earth. It is hard to throw off the cuddling, old faith of Superabundance and

8 Robert W. Merry, *Sands of Empire: Missionary Zeal, American Foreign Policy, and the Hazards of Global Ambition* (Simon & Schuster, New York, 2005), 7.

9 Eugene Linden, *The Future In Plain Sight: Nine Clues To The Coming Instability* (Simon & Schuster, New York, 1998), 140.

10 I further delve into the Myth of Superabundance in *Conservation vs. Conservation* and *The Nature Haters.*

think about population limits when you are unschooled in science—as are most economists (and, sadly, many environmentalists).

CORNUCOPIAN MYTH

Two generations ago, the American and world Establishment was caught up in "the golden optimism of the 1950s." One report from the Rockefeller Panel foresaw, "New technologies, more efficient extraction processes, new uses may open up new worlds. Even now we can discern the outlines of a future in which, through the use of the split atom, our resources of both power and raw materials will be limitless . . . ."[11]

Ahh, yes! We crowed that power from nuclear plants would be "too cheap to meter!"

Time magazine fawned over Bureau of Reclamation engineers in 1951. One article with the bullish title "Endless Frontier" gushed that "irrigation experts are now convinced that the rapidly growing U.S. can expand almost indefinitely within its boundaries."[12] In 1966, *Time* whooped that everyone in the U.S. would be independently wealthy by 2000 and that only ten percent of the population would have to work. (How did Nancy and I get stuck in that unlucky ten percent?) The breathless magazine quoted Rand Corporation scientists who blissed how "Huge fields of kelp and other kinds of seaweed will be tended by undersea 'farmers'—frogmen who will live for months at a time in submerged bunkhouses. . . . This will provide at least a 'partial answer' to doomsdayers who worry about the prospects of starvation for a burgeoning world population."[13]

11 William R. Catton Jr., *Overshoot: The Ecological Basis of Revolutionary Change* (University of Illinois Press, Urbana, 1982), xii.

12 Henry Luce, "Endless Frontiers," *Time*, July 30,1951; quoted in Jon M. Cosco, *Echo Park: Struggle for Preservation* (Johnson Books, Boulder, Co, 1995).

13 Rose DeWolf, "Yesterday's Tomorrow," *The New York Times Magazine*, December 24, 1995. As an aside, I think we scuba divers should start calling ourselves frogmen and frogwomen again, or maybe just frogfolk.

However, the cornucopians did not have the floor to themselves. It was a rough and tumble time. In 1960, Edward S. Deevey, Jr., took a sweeping look at population in *Scientific American.* As for those with wild-eyed dreams of much, much bigger human populations on Earth, he wrote:

> *If my new figures are correct, the population could theoretically increase by 30 to 40 times. But man would have to displace all other herbivores and utilize all the vegetation with the 10 percent efficiency established by the ecological rule of tithes. No land that now supports greenery could be spared for nonagricultural purposes; the populace would have to reside in the polar regions, or on artificial "green islands in the sea…"—scummed over, of course, by 10 inches of Chlorella Culture.*[14]

In 1967, *Time* magazine made the "25 and Under" generation "Man of the Year," and brayed, "He is the man who will land on the moon, cure cancer and the common cold, lay out blight-proof, smog-free cities, enrich the underdeveloped world and, no doubt, write finis to poverty and war."[15] Well, "he" did land on the moon.[16]

Such was the coming utopia for which the establishment was beating the drums when the Sierra Club brought out Paul Ehrlich's *The Population Bomb.* Ehrlich's 1968 book can be nit-picked on some grounds today. But why are not the cornucopians held to their cheery forecasts the way they hold Paul Ehrlich to his dreary scenarios (not "forecasts")? To be fair, editors should make every writer who waves a "prediction" from Ehrlich that didn't come true do the same with one

14 Edward S. Deevey, Jr., "The Human Population," *Scientific American* 203(3), September 1960, 195-204; reprinted in Paul Shepard and Daniel McKinley, editors, *The Subversive Science* (Houghton Mifflin, Boston, 1969), 52.

15 *Time,* January 6, 1967. This same gee-whiz optimism shows up in more recent issues of *Time* that look to the future. *Time,* November 8, 1999, and June 19, 2000, for example.

16 However, everyone who has landed on the moon was already older than twenty-five in 1967.

from the cornucopian optimists. In Chapter 7, I show how Ehrlich was amazingly right on most things.

For me to be fair, though, I have to give a nod to uber-optimists Herman Kahn and Anthony Weiner in 1967 for getting one thing right out of "One hundred technical innovations very likely in the last third of the twentieth century": "31. Some control of weather and/or climate."[17] Unfathomably, though, Kahn's Pollyannan heirs now gainsay that we have gained this might as they huffily spurn what we know about greenhouse gases and climatic weirdness.

In 1974, Nobel Laureate in Economics Robert Solow wrote, "It is very easy to substitute other factors for natural resources, then.... The world can, in effect, get along without natural resources, so exhaustion is just an event, not a catastrophe."[18] I wonder if he would have switched his mind had he stepped out of the abstract and into the real? Would he have thought dying of hunger or thirst was an event, not a catastrophe? Solow's world that could get along without natural resources was a world only of Men. Utterly unknown to him was the world of other Earthlings, in which, as Phillip Cafaro of Colorado State University wrote me, "Other species cannot substitute one resource for another: lose snail populations, and lose the Everglades kite; lose large cavity-nesting trees, and ivory-billed woodpeckers go extinct. Concern for other species is not a requirement for winning the Nobel Prize in Economics."

The cornucopian mood was well put by economist George Gilder in 1981 when he wrote, "The United States must overcome the materialistic fallacy: the illusion that resources and capital are essentially

17 Herman Kahn and Anthony Weiner, *The Year 2000* (Macmillan, New York, 1967), quoted in Ehrenfeld, *Arrogance of Humanism,* 45.

18 Robert Solow, "The economics of resources or the resources of economics," *American Economics Review,* 64, 1974, 1-14, quoted in William E. Rees and Mathis Wackernagel, "Ecological Footprints And Appropriated Carrying Capacity: Measuring The Natural Capital Requirements Of The Human Economy," *Focus,* Vol. 6, No. 1, 1996, Carrying Capacity Network, 47.

things which can run out . . . ." A more rational economist, Allen Kneese, recognized in 1988 that Gilder's kind of economics was "a perpetual motion machine."[19] Kneese wasn't the first to see this. After the 1972 United Nations Conference on the Human Environment in Stockholm, Paul Ehrlich wrote about the back-and-forth between economists and scientists there on sustainability, "As each new perpetual-motion-machine was propounded, one of the biologists or physicists would simply point out that it violated the second law. Finally, in frustration, one of the economists blurted out, 'Who knows what the second law of thermodynamics will be like in a hundred years?'"[20]

It's bad enough that neoclassical economists do not believe in biology, but they do not even believe in physics! Or, as Kenneth Boulding, once president of the American Economic Association, said, "Only madmen and economists believe in perpetual exponential growth."[21] I daresay that some investors and homeowners who believed in perpetual exponential growth in 2008 have rethought their beliefs.

Some cornucopians, however, do believe in resources and even that they can be exhausted. But, so what? In 1986, the U.S. National Research Council wrote in a panel report, "Unless one is more concerned with the welfare of people born in the distant future than those born in the immediate future, there is little reason to be concerned about the rate at which population growth is depleting the stock of exhaustible resources."[22] Long live shortsightedness! To hell with the grandkids!

19 Hardin, *Living Within Limits,* 44-45.

20 Paul R. Ehrlich, "An Ecologist Standing Up Among Seated Social Scientists," *CoEvolution Quarterly* 31 (1981), 28, quoted in Hardin, *Living Within Limits,* 193.

21 Hardin, *Living Within Limits,* 191.

22 U.S. National Research Council, *Population Growth and Economic Development: Policy Questions* (National Academy Press, Washington, D.C., 1986), 15-16.

One of today's cornucopians who overgushes with happy news is Gregg Easterbrook. Because, I guess, he makes people feel good about themselves, he is thought one of America's "public intellectuals" and is handed column inches in top publications. A piece he wrote for the *Los Angeles Times* in 2006 to celebrate the coming of the 300 millionth American shows how matchless he is as a lover of population growth: "But the rising population also is a fantastic achievement. It means ever-more people are alive to experience love, hope, freedom and the daily miracle of the rising sun. None of us who today enjoy the privilege of being Americans should want to deny this privilege to the many more to come."[23] Now that is cornucopianism, but with a guilt trip added on for not making even more Americans.

Arithmetic and Julian Simon

Julian Simon's careless swagger in 1994, "We now have in our hands—in our libraries, really—the technology to feed, clothe, and supply energy to an ever-growing population for the next 7 billion years," is the most straightforward utterance of irrational exuberance among cornucopians.[24] Well, let's talk a little arithmetic. Seven *billion* years, he said. The planet Earth came into being only about four-and-a-half billion years ago. Life first wriggled no more than four billion years ago. Most animal phyla evolved less than 600 million years ago, and hominins split off from chimpanzees about five million years ago. Farming and settled life did not sprout until 10,000 years ago. The first civilization started less than seven thousand years ago. Yet, Simon believed that human population could keep growing for seven billion years.

Seven billion years is *one million times the length of time human civilization has lasted so far.*

---

23 Gregg Easterbrook, "Living Large; There'll soon be 300 million of us. But don't worry, there's plenty of room." *Los Angeles Times,* October 8, 2006.

24 Myers and Simon, *Scarcity or Abundance*, 65.

In 1994, the year in which Simon crowed about seven billion years, world population was doubling every forty-three years. At this speed in only 774 years there would be "*ten human beings for each square meter of* ice-free land on the planet," write Paul and Anne Ehrlich. To get a feeling for this, get four yardsticks and nine friends. Make a square with the yardsticks. Then stand inside with your friends.[25] Furthermore, "After 1900 years at this growth rate, the mass of the human population would be equal to the mass of the Earth; after 6000 years, the mass of the human population would equal the mass of the universe."[26] I know the Ehrlichs and they are kind and fair. So, they cut Marketing Professor Simon a great deal of slack and reckoned with a growth rate "*one million times* smaller than the actual 1994 value—that is, if it were only an infinitesimal 0.0000016 percent per year—Earth's population would still reach a mass exceeding that of the universe before the end of the 7-billion-year period Simon mentioned."[27] Simon's belief, then, is witless. Even feckless.

University of Colorado physics professor emeritus Al Bartlett writes that some of his friends quizzed Julian Simon after his seven-billion-year wisecrack and Simon backtracked that he meant only seven *million* years. (Be glad this guy wasn't doing your taxes!) A billion years is one thousand million years, so Simon was off a bit. Bartlett whipped out his calculator and reckoned what would happen if we grew only one percent for seven million years. He got 2.3×10^{30410}. He says, "This is a fairly large number!" The number of atoms in the universe is only about 3×10^{85}. The first number is thirty kilo-orders of magnitude bigger than the number of atoms in the universe. So, if

25 The Ehrlichs wrote this before we understood how quickly much of the ice might melt from greenhouse gases, so one of your friends can put one foot out of the square.

26 Paul R. Ehrlich and Anne H. Ehrlich, *Betrayal of Science and Reason: How Anti-Environmental Rhetoric Threatens Our Future* (Island Press, Washington, D.C., 1996), 66. In case you don't want to do the math yourself, the Ehrlichs do it on page 264.

27 Ehrlich and Ehrlich, *Betrayal of Science and Reason,* 66-67.

Simon only wanted the number of people to equal the number of atoms in the universe, how long would it take to get there at a growth rate of one percent? All of 17,000 years.[28]

Were you to hear some bedraggled street-corner prophet telling a lamppost that we could keep growing for seven billion (or million) years, you would chuckle and keep on trucking. However, Julian Simon was not a homeless schizophrenic. He was (and still is) the most gushed-over no-limits-to-growth economist for the *Wall Street Journal* tassel-loafer crowd. Such folks have no understanding of time or limits, or, it would seem, of numbers. The sheer silliness of Simon's seven-billion (or million, who cares?) big-talk shows that the cornucopians are dwelling in a dream world inside their heads and not in the world of earth, fire, air, and water. Long before there were make-believe worlds inside the Internet in which gamers could dwell, cornucopians had made up their own. It's hopeless to try to show faith-based cornucopians how they are wrong, but we do need to show others just how far from Earth the Mad Simonites are.

Now, I am no whiz at arithmetic. However, even I can understand Al Bartlett when he teaches simple math to the cornucopians. I don't know anyone smarter, but he is smart in a summer barbeque and beer way. Bartlett writes that a round Earth is a problem because a "sphere is bounded and hence is finite." He sees "a new paradigm... emerging which seems to be a return to the wisdom of the ancients." "The pro-growth people say that perpetual growth on this earth is possible. If the pro-growth people are correct, what kind of earth are we living on?"

Bartlett answers that:

> *[A] flat earth can accommodate growth forever, because a flat earth can be infinite in the two horizontal dimensions and also in the vertical downward direction. The infinite horizontal dimensions*

28 Albert A. Bartlett, "The Exponential Function, XI: The New Flat Earth Society," *Focus,* Carrying Capacity Network, Vol. 7, No. 1, 1997, 34-36.

> *forever remove any fear of crowding as population grows, and the infinite downward dimension assures humans of an unlimited supply of all of the mineral raw materials that will be needed by a human population that continues to grow forever.*[29]

So, the cornucopians are flat-Earthers.

Bartlett also warns of the *Flying Leap Syndrome*: jumping from a high building, an anti-Malthusian is thrilled and, for a second or two or three, thinks everything will be peachy keen forever. The ground is the truth the jumper ignored.[30] Splat. Bartlett lines up the kinds of anti-Malthusians in his essay "Malthus Marginalized," which should be widely read. He says that many of them "put their faith in Walt Disney's First Law: wishing will make it so."[31] As a realist, however, I go with the Iron Law of Traven: *This is the real world, muchachos, and you are in it.*[32]

Leftist Cornucopianism

For those who believe we will soon be able to shoot our too-many off into space to settle unknown planets, Garrett Hardin long ago threw cold water on that hope: "As of 1991 more than a quarter of a million people would have had to be shot off the earth *each day* just to keep earth's population constant at 5.3 billion."[33] I don't think that all of the nations of the world could even shoot one person a day off Earth nowadays. And we sure don't have anywhere to send them.

So far, I've been using my cudgel to beat up the cornucopians of the right. As I wrote at the beginning of this chapter, though, the left has a wealth of cornucopians, too. Let's take a look now at this other side. Some on the left say all we have to do for sustainability is to spread wealth better. Sandy Irvine brings them down to Earth in "The Great

29 Bartlett, "The New Flat Earth Society," *Focus*, 34.

30 Albert A. Bartlett, "Malthus Marginalized: The massive movement to marginalize the man's message," *The Social Contract*, Spring 1998, 241.

31 Bartlett, "Malthus Marginalized," 240.

32 B. Traven, *Treasure of the Sierra Madre.*

33 Garrett Hardin, *Living Within Limits*, 299.

Denial." He writes, "Studies in Guatemala, for example, show that the benefits of land redistribution would disappear within a generation simply because of population growth."[34] This is not a brush-off of the fairness and need for land redistribution, just an acknowledgment that poverty-alleviation and social-justice reforms are hopeless without population stabilization. I'll poke about more in this thicket later when I look at the immigration bugbear. However, we need some folks who are more or less on the left to take on leftist cornucopianism better than I can do. I'm glad that Phil Cafaro and other progressives are going to be doing this.

In 1994, Hardin showed the blunder of the social-justice foes of population stabilization:

> *Promoters of "ethnic power" love to scold rich countries for urging a lower birth rate in poor countries; the ethnics call this "genocide." But if a country is poor and powerless because it already has too many children for its resources, it will become even poorer and more powerless if it breeds more. If ethnic pronatalists have their way, poor countries will be ruined.*[35]

And what Hardin foresaw in 1994—too many children—has wrecked poor countries. Think of Niger, Rwanda, Mali, Ethiopia, Sudan, Bangladesh, Yemen, Somali, Honduras.... All sad lands with too many babies tumbling down from the storks flying overhead, babies swaddled in hopelessness for tomorrow.

Maybe the thought of scarcity itself is what's wrong. Hardin writes, "The idea of scarcity also needs examining, if we are not to be bewitched by words. The problem of poverty is almost invariably seen as one of *shortages*—shortages of supply. But note: poverty can just as logically be seen as a problem of *longages*—longages of demand."[36]

---

34 Irvine, "The Great Denial," 12.

35 Hardin, *Living Within Limits,* 307.

36 Garrett Hardin, "An Ecolate View of the Human Predicament," XI, 25.

We conservationists must keep our feet grounded in the true world. We must teach others about Simon's 7-billion-year make-believe, and show how simple math shows it to be a Xanadu-dreamworld for Blackberry-toting Ozymandiases. We must time and again remind others of the true world when they drift off into dream worlds with Tinkerbelle and Julian Simon—at least when they are fellow conservationists and environmentalists who have fallen for the big lie that Simon was right and Ehrlich was wrong. Not on your life. We must teach about the might of exponential growth, how even seemingly tiny yearly growth rates of one percent quickly swell into hungry throngs clawing at the wildworld for a bite and a sip.

The cornucopian myth rests upon not knowing much about Man's history and prehistory. Archaeologist Steven LeBlanc writes that "there is no evidence—not in the archaeological, ethnographic, or historical records—that humans have ever attained [ecological] balance for more than a couple of centuries anywhere on Earth. All humans grow, impact their environment, and, sooner or later, exceed the carrying capacity."[37]

Given all this, why don't today's environmentalists and conservationists bear down on overpopulation as they did in the 1960s and 1970s? I'll sing that woeful saga around our campfire in Chapter 9. There I'll also shed further light on left-wing cornucopianism. After all, it is the cornucopian left, not the Simonista right, that has sapped the hearts of conservationists and environmentalists on dealing with overpopulation.

37 Steven A. LeBlanc with Katherine Register, *Constant Battles: The Myth of the Peaceful, Noble Savage* (St. Martin's Press, NY, 2003), 54.

Chapter 6

Birth Dearth Follies

We geezers can still work.

—Susan Morgan

Just when I thought that cornucopianism couldn't get any dafter, along came a fellow by the name of Phillip Longman. In 2004, he wrote in *Foreign Affairs,* "Most people think overpopulation is one of the worst dangers facing the globe. In fact, the opposite is true. As countries get richer, their populations age and their birthrates plummet. And this is not just a problem of rich countries; the developing world is also getting older fast. Falling birthrates might seem beneficial, but the *economic* and *social* price is too steep to pay. The right policies could help turn the tide, but only if enacted before it's too late."[1] (My italics.)

Some countries (Japan and a few in Europe) have not only slowed how fast their populations are rising but also have brought them down to replacement or even to where their many footprints will slowly

1 Phillip Longman, "The Global Baby Bust," *Foreign Affairs,* May/June 2004.

ebb. In other words, they have gained what many conservationists, environmentalists, and others have long worked for. But, instead of marking this wonderful fulfillment with thousands of popping champagne corks raining down as condoms, the birth dearthers are warning of doom.

Longman's is not a lonely keening. Other shortsighted analysts and government leaders are overwrought with what they see as the economic and social woes of fewer births. From Italy and Greece to South Korea and Japan, governments are offering cash and other goads to women for having more than two children. With all this breathless screeching, the devil Longman foresees must be something truly awful. But, gee, it's not even up to the creepy-crawlies in the old movies on the late-night horror channel on your television. What are Longman and the others in a cold sweat about? There may be fewer working-age people to underwrite pension plans for retirees. Schools overbuilt from the Baby Boom may shutter. Hinterland villages might become emptier. And heavy-breeding clans might overrun lower-breeding clans. Are these nightmares the whole of it? I'm afraid so. That's all there is. And when we look more sharply, we might even say that there is no there there.

Worry about slowing growth is not wholly owned by the right; some progressives are also in a lather. Stewart Brand is. But the Merry-Prankster founder of *The Whole Earth Catalog* has always been the counterculture's answer to Julian Simon. *The Whole Earth Catalog* fairly gushed about technology, as Brand played the know-it-all, been-there-done-that, cool older brother of the hippies. There's also *National Geographic*. That gray, plodding, and unruffled old lady, flips out, using words like "dire" and "troubling" for birth slowdown on her map of Europe. She calls for bumping up births and opening the doors to more immigration to Europe.[2]

2 June 2005 map of Europe, *National Geographic*.

The birth-dearth worry is breathtaking in its narrowness and shallowness. Birth dearthers sweat over a slight shift in age within wealthy societies and how that might make it tougher to underwrite fat retirement policies for oldsters. Therefore, they want more births so there will be more workers to put up the money for retirees. Or, they want loads of young immigrants to tilt the age ratio. In other words, swell all the ills of overshooting carrying capacity to deal with a little, bitty accounting bump.

Nor are *Foreign Affairs* and like journals Longman's only soapbox. He also wrote a birth dearth article for *Conservation in Practice. Conservation in Practice,* for crying out loud, published by the Society for Conservation Biology. One would think that conservation biologists would at least know the first thing about carrying capacity and about how Man is sucking up over 40 percent of Net Primary Productivity already. Nary a thought is given to how more of us make more greenhouse gases. I guess all the awful outcomes from greenhouse gases are small potatoes up against plush retirement accounts. How the Society for Conservation Biology can publish such shortsighted trash is beyond me.

The first thing to understand about birth-dearth fears is that they are only economic and social. They are not *ecological.* Not even a teeny bit. They are about a world that has no life other than Man. Sitting back and thinking things through should make one understand how much more hopeless the ecological plight will be with billions more hungry mouths. Dealing with the economic and social plights tied to slowing births is child's play alongside the ecological Ragnarok that will be brought by through-the-roof populations and overshooting carrying capacity. All we need to do is to cut benefits a tad or raise retirement ages a year or two. Those who are bug-eyed and flushed about dealing with the overblown hassle brought by population stabilization are men and women of small cleverness and shuttered thoughtfulness. The out-of-doors to them must be only the sidewalks on Wall Street.

It is far better to work out the answers for such straightforward social and economic tweaks now than when we are faced with many more people and the even-more ghastly ecological woes of tomorrow brought by a landside of cooing babies. Phil Cafaro writes me, "The alternative, ever larger age-cohorts to preserve benefits without paying the piper ourselves, has all the markings of a classic Ponzi scheme."

None of the birth-dearth wailers weigh ecological outcomes; theirs is a world only of Man. Other Earthlings do not exist for them. However, owing to the bewildering way the too-few-babies drumbeat has been broadcast and bandwagoned, we must take this phony fear on. When we conservationists rumble with the birth dearthers, we should do two things: (1) belittle the chore of dealing with the social and economic hiccup of fewer births, and (2) underline the ecological nightmare brought by the ongoing population explosion. If conservationists spend too much time dealing with the economic and social worries from slowing birth rates, we will seem to go along with the Weltanschauung and standards of those who shun wild things. We would be, then, fighting on their turf, not ours. Instead, we must over and over again highlight the ecological impact of the population explosion. That is where our knowledge lies and that is where we can show the gruesome outcomes of overpopulation now.

Therefore, we need to talk about the following:

- Women are choosing to have fewer children for their own life's good and economic wellbeing. It is a big step backward for governments to once again see women as brood-moms for more taxpayers.
- Dreamed-up fears about steady or even slowly ebbing populations are economic, social, and political, not ecological.
- The whole birth-dearth teapot storm may be best seen as a clever scam run by those who get rich from growth. I am loath to see conspiracies, but given the devilish cunning of some industries in misleading folks and their leaders, we need to look at this with a

sharp eye. Cigarette tobacco, the ozone hole, and greenhouse gases are a few earlier plays of this kind.[3]

- Oldsters are not the only ones who lean on working-age men and women. Babies and children do, too. For reckoning percentages of working-age and nonworking-age folks, the birth dearthers leave out children. This shows how shallow their thinking is. Or maybe it shows how cunning and underhanded they are.
- Worries about lopsidedness between retirees and those paying into pensions can be straightforwardly dealt with now by raising the retirement age a few years. As Susan Morgan says, "We geezers can still work." Steve Camarota, Director of Research at the Center for Immigration Studies, takes the same tack. Instead of raising immigration to deal with the "dependence ratio" plight, Camarota says a slight raising of the retirement age would do it.[4] So, a little number crunching shows what a phony plight the birth dearthers have brewed up in their gurgling vat of overwrought fear.
- At some time in the true world, growth must stop. It will be much harder to deal with the economic shift later when there are even more bodies to feed and house, and to care for in old age. I have seen nothing from the birth dearthers that shows they have thought this far into tomorrow.
- The worst outcomes of population growth are ecological. Climate weirdness, habitat withering, and mass extinction are far harder to work out when there are more Men.

---

3 Chris Mooney, *The Republican War on Science* (Basic Books, New York, 2005). Mooney does a tip-top job of showing how the right-wing lynching of science and scientists from the health threat of tobacco to global warming is a clever public-relations game for big business.

4 Steve Camarota, "100 million More—Projecting the Impact of Immigration on the U.S. Population, 2007-2060," http://www.cis.org/articles/2007/back707.html.

- If we want to weigh social and economic plights, then feeding, housing, and caring for billions more is tougher than the phony retirement woe.
- Lastly, we can pitch the overwrought worries of the birth-dearthers as being not about a true threat, but rather as a soft puzzle to be worked out by the genius of the free-market system.

Man has already overshot ecological carrying capacity on Earth. The atmosphere and oceans no longer have the wherewithal to suck up the greenhouse gases we belch. Earth's carrying capacity at a European standard of living is at best five billion fewer people than live today—or less than two billion. (Don't get shook; two billion was Earth's population in 1927.) One of the few bright spots on the skyline is that growth in many of the wealthiest countries—which are those that do the worst harm to worldwide carrying capacity and the health of wild things—has stopped and in a few is beginning to slightly ebb. This is wonderful; something to be cheered, not dreaded. What better, happier job could we have than to reckon out how a no-growth society should work, to reckon what landscapes to rewild? What a top-notch puzzle for the sharp minds of free-market whiz kids!

In the end, what plight would fewer Men not lessen? The birth-dearth fears and calls for more babies are truly much ado about nothing. But they click with something in the mind of Man. Something in there is afraid of a population running flat. If our community doesn't grow, we feel that we have failed. Thus, the birth-dearth foolishness finds warm lodging in our heads. Even in otherwise good heads. On New Year's Day, 2007, *The New York Times* ran an article that read, "Japanese births rose for the first time in six years in 2006, according to government statistics announced Monday, offering a glimmer of hope for a rapidly aging society."[5]

5 "Japan Births Rise for 1st Time in 6 Yrs.," *The New York Times,* January 1, 2007.

What shortsighted madness drove them to write that?

Since that time, I have found scores of other articles and essays prattling the same nonsense. This tells me that the birth dearth has become a slice of the popular wisdom among public intellectuals, who, in their ecologically shallow braininess, never think of asking bedrock questions about carrying capacity or about the welfare of other Earthlings.

Those of us who understand carrying capacity and love wild things need to knock down birth-dearth fears whenever we hear them.

Chapter 7

Was Ehrlich Wrong?

During the 1980s, some of the worst famines in history afflicted large parts of Africa and South Asia, under the very noses of the United Nations and other international agencies. In absolute numbers, more illiterate, impoverished, and chronically malnourished people live in the world at the end of the twentieth century than at the beginning.[1]

—Marvin Harris

When I first thought to write a book about overpopulation and biodiversity—or the Man swarm and wild things—sometime in the late 1990s, I reckoned that the book would have more than a few words backing up Paul Ehrlich, *The Population Bomb,* and the other so-called doomsayers and their warnings. But after chewing over Eileen Crist's insights, I thought that I could overlook the squabbling about whether or not Ehrlich and his fellows were right or wrong. The more I've worked on *Man Swarm,* though, and thought about why conservationists and

1 Marvin Harris, *Our Kind* (Harper & Row, New York, 1989), 497.

environmentalists have backed off on caring about or working on overpopulation, the more I see the weight of the misunderstanding that "overpopulation has been proved not to be a problem."

One way cornucopians sweep away worry about overpopulation is by targeting Paul Ehrlich's 1968 book, *The Population Bomb,* and saying that because his warnings about a great starvation did not come true, fear about overpopulation is bunk.[2] Many folks are taken in by this thinking—even some environmentalists and conservationists. But, truly, was Ehrlich blowing smoke? I'll do my best here to answer that. I'm not going deep, though, only enough to shed some light on the misunderstanding. If you want to go deeper, read Paul Ehrlich's 1996 book with his wife Anne, *Betrayal of Science and Reason.*

Consider the times when Ehrlich wrote

First of all, recall that *The Population Bomb* was written in 1968. It was a book of its time and should be read in that light.

In 1968, family planning and much of what we take for granted in birth control today was not widespread and was still a hot potato. Abortion was still unlawful in most states. Heck, in some states contraception was illegal in the 1950s.

In 1968, widespread starvation was seen as something that could happen, and population growth was outstripping food growing. This was before the "Green Revolution," which goosed up how much food could be grown worldwide thanks mostly to fossil fuels and more irrigation. Better kinds of crops helped, but their weightiness has been overstated. More fertilizers and pesticides were key, and they are mostly made from petroleum. Thousands of irrigation dams have been built all over the world and the building has been done with fossil fuels. Gasoline-powered well drilling and water pumps have irrigated millions of acres. Tractors and other farm machinery running on gasoline and diesel have become much more widespread since 1968.

2 Paul R. Ehrlich, *The Population Bomb* (Sierra Club-Ballantine Books, New York, 1968).

When I reread *The Population Bomb* last year, I was somewhat taken aback by its apocalyptic feeling. But then I recalled: 1968. This was an apocalyptic time. A world war was much worried about then. The Cuban Missile Crisis had happened only a few years earlier. The Vietnam War was going badly, and there was fear of Chinese swarming in from the north. Red China was thought a great threat; Nixon had not yet opened the door to diplomatic relations. Fifteen years earlier we had been in a major land war with Red China in Korea.

And, in 1968, population growth had not yet slowed down anywhere; it was still raining babies in the United States, Europe, and Japan.

Millions were starving in China owing to shortfalls in food growing.

Understanding what the world was like in 1968 sheds light on the scenarios in *The Population Bomb* about widespread, deadly starvation leading to world war with Red China. This was seen as something that could easily happen.

Ehrlich wrote scenarios not predictions

We need to understand that Ehrlich's scolders make up forecasts from *The Population Bomb* to take down. Few books have been more misquoted or misunderstood. I wonder how many of those who "put it down" have ever picked it up, to read it? Cornucopians say that Ehrlich was making hard predictions when he was only throwing onto the table a handful of possible scenarios for the future. His scenarios, and those of other population writers, were for the worst outcomes if we didn't do anything to head them off. *If we didn't do anything to head them off.* That is key. Ehrlich and others weren't writing only to scare folks; they were writing to wake up everyone so they would do something to head off the worst. Others need to understand that we doomsayers want to be wrong. Cornucopians want to be right. Nothing could make me happier than for the woes I've written about not to happen. Much of the drive for the strong work undertaken worldwide to get birth control into the hands of women was thanks to Ehrlich and others waking world leaders and all kinds of folks. Without *The Population Bomb* and other "doom and gloom" warnings, things would be much worse for people today, and we could have already cracked the ten billion mark.

Ehrlich and everyone else, markedly foes, were shortsighted

Again, 1968 was an apocalyptic time. Many thought the shit would hit the fan soon (whatever the shit was, and that shifted with the doomsayer). Moreover, it is likely that bad things will still happen. Michael Klare's books are cool, thoughtful analyses of the likelihood of "resource wars."[3] Some of the worst scenarios in *The Population Bomb* could *yet* happen. *Yet* is the key word.

Where *The Population Bomb* and others went wrong was in shortsightedness. We naked apes—even the smartest and wisest—are often shortsighted. This is a glitch in our minds, I think. So, the worst of the ugsome overpopulation scenarios haven't happened—yet. Nonetheless, tens of millions have died or have been made wretched thanks to population growth since 1968. More starvation may be on the way. When? I don't know. But I do know that right now we are scalping millions of acres of wildlands that are the homes for thousands of kinds of threatened wildeors and worts. I know that right now we are sucking the oceans clean of fish for our snowballing populations to eat. The worst for Man is still up ahead. The worst for all the other Earthlings is right now—though it will get even worse.

3 Michael T. Klare, *Resource Wars: The New Landscape Of Global Conflict* (Henry Holt, New York, 2001); and *Blood and Oil: The Dangers And Consequences Of America's Growing Dependency On Imported Petroleum* (Henry Holt, New York, 2004).

Ehrlich offered answers and many were followed

Widely overlooked by those who snort at *The Population Bomb* is that Ehrlich offered a ladder of steps to head off starvation. Among them was all-out work to jump up agricultural productivity. This—the Green Revolution—was done and crop yields per acre rose. Again, much of the Green Revolution came from petroleum: fertilizer, pesticides, herbicides, and fuel to run irrigation pumps and tractors. Improved crops helped, but not as much as technological optimists want to believe. All together, improved crops from scientists such as Norman Borlaug, and the heavy use of fossil fuels and artificial fertilizer led to a rise of two percent a year in grain yield per acre all over the world from 1950 to 1990. In the last twenty years, though, yield has been going up only one percent a year or has flatlined. Technological optimists think that genetic reengineering will lead to another Green Revolution, but Lester Brown pricks their hope-bubble, writing, "Unfortunately, however, no genetically modified crops have led to dramatically higher yields ... Nor do they seem likely to do so, simply because conventional plant-breeding techniques have already tapped most of the potential for raising crop yields."[4]

Ehrlich and others called to make family planning widespread worldwide. Those of us then alive will recall that international birth control became a big deal. Not only in Europe and Japan and North America did birth rates come down sharply thanks to this campaign, but so did birth rates in many third-world countries as well. China, perhaps, showed the most gumption of any country in this undertaking (they had the worst threat staring them in the eyes, too) and cut births back amazingly. If you look at the third-world countries that worked hardest at lowering births in the 1960s and 1970s, you will also see those that have done much better economically.

4 Lester Brown, "Could Food Shortages Bring Down Civilization?" *Scientific American,* April 22, 2009.

Cornucopian predictions and scenarios of the time were much more wrong

In Chapter 4, I offered just a few of the cornucopian predictions from that era that I've found. Line them up alongside the *scenarios* from Ehrlich and others and see which are the most laughable today. Also think about which could still come to pass.

Famine has happened and is still happening

Some who pooh-pooh *The Population Bomb* and the writings of other "doomsayers" make it seem as though everyone is well fed in today's world and that there have been no bad famines. This isn't so. Starvation has struck time and time again since 1968. Remember Ethiopia? Remember Somalia? How about North Korea? Afghanistan? China? In truth, between 1968 and 1996, 250 million people died from starvation. This is about what the population of the United States was in 1996. Nearly ten million children a year have died from "hunger and hunger-related diseases" since *The Population Bomb* was written.[5] More than fifty countries that had fed themselves in the 1930s were net importers of food by the 1980s.[6] That statistic stands as one of the most hard-hitting truths about population growth and food production. Cornucopians utter not a word about these fifty. The hallowed leap in crop yield has happened in only some lands. In these other fifty, Malthus rules, with population growing faster than crop production during the Green Revolution. Insofar as tomorrow goes, if you want to know why the world shortly will be a hungry, oh, so hungry world, read Lester Brown's book, *Outgrowing The Earth.*[7] It is full of facts and figures, not feel-good fantasies.

5 Paul R. Ehrlich and Anne H. Ehrlich, *Betrayal of Science and Reason: How Anti-Environmental Rhetoric Threatens Our Future* (Island Press, Washington, DC, 1996), 71-76.

6 Clive Ponting, *A Green History Of The World* (St. Martin's Press, New York, 1991), 252.

7 Lester R. Brown, *Outgrowing The Earth* (W.W. Norton, New York, 2004).

After listing a few of the wars and internal fights wracking the world at the end of the twentieth century, distinguished anthropologist Marvin Harris wrote, "As one of these conflicts ends, another begins: Nothing warrants the hope that the rate of carnage is about to slacken."[8] Furthermore, "During the 1980s, some of the worst famines in history afflicted large parts of Africa and South Asia, under the very noses of the United Nations and other international agencies. In absolute numbers, more illiterate, impoverished, and chronically malnourished people live in the world at the end of the twentieth century than at the beginning."[9]

What Harris writes is key for understanding today's lay of the land. Thanks to the hard work, heart-felt caring for others, billions of dollars from wealthy countries, and the Green Revolution... well, hundreds of millions more are now threatened by starvation than in 1968. This is the sad thing. Doing good for those alive today sometimes sets up tomorrow to be worse than it would have been if nothing had been done. When I've written such things before, I've been damned as a hardhearted, mean, old man. In truth, however, I'm a realist with hard eyes and a soft heart. Too many do-gooders do good for their own self-esteem without thinking through tomorrow's outcomes of their boundless "love" for the needy.

Moreover, the Green Revolution with its leaning on fossil fuels helped lead to greater greenhouse gas pollution. So did other technological "fixes" that helped us to further overshoot carrying capacity. Such bad "side effects" will harm hundreds of millions of the world's poorest folks. Whichever way we turn, it seems that humanitarian and managerial successes can only make things better if they are wrapped up in work for population stabilization.

8 Harris, *Our Kind*, 497-498.

9 Harris, *Our Kind*, 497.

The Population Bomb was a roaring success

The Population Bomb and like books and warnings woke people up to the threat of overpopulation. By doing that, such warnings helped lead to workable population control and helped lead to growing more food.

Would these have happened without *The Population Bomb?* I think not.

So, those like Paul Ehrlich who warned of the threat of overpopulation in the 1960s and are now pooh-poohed may be the ones most responsible for their frightening scenarios not coming true. Chew on that.

The Great Bet myth

Those who say population growth is nothing to worry about, bring up a bet between Paul Ehrlich and Julian Simon, which Ehrlich "lost." This bet has become mythic and is often brought out to gainsay Ehrlich and all who have warned about overpopulation and overshooting carrying capacity. In truth, however, the bet had nothing to do with carrying capacity. It was about whether the price of five metals would go up or down over a set time of ten years. For the life of me, I don't understand why Ehrlich made the bet. I guess it was a belief that with rising population, all raw goods would become dearer and thus become worth more. Simon, believing in the endless cleverness of Man, thought everything would become cheaper. Again, it had nothing to do with whether or not Earth could house greater and greater swarms of Man.

Paul and Anne Ehrlich thoroughly debunk the bet myth in their 1996 book, *Betrayal of Science and Reason.* This is a top-notch book, by the way, and should be read by all conservationists and environmentalists. Indeed, for worthiness today, I'd say that it might be the Ehrlich's best book. The subtitle, *How Anti-Environmental Rhetoric Threatens Our Future,* tells what it is about. Paul and Anne go through the antiscientific myths, lies, and blather from the Nature haters one by one and slay each.

Anyway, prices for three of the metals went down somewhat and two went up, so, since the bet was $200 for each, Simon owed $400 and Ehrlich owed $600. Ehrlich and his fellows lost $200 in all. And that is all there is to the bet.

A few years later (in 1995), Julian Simon wrote in the *San Francisco Chronicle,* "Every measure of material and environmental welfare in the United States and in the world has improved rather than deteriorated. All long-run trends point in exactly the opposite direction from the projections of the doomsayers."[10] Simon was so sure of himself that he offered to bet on his belief. Paul Ehrlich and climatologist Stephen Schneider took on Simon and made fifteen predictions of things getting worse, from per capita cropland decline to buildup of greenhouse gases to per capita firewood decline to extinction to AIDS deaths.[11] Simon wouldn't take the bet. A full list of the fifteen is in *Betrayal* along with further explanation.[12] Whenever someone brings up the metal-price bet, the later bet should be thrown in their face.

And so, overall *The Population Bomb* is far more on target than otherwise. In no way, can one say that Ehrlich and others have been disproved. It is an outlandish myth. Don't believe it. And please shoot it down when you hear it.

However, Eileen Crist is right, as I showed in Chapter 2, that the weakness of *The Population Bomb* and most other overpopulation warnings is that they don't deal with how population growth wrecks the wildworld.

And that is the really big deal.

10 Julian Simon, "Earth's Doomsayers are Wrong," *San Francisco Chronicle,* May 12, 1995.

11 Paul R. Ehrlich and Stephen H. Schneider, "Bets and 'Ecofantasies,'" *Environmental Awareness,* Vol. 18, No. 2, 1995, 47-50.

12 Ehrlich and Ehrlich, *Betrayal of Science and Reason,* 100-104.

Chapter 8

A History of Thinking About Man's Limits

Man stalks across the landscape, and deserts follow in his footsteps.

—Herodotus

Growth for the sake of growth is the ideology of the cancer cell.

—Edward Abbey

In Chapter 2, I wrote how warnings of overshoot can be dealt into five broad outcomes: (1) hunger and starvation because we can't grow enough food; (2) squandering natural resources (raw goods) until we run out; (3) landscalping and the loss of land fertility; (4) cultural, economic, and political upheaval; and (5) wounds to wild things. As I said then, most of those writing about overshoot have targeted the first four outcomes, which hit Man, and have given little heed to how our population explosion harms wild things. In this chapter, I'll sweep through 2,500 years of warnings and worries about overshoot. The thinkers I showcase wander about in which outcomes they underline.

They also wander about in how much they bring Man's population growth to the forefront as the driver of landscalping and the other plights, but whether said or unsaid, population growth lurks in the history they unfold and the warnings they draw from it. Those coming from a resourcist bent believed and yet believe that better management and technological breakthroughs could help solve the curses of landscalping and overshoot. A good thesis or dissertation topic would be to delve into all of these warnings of overshoot to find how much they see population growth as a key driver.

Modern talk about limits began in 1798 when English clergyman and economist Thomas Robert Malthus wrote an "Essay on the Principle of Population," in which he reckoned, "Population, when unchecked, increases in a geometrical ratio. Subsistence increases only in an arithmetical ratio."[1] (World population would not hit one billion until 1804; it's now nearly seven billion.) Malthus's thinking poured the floor for all later thinking and writing about the swelling tide of Man. Among cornucopians, there is no worse sneer than *"Malthusian!"* Bury the good reverend though they would, his wisdom yet creeps out of the crypt to waylay them. We already looked at the Malthusian outlook in Chapter 3.

Watchers and thinkers long before Malthus saw the same, though. Twenty-five hundred years ago, the Greek historian Herodotus wrote, "Man stalks across the landscape, and deserts follow in his footsteps."[2] Plato also saw fingerprints from the withering hand of Man on the land. In *Critias,* he wrote that after logging and goat browsing in the high hills of Attica, "What now remains compared with what then existed is like the skeleton of a sick man, all the fat and soft earth having been wasted away, and only the bare framework of the land being left."[3]

1 William R. Catton Jr., *Overshoot: The Ecological Basis of Revolutionary Change* (University of Illinois Press, Urbana, 1982), 126.

2 Garrett Hardin, *Living Within Limits: Ecology, Economics, and Population Taboos* (Oxford University Press, New York, 1993), 17.

3 Quoted in H. C. Darby, "The Clearing of the Woodland in Europe," in

Right before and after the time of Malthus, scientists such as Comte George-Louis Leclerc de Buffon and Alexander von Humboldt worried about the harm done by swelling swarms of Men. George Perkins Marsh, Abraham Lincoln's ambassador to Italy and Turkey, wrote his path-finding book *Man and Nature* about the scalped landscapes he saw in the Mediterranean. He believed that the downfall of earlier civilizations came from the flaying of their land.[4] Following Marsh's lead in weighing land-blighting by Middle Eastern, Egyptian, Greek, Roman, and North African empires, and spurred by the god-awful Dust Bowl of the 1930s (little recalled today it seems), between 1935 and 1955 scientists and conservationists carefully looked at soil erosion over thousands of years and warned the living.

In 1935, Yale botanist Paul Sears, one of America's leading scientists, eyed the loss of topsoil in the United States in his book *Deserts on the March.* Writing during the height of the Dust Bowl, Sears asked, "Is the human race digging its own grave in North America?" He went on to warn,

> *Man has become the sponsor of a biological experiment without known parallel in the history of the earth and its inhabitants. He is the first example of a single species to become predominant over the rest.... He no longer accepts, as living creatures before him have done, the pattern in which he finds himself, but has destroyed that pattern and from the wreck is attempting to create a new one. That, of course, is cataclysmic revolution.*[5]

Sears saw population growth as the driver behind desertification. In a Preface to the Fourth Edition of *Deserts On The March*

William L. Thomas Jr., ed., *Man's Role In Changing The Face Of The Earth* (The University of Chicago Press, 1956), 185.

4 Clarence Glacken, "Changing Ideas of the Habitable World," in *Man's Role In Changing The Face Of The Earth*, 70-92.

5 Paul B. Sears, *Deserts On The March* (University of Oklahoma Press, Norman, 1980 (1935)). Sears retired to northern New Mexico. I was thrilled in 1972 when he wrote me to back my work against building Cochiti Dam on the Rio Grande.

written in 1980, Sears told how demographers had earlier guessed that "the population of the United States would stabilize at around 160 million by 1960."[6] If only it had. (It's over 300 million today and it could hit 800 million by 2100 if we don't do something.)

Carl O. Sauer, the leading geographer of the mid-1900s, wrote in 1938, "In the space of a century and a half—only two full life-times—more damage has been done to the productive capacity of the world than in all of human history preceding." He saw it as "a reckless glutting of resource for quick profit."[7]

In 1938, the assistant chief of the United States Soil Conservation Service (SCS), W. C. Lowdermilk, was asked by the Department of Agriculture to make an on-site "survey of land use in olden countries for the benefit of our farmers and stockmen… in this country." For eighteen months, Lowdermilk and his fellows roamed through western and southern Europe, North Africa, and the Middle East. The Soil Conservation Service published his report with photographs in a thirty-page bulletin, *Conquest of the Land Through 7,000 Years.* Lowdermilk found "tragedy after tragedy deeply engraved in the sloping land throughout the lands of early civilizations." He ended *Conquest of the Land* with the "Eleventh Commandment" that he had first given in a talk in Jerusalem in 1939, "If any shall fail in this stewardship of the land thy fruitful fields shall become sterile stony

6 Sears, *Deserts On The March,* vi.

7 Carl O. Sauer, "Theme of Plant and Animal Destruction in Economic History," *Journal of Farm Economics* 20 (1938), 765-775, reprinted in Paul Shepard and Daniel McKinley, editors, *Environ/Mental: Essays on the Planet as Home* (Houghton Mifflin, Boston, 1971), 54.

ground and wasting gullies, and thy descendants shall decrease and live in poverty or perish from off the face of the earth."[8] If only we had heeded his wisdom then and since worldwide.

In 1948, Fairfield Osborn, President of the Conservation Foundation and a well-known scientist, wrote *Our Plundered Planet*, which also drew on fallen civilizations that had grubbed the wealth out of their lands. Osborn showed how a swiftly growing population was a threat. He warned that the world's human population could double in seventy years. The world population in 1948 was about 2.3 billion.[9] Many brushed him off as a fearmonger. Was he? Well, it is now about sixty years later and the world's population is nearly seven billion: *Three times as much.* Osborn worried that world population would reach 4.6 billion in 2018. Eight years before his date, there were 2.4 billion more people than he foresaw! We need to keep his forecast in mind when we hear cornucopians sneer at other warnings about population growth. (Not long ago I reread *Our Plundered Planet* and was taken by how good it still is. Nothing outdated or milquetoast about Osborn.)

Another leading conservationist of the time, William Vogt, wrote *Road To Survival* in 1948, wherein he warned, "By excessive breeding and abuse of the land mankind has backed itself into an ecological trap." He wisely brought overpopulation and bad stewardship

8 W. C. Lowdermilk, *Conquest of the Land Through 7,000 Years*, Agriculture Information Bulletin No. 99, U.S. Dept. of Agriculture, Soil Conservation Service, August 1953. The Department of Agriculture was yet handing out copies of Lowdermilk's report in the early 1970s when I got my copy. Soil conservation was still a crusade then. We don't seem to think much about it today. We will pay for that. A PDF of *Conquest of the Land* for reading or downloading is at www.rewilding.org. I strongly recommend it. SCS is now NRCS, or Natural Resources Conservation Service.

9 Fairfield Osborn, *Our Plundered Planet* (Little, Brown and Company, Boston, 1948).

together as drivers of ecological breakdown. Conservation historian Roderick Nash sees Vogt and Osborn as laying the groundwork for Paul Ehrlich and Garret Hardin.[10]

About this time, Aldo Leopold wrote in his insightful essay, "Round River," "One of the penalties of an ecological education is that one lives alone in a world of wounds."[11] In this, I believe, the great conservationist was mulling over the harm we do to wildlife and wildlands, not just how we chugalug raw goods.

Some of the best and toughest thinking about overpopulation was offered in articles and scientific papers in academic journals in the 1950s and 1960s. It's hard to track these down now, but some of them found their way into "environmental studies" anthologies beginning in the late 1960s with Paul Shepard and Daniel McKinley's wonderful stock of papers, *The Subversive Science: Essays Toward an Ecology of Man.*[12] *When I read Subversive Science* in 1972, I was gripped by it. Few books shaped me as it did. I just reread it, trolling for goodies for this book, and recalled why I liked it so much the first time. What a wealth of thoughtful wisdom is between its covers. I don't know if one can find it today, but it would be a good text for college courses yet and a worthwhile read for any conservationist. Indeed, if you want to understand the history of how we talked about overpopulation in the middle of the last century, which was the key time after all, you need to know some of the scientists and their papers squirreled away in *Subversive Science, Environ/Mental,* Rod Nash's *American Environmentalism,* and other academic anthologies.

10 William Vogt, *Road to Survival* (William Sloane Associates, New York, 1948), 284. Excerpted as "The Global Perspective" in Roderick Frazier Nash, ed., *American Environmentalism: Readings in Conservation History* Third Edition (McGraw-Hill, New York, 1990), 166. Vogt strongly backed the campaign against the Sagebrush Rebellion's attempt to steal the public lands in the late 1970s (in which campaign I was a player).

11 Luna B. Leopold, ed., *Round River: From the Journals of Aldo Leopold* (Oxford University Press, New York, 1953), 165.

12 Paul Shepard and Daniel McKinley, editors, *The Subversive Science: Essays Toward an Ecology of Man* (Houghton Mifflin, Boston, 1969).

In 1955, Tom Dale of the Soil Conservation Service and Vernon Gill Carter of the National Wildlife Federation wrote the most thorough work up to that time of Man's wounding of the land: *Topsoil and Civilization*. After carefully sifting through the archaeology and history of the world's civilizations, they wrote, "The fundamental cause for the decline of civilization in most areas was deterioration of the natural-resource base on which civilization rested."[13]

A pet peeve of mine is that today's writers overlook the work of Sears, Lowdermilk, Osborn, Vogt, Dale and Carter, and others like them, and come up with cultural or political grounds for the fall of civilizations, overlooking population growth and landscalping. In many ways, these older works are still the best for grasping why civilizations slump and crash, but I don't see them cited. Modern scholarship is weak in its lack of knowledge about trailblazing scholarship fifty to one hundred years ago, and uppity about overlooking worthwhile writing not in a handful of peer-reviewed journals today. Good as some of today's books like Jared Diamond's *Collapse* may be, I still think the older books are more straightforward and should be read first. We know-it-all brats today do not look up to the wisdom of our elders, and such churlishness hurts our understanding of the world.

In 1955, the year *Topsoil and Civilization* came out, wise and learned men (but no women—times have changed, thank goodness) from all over the world gathered for a week in Princeton, New Jersey, to chew over "Man's Role in Changing the Face of the Earth." The great American geographer Carl O. Sauer was co-chair along with the free-roaming scholars Lewis Mumford and Marston Bates. A year later, the two-volume proceedings were published.[14] Although little known

13 Vernon Gill Carter and Tom Dale, *Topsoil and Civilization* Revised Edition (University of Oklahoma Press, Norman, 1974), 20.

14 Thomas, *Man's Role in Changing the Face of the Earth*. A couple of years ago, I read this mighty work again and found it still loaded with sharp insights and sorely needed information. In some academic fields, work done decades ago has not been bettered. *Man's Role* is proof of that.

today, this meeting laid the broad scholarly background for talking about carrying capacity and how we harm Earth. Meeting-goers ran the ladder from cheerleaders for mining and other kinds of landscalping to farsighted conservationists. I find it bewitching that Charles Darwin's grandson Sir Charles Galton Darwin and Aldo Leopold's son Luna Leopold were there.[15] In an ending session, Darwin said that he was "an absolutely convinced Malthusian."[16] Although he believed that we would not stop population growth, he steadfastly called out to his fellows, "Do not let us be blamed by our descendants for not trying."[17] Though I have no offspring, Sir Charles has given me the path down which I walk when ere I've thought of giving up. To be damned for woodenheadness and gutlessness by those who come after us would be a scalding kind of hell.

In 1956, Shell Oil Company geologist M. King Hubbert "predicted that the peak of crude-oil production in the United States would occur between 1966 and 1972." (It peaked in 1970.)[18] Hubbert's work gave bedrock to thinking about resource depletion.

So, long before what many believe to be the beginning of today's conservation movement—or of "The Environmental Movement"—in the 1960s, thoughtful scientists and historians were looking to yesterdays to understand today. There they found deserts in the footsteps of civilizations. Rutgers biologist David Ehrenfeld, whose book *The Arrogance of Humanism* needs to be read by everyone, wrote, "'Desert-makers' is truly as appropriate a title for humans as 'tool-users.'"[19]

15 Luna Leopold, a great hydrologist, died in early 2006. I wonder if any of the symposium's other participants yet live?

16 Thomas, *Man's Role,* 1115.

17 Thomas, *Man's Role,* 1117.

18 Richard Heinberg, *The Party's Over: Oil, War and the Fate of Industrial Societies* (New Society Publishers, Gabriola Island, British Columbia, Canada, 2003), 88.

19 David Ehrenfeld, *The Arrogance of Humanism* (Oxford University Press, NY, 1978), 115.

David Brower, while executive director of the Sierra Club, shoved human population growth into the forefront of "The Environmental Movement" when he published Paul Ehrlich's *The Population Bomb* in 1968. In his foreword to the book, Brower wrote,

It was only twelve years ago [1956] that we even suggested, in any Sierra Club publication, that uncontrolled population was a menace. We went far enough to write: "People are recognizing that we cannot forever continue to multiply and subdue the earth without losing our standard of life and the natural beauty that must be part of it....These are the years of decision—the decision of men to stay the flood of man."[20]

In *The Population Bomb*, Paul Ehrlich warned,

[T]he world's population will continue to grow as long as the birth rate exceeds the death rate; it's as simple as that. When it stops growing or starts to shrink, it will mean that either the birth rate has gone down or the death rate has gone up or a combination of the two. Basically, then, there are only two kinds of solutions to the population problem. One is a "birth rate solution," in which we find ways to lower the birth rate. The other is a "death rate solution," in which ways to raise the death rate—war, famine, pestilence—find us.[21]

Hundreds of thousands of copies of *The Population Bomb* sold.[22] Overpopulation was brought up to the front burner. More than once, Paul Ehrlich was a guest on Johnny Carson's *The Tonight Show.*

In the year *The Population Bomb* came out, leading Italian industrialist Dr. Aurelio Peccei gathered a small worldwide bunch

20 David Brower, "Foreword" in Paul R. Ehrlich, *The Population Bomb* (Ballantine Books/Sierra Club, New York, 1968).

21 Paul R. Ehrlich, *The Population Bomb* (Ballantine Books/Sierra Club, New York, 1968), 34.

22 I helped pass out a hundred or more copies of *The Population Bomb* (printed as a cheap pocketbook) at the University of New Mexico. I still have six copies in my library.

of businessmen and scientists to talk about tomorrow. Out of that meeting grew The Club of Rome, which asked a team of scientists at the Massachusetts Institute of Technology (MIT), led by Donella Meadows, to study exponential growth of human population and industrialization. That work, with early computer models, was published in 1972 as *The Limits to Growth,* and ended with a cold-water-in-the-face warning:

> *If the present trends in world population, industrialization, pollution, food production, and resource depletion continue unchanged, the limits to growth on this planet will be reached sometime within the next one hundred years. The most probable result will be a rather sudden and uncontrollable decline in both population and industrial capacity.*[23]

Limits to Growth was a key step in reckoning how we harm Earth's wherewithal to keep us alive and healthy, although the no-limits establishment pissed on it from a great height. Meadows's follow-up study in 1992, *Beyond the Limits,* was a more thorough work, and *Limits to Growth: The 30-Year Update* even more so.[24] These are resource conservation books, however, and none give much heed to wild things. Even so, it is telling that a study looking only at the well being of Mankind can come out so strongly on the need to limit growth. One doesn't need to be a lover of wild things to worry about the outcome of the population explosion, to see that there are too many of us.

David Brower kept up his work on population with Friends of the Earth (FOE), which he started after he was fired from the Sierra Club. Friends of the Earth rushed *The Environmental Handbook* into

23 Donella H. Meadows, Dennis L. Meadows, Jorgen Randers, and William W. Behrens III, *The Limits to Growth* (Universe Books, New York, 1972), 23. Sadly, Donella Meadows passed away in 2001, after a distinguished career of warning people of the folly of unlimited growth.

24 Donella H. Meadows, Dennis L. Meadows, and Jorgen Randers, *Beyond the Limits: Confronting Global Collapse, Envisioning a Sustainable Future* (Chelsea Green Publishing Company, Post Mills, VT, 1992); Donella Meadows, Jorgen Randers, and Dennis Meadows, *Limits to Growth: The 30-Year Update* (Chelsea Green Publishing Company, White River Junction, VT, 2004).

print in time for the First National Environmental Teach-In on April 22, 1970. The Teach-In became better known as Earth Day. This mass-market paperback was a quick paste-up of new and reprinted articles along with wide-roaming thoughts on how to get out of our plight. It didn't beat around the bush on population and called for making population stabilization a national policy and giving foreign aid "only to countries with major programs to curb population growth." We need to bring back this goal today and make it a key plank in a population stabilization platform. Furthermore, we should halt immigration from any country that does not have a strong population stabilization program. *The Environmental Handbook* also set as a long-term goal "half of the present world population, or less." In 1970, there were fewer than four billion of us, so some environmentalists and conservationists were calling for a world population of fewer than two billion humans. Gad, what a time that was. We have fallen so far. Overpopulation was a plight strongly acknowledged at the time within the radical "ecology" movement.[25] All this should give some feeling for how widespread worry about overpopulation was in 1970 and how it was not "politically incorrect" to earnestly call for lowering worldwide population, or—my goodness—for giving aid only to countries working to lower their populations. What if progressives still had such a backbone?

At an Earth Day 1970 rally at the University of Michigan, University of Wisconsin botanist Hugh Iltis warned that we were bringing on a mass extinction—and that overpopulation was making it happen.[26]

Since the 1970s, there has been a small flood of books about population growth, resource depletion, and carrying capacity. In *Living Within Limits* and *The Ostrich Factor,* lion-hearted Garret Hardin slew

25 Keith Murray, Berkeley Ecology Center, "Suggestions Toward an Ecological Platform" in Garrett de Bell, Editor, *The Environmental Handbook* (Ballantine/Friends of the Earth, New York, 1970), 317-324.

26 Dave Foreman, *Rewilding North America* (Island Press, Washington, DC, 2004), 20.

the sacred cows of today's beliefs right and left. The Ehrlichs lay out why they think (rightly) that the population bomb has exploded in their strong, sound, sweeping *The Population Explosion,* which also stands out for its early eyeballing of global warming.[27] However, the best of the books on overpopulation and the key one for lovers of wild things is *Overshoot* by William R. Catton, Jr.[28] I draw on it deeply in this book and in my other writings. I won't list other books about overpopulation here, but I give some of them short reviews in "Books of the Big Outside" at www.rewilding.org.

Of the many books I have read about our plight, one stands out for its tough truthfulness and fearless seeking of understanding. It is *The Spirit In The Gene* by Australian photojournalist Reg Morrison.[29] Wide-thinking biologist Lynn Margulis wrote the Foreword, and Harvard's E. O. Wilson blurbed on the back, "Reg Morrison offers varied and often fascinating documentation from ecology, economics, and natural history to portray human history for what it is, a Greek tragedy in which our greatest strengths are no less than our most dangerous flaws."[30] Morrison writes, "The graph of human population growth over the past ten thousand years is disturbingly similar to the population graph of an animal entering what we would commonly describe as a plague phase."[31] *The Spirit In The Gene* is an unsettling book, and may be only for those with a daring mind and a leather soul.

Lately, a few historical and geopolitical overviews belly up to the bar in their willingness to look at human population growth and the shadows where it may lead. *The Human Web: A Bird's-Eye View Of World*

---

27 Ehrlich and Ehrlich, *The Population Explosion.* Garrett Hardin, *Living Within Limits: Ecology, Economics, and Population Taboos* (Oxford University Press, New York, 1993); and *The Ostrich Factor: Our Population Myopia* (Oxford University Press, New York, 1999).

28 William R. Catton, Jr., *Overshoot: The Ecological Basis of Revolutionary Change* (University of Illinois Press, Urbana and Chicago, 1982).

29 Reg Morrison, *The Spirit In The Gene: Humanity's Proud Illusion and the Laws of Nature* (Cornell University Press, Ithaca, New York, 1999).

30 E. O. Wilson, back cover blurb, Morrison, *The Spirit In The Gene.*

31 Morrison, *The Spirit In The Gene,* xi.

History by the son-father pair of J. R. McNeill and William McNeill may be the best short overview of world history. William McNeill, author of the mighty *The Rise of the West,* in 1976 wrote *Plagues and Peoples,* a trailblazing work that showed how epidemic disease has often steered world history (it was smallpox, not guns, horses, and Spanish military genius, that smashed the Aztec Empire).[32] J. R. McNeill, his son and author of *Something New under the Sun: An Environmental History of the Twentieth Century World,* is also a top historian. In *The Human Web,* they see global civilization rising over the last 5,000 years as local and regional civilizations slowly spun "webs" of trade, travel, and takeover among one another. Far-flung civilizations had their own kinds of epidemic diseases that became set as populations grew big enough to keep the germs always alive in someone's body. (To wit: about half a million people in one web was needed to keep a pool of measles happy.) Among their host humans, such ills became less deadly as years went by; adapting human populations thereby climbed. But when webs met and overlapped, diseases killed millions as they flowed into new, unexposed populations. World population growth could not truly take off until Europe, India, China, and lands in-between were brought into the same epidemiological world, about 1800 C.E. when "the world's separate webs fused."[33] The weaving together of the great webs left no big epidemic-naive populations. The McNeill's insightful breakthrough has long been needed to help us understand why population growth shot up in the last two hundred years. (We seven billion, worldly with all the old ills, now find at our door new diseases to which we may be nightmarishly naked.)

A gusher of books on the coming oil shortage has come out in the last few years. I find Richard Heinberg's *The Party's Over* most sound because he draws on petroleum geologists and doesn't fall into

32 William H. McNeill, *Plagues and Peoples* (Anchor Press/Doubleday, New York, 1976).

33 J. R. McNeill and William McNeill, *The Human Web: A Bird's-Eye View Of World History* (W.W. Norton & Company, New York, 2003), 210-211.

conspiracy theories. He also pops the rosy bubbles of alternative-energy and organic-farming boosters, showing that we've overshot carrying capacity and there are no silver bullets. He writes, "Both leftist and rightist ideologies contain an element of unreality or even denial concerning population and resource issues."[34] Given that a progressive—even countercultural—Canadian publisher, New Society Publishers, published his book, Heinberg is forthright about overpopulation and how immigration drives growth in the United States. Environmentalists and progressive conservationists should read *The Party's Over,* because it cannot be brushed off as right-wing or nativist, at least not among folks who can think.

On the other hand, world security expert Michael Klare's *Resource Wars* should ring true with foreign policy realists and those worried about American security. He is more straightforward in looking at how population growth plays in world happenings than are most environmental and conservation leaders. He writes, "The growing demand for resources is driven, to a considerable degree, by the dramatic increase in human numbers." He also gives weight to "the spread of industrialization to more and more areas of the globe and the steady worldwide increase in personal wealth...."[35] He sees most bickering in the world today and tomorrow as "*resource wars*—conflicts that revolve, to a significant degree, over the pursuit or possession of critical materials."[36] He carefully weighs the threat of greater and greater water shortages in hungry lands that have booming crowds and that are hobbled to irrigated farming. Climate breakdown now swells an even bigger wave of hunger and thirst toward them.

---

34 Richard Heinberg, *The Party's Over: Oil, War and the Fate of Industrial Societies* (New Society Publishers, Gabriola Island, British Columbia, Canada, 2003), 187. I wholeheartedly believe in and back organic farming, but it isn't going to feed our growing swarm.

35 Michael T. Klare, *Resource Wars: The New Landscape Of Global Conflict* (Henry Holt and Company, New York, 2002), 15.

36 Klare, *Resource Wars,* 25.

The late Samuel Huntington, in *The Clash of Civilizations and the Remaking of World Order,* looked at population growth as a slide to a wobblier world. He wrote that "the Resurgence of Islam has been fueled by equally spectacular rates of population growth."[37] When I see news photos of shouting, fist-pumping, shoulder-to-shoulder mobs of horny, hungry, young men in the Moslem world, I shake my head in disbelief at the Pollyanna angels who think there will be peace. God love 'em for their righteous work, but without population stabilization, the peacemakers may as well part the Red Sea with the wave of a stick. The sad truth is that fast population growth unleashes a chain of outcomes: high unemployment among young men, which leaves them frustrated and unsettled, unable to start their lives and families, and prey to radicals and to hatred of others who seem to have what they can't have.

Lester Brown, through the organizations he has started, Worldwatch Institute and Earth Policy Institute, has long been the foremost thinker about whether the growing world crowd can feed itself tomorrow. His 2004 book, *Outgrowing The Earth: The Food Security Challenge In An Age Of Falling Water Tables And Rising Temperatures,* is a wakeup! slap to the jowls of all cornucopians. By pulling in the whole puzzle—erosion, withered soil fertility, pricier and dearer fossil-fuel-based fertilizers and herbicides/pesticides, dropping groundwater, drying rivers and snowpacks and mountain glaciers, climatic weirdness, crashing seafood stocks, fatter diets, and population growth—Brown should sober up the worst optimism-drunk. If you want to understand why we are looking at an awfully hungry and unsettled tomorrow, you must read *Outgrowing the Earth.*[38]

37 Samuel P. Huntington, *The Clash of Civilizations and the Remaking of World Order* (Simon & Schuster, New York, 1996), 116.

38 Lester R. Brown, *Outgrowing The Earth: The Food Security Challenge In An Age Of Falling Water Tables And Rising Temperatures* (W.W. Norton & Company, New York, 2004).

Archaeologist Stephen LeBlanc, after sifting through lessons in the dirt, lays out in his landmark book *Constant Battles* how our long tale is about struggle between neighboring bands over scant resources. His book is so key to understanding our plight that I'll look at it more fully later.

No other writer, however, has done better than Ed Abbey in shining a light on the truth:

> *Growth for the sake of growth is the ideology of the cancer cell.*

A poster or plaque with those words should hang on the wall in the reception area of every conservation and environmental office.[39]

The ideology of the cancer cell has dogged followers among economists, politicians, and social activists of the left, liberal, and conservative political spectrums, among radicals and moderates, among corporate CEOs and peasants. We seem to have a deep-seated loathing to acknowledge limits; we may be genetically wired to be optimists with the kind of deathless nothing-can-stop-us rush found in a bunch of teenagers with a hot car and a case of beer. From street rap to NASCAR engines' roar to Wall Street's bell, the shout is, "Don't tell us about limits!"

39 The Rewilding Institute has a bumpersticker with those words. www.rewilding.org

Chapter 9

The Great Backtrack

Unlike plagues of the dark ages or contemporary diseases we do not yet understand, the modern plague of overpopulation is soluble by means we have discovered and with resources we possess. What is lacking is not sufficient knowledge of the solution but universal consciousness of the gravity of the problem and education of the billions who are its victims.[1]

—Rev. Martin Luther King, Jr., 1966

Over the last thirty years, there have been many shifts in the conservation, environmental, and resource camps. Maybe the most striking and deep-rooted is that these camps worked hard to spotlight the booming Man swarm in the 1960s and 1970s, yet today overpopulation worry is kicked into the corner and shunned like an old, smelly dog. This is a tectonic shift.

1 Martin Luther King, Jr., Speech given after getting Margaret Sanger Award in Human Rights, 1966. Quoted in Paul R. Ehrlich and Anne H. Ehrlich, *Population Resources Environment: Issues in Human Ecology* (W. H. Freeman and Company, San Francisco, 1970), 211.

In today's world, population growth is overlooked as the mainspring of ecological and social woes. I've been clipping news stories about wretchedness and starvation in Africa for a long while. Most of these reports don't tip a hat to population growth as the root (or even a rootlet) or look at how population stabilization could help lessen the woes. In the fall of 2005 there was much ado about starvation in Niger. Left unsaid about this forlorn land was that the United Nations says it has the highest birthrate in the world. The beaten-down souls highlighted in the news all seemed to have nine kids more or less. Could this have anything to do with why Niger was a heartbreaking, hopeless, hungry wreck? It didn't seem as though any of the reporters were asking.

Likewise, environmentalists in the United States lambaste suburban and exurban sprawl (as they should). But do they acknowledge that over half of sprawl is driven by population growth, that the United States is the only big, wealthy land with third-world growth rates, and that our growth is mostly goosed along by immigration? Not that I've heard lately. This head-in-the-sand mood showed itself further in the fall of 2006 when the United States snapped the 300-million-head wire. Environmentalists and conservationists should have been marching in the streets to warn that we must freeze our population and stop growth. But those who should understand that there are limits to growth mostly overlooked this frightful benchmark. When environmentalists did say something about it, they seemed to shrug it off as small potatoes. For one, a spokesman for the Environmental Defense Fund said that population growth itself wasn't what was wrong, that it was where people chose to live.[2] I shook my head in disbelief. No, that's not true. I yelled at the paper, balled it up in my hands, and threw it against the wall, cussing up a blue streak all the while. Later, I smoothed it out so I could clip the article. There are more than one or two articles in my files that look like they've gone through the same.

2 "U.S. Population on Track to 300 Million," *The New York Times,* October 14, 2006.

When we snapped the 200-million wire 'way back in 1968, scientists and leading antiwar do-gooders such as Linus Pauling and Jonas Salk put their names on a full-page newspaper ad about the milestone/millstone. The ad splashed a few words across a photo of bouncing, diapered, smiling baby. The words? "Threat to Peace." In smaller type, they explained, "It is only being realistic to say that skyrocketing population growth may doom the world we live in."[3]

In Great Britain, the new Ecology Party (Greens) worked on what a sustainable population would be; Oxfam (the international antipoverty foundation in England) called for zero population growth; and Greenpeace in the United Kingdom was shouting, "Stop at Two." Today, the Greens, Oxfam, and Greenpeace have dropped population stabilization to where none of them even breathe a word about it. A once-hardhitting British group, Population Countdown, "worried about alienating funders, became Population Concern and, more recently, Interact Worldwide."[4]

How far conservationists and environmentalists have fallen from what now seem to me to be the Golden Years of the 1960s and 1970s. No wonder I'm such an old sorehead.

If conservationists are going to keep the wildworld, we must deeply and truthfully ask why we've backed away from the overpopulation fight.

Historian Samuel Hays, in his landmark book *Beauty, Health, and Permanence,* wrote that in the 1970s, "It was rather widely agreed that population growth should be limited."[5] Widely, indeed; good heavens, former President Eisenhower in 1968 said, "Once, as president,

3 John Tierney, "The Kids Are All Right," *New York Times,* October 14, 2006.

4 David Nicholson-Lord, "Whatever happened to the teeming millions?" Optimum Population Trust, November 2005.

5 Samuel P. Hays, *Beauty, Health, and Permanence: Environmental Politics in the United States, 1955-1985* (Cambridge University Press, New York, 1987), 224.

I thought and said that birth control was not the business of our Federal Government. The facts changed my mind ... I have come to believe that the population explosion is the world's most critical problem." Keep in mind that Ike said this in 1968 as Vietnam was blowing up in our hands and when the Cold War was about as hot as it got. Three years earlier, President Lyndon Johnson had told the United Nations that "five dollars invested in population control is worth one hundred dollars invested in economic growth."[6] That wisdom should be etched into marble above the main door of the World Bank. A Gallup poll in 1976 showed that in North America "84 percent said that they did not want more people in their country and 82 percent not in their community."[7] Today we seem happy to wallow together cheek to jowl, butt to butt in an endless sardine can. U.S. population in 1976 was a little over 200 million; now it is about 310 million. Juggle those two numbers in your head and think through what they mean.

Why the Retreat?

Leon Kolankiewicz and Roy Beck, in their two papers, "The Environmental Movement's Retreat From Advocating U.S. Population Stabilization" and "Forsaking Fundamentals," have undertaken the most thorough look at why U.S. environmental and conservation bodies have shunned population quandaries.[8] William Ryerson, president of the Population Media Center, wrote in *Wild Earth* in 1998/99 how political correctness led to the international backing-off on overpopulation.[9]

6 Quoted in Ehrlich and Ehrlich, *Population Resources Environment*, 259, 295.

7 Hays, *Beauty, Health, and Permanence*, 224.

8 Roy Beck and Leon Kolankiewicz, "The Environmental Movement's Retreat from Advocating U.S. Population Stabilization (1970-1998): A First Draft of History," and Leon Kolankiewicz and Roy Beck, "Forsaking Fundamentals: The Environmental Establishment Abandons U.S. Population Stabilization," Center for Immigration Studies, April 2001. Both papers as pdfs are available at www.rewilding.com.

9 William N. Ryerson, "Political Correctness and the Population Problem," *Wild Earth*, Winter 1998/99, 100-103.

These researchers are unsparing truth seekers and unafraid of spooking a stampede of frothing, red-eyed sacred cows. Kolankiewicz and Beck see five drivers behind the "American environmental movement's retreat from population advocacy": (1) Dropping Fertility; (2) Anti-Abortion Politics; (3) Emergence of Women's Issues as Priority Concern of Population Groups; (4) Rift Between Conservationists and New-Left Roots; and (5) Immigration Becomes Chief Growth Factor.[10] In his weighing of how international population stabilization work was torpedoed and left to sink, Ryerson spotlights lowering of U.S. fertility rates, the Catholic stand against contraception and abortion, the feminist shift to pronatalism, and how the Reagan Administration dropped U.S. leadership.[11] The Optimum Population Trust in Great Britain sees fears that worrying about immigration is racist, and that consumption is the threat, not population growth.[12] There are deeper roots yet, having to do with Man's nature. And then there is how population Cassandras have warned about the wrong things.

Fertility Rate Drop in Wealthy Countries

Although population had been growing by frog-leaps in the West since 1800 and the world over after 1900, soldiers coming home after World War Two lit the fuse of the population bomb in the United States and other wealthy countries—the Baby Boom. The Total Fertility Rate (TFR—the average number of children per woman) for American women in the 1950s was 3.5, whereas 2.1 is the TFR to keep a population stable. We were bustin' our britches with that 3.5 TFR. I was born in 1946, the first year of the Baby Boom, and I recall that my class throughout school was always twice as big as the year before us and much smaller than the year after us. By 1969, President Richard Nixon warned, "One of the most serious challenges to human destiny

10 Kolankiewicz and Beck, "Forsaking Fundamentals," 3-4.

11 Ryerson, "Political Correctness."

12 Nicholson-Lord, "Teeming Millions."

in the last third of this century will be the growth of the population. Whether man's response to that challenge will be a cause for pride or for despair in the year 2000 will depend very much on what we do today."[13] Knock Nixon all you want, but in this he was a great, farsighted statesman, brimming with wisdom, and the world's leaders today are chicken-hearted, head-in-the-sand pipsqueaks handing us sweet little lies bubbling in golden champagne flutes. And now, were Nixon still with us, he would be overflowing with despair, not pride. As am I.

Also in 1969, Stephanie Mills, in her commencement address at Mills College on the east side of the bay from San Francisco, said that "the most humane thing for me to do is to have no children at all."[14] Stephanie was thrust into national celebrityhood for her selfless oath. She was not alone in her feelings, as I and others of our generation picked childlessness, too.[15] Others chose to have only one or two children.

Thereby something striking happened: "[T]he birth rate in the United States dropped dramatically....By 1973, the fertility rate had fallen to replacement level." In 1975, the TFR was only 1.7. The news media ballyhooed the drop with headlines blaring "Population Problem Solved" and "US Arrives at Zero Population Growth."[16] However, it was a sweeping misunderstanding that getting to replacement-level fertility meant that zero population growth had been gained. "Population momentum" keeps the population climbing for "up to 70 years after the

13 Kolankiewicz and Beck, " Forsaking Fundamentals," 12.

14 Stephanie Mills, *Whatever Happened To Ecology?* (Sierra Club Books, San Francisco, 1989), 51.

15 Off the top of my head I can name nearly one hundred friends within fifteen years of my age who have never had children. Then there is my family. My grandmother had four children and eleven grandchildren. But those eleven grandkids have had only fifteen children—less than replacement by far (it takes two to make a baby, so the eleven grandkids had eleven bedmates—twenty-two folks in all—to make fifteen great-grandchildren).

16 Ryerson, "Political Correctness," 101.

replacement-level fertility is reached," write Kolankiewicz and Beck.[17] Recall that we earlier learned that happens owing to the many more women giving birth at the lower rate. Moreover, it was only wealthy countries that had gained replacement-level fertility. Elsewhere, babies were still coming down like hailstones in a High Plains thunderbuster. However, many folks in the United States and other wealthy lands believed the population threat was over. Even many environmentalists and conservationists so believed and shoved population to the back burner.

Nonetheless, lowering the birth rate in the U.S., Europe, Japan, and elsewhere was an awesome deed. Have you thanked a nonbreeder today?

A stabilized U.S. population of no more than 250 million was in our grasp in 1975. As we shall see shortly, though, we let that hope fall through our fingers. Without taking strong steps now, the U.S. will have a population in 2100 that is over 750 million—three times at which our population could have stabilized had we not stumbled since the late 1970s. I sit here in my recliner chair with a stiff drink in my hand. Even that, the fire crackling in the fireplace, the snow swirling outside, and a big, ol' gray tabby cat purring in my lap can't chase away the gloom and the shame that in my conservation life this happened. We failed. What else can I say? As we shall see shortly, we failed because we didn't pay enough heed to what was happening in Washington, D.C., with immigration legislation at the time.

Anti-Abortion Politics

The Catholic Church sneered at worry about population growth owing to their gruesome belief that contraception is a sin. When the Pope of Rome finally okayed the rhythm method in 1930, H. L. Mencken wrote, "It is now quite lawful for a Catholic woman to avoid pregnancy by resort to mathematics, though she is still forbidden

17 Kolankiewicz and Beck, "Forsaking Fundamentals," 16.

to resort to physics or chemistry."[18] With the Supreme Court's Roe vs. Wade ruling in 1973 making abortion lawful, the Catholic Church heaped up wrath about "baby killing" to their spurning of family planning. Catholics got into bed with their erstwhile blood-foes, fundamentalist Protestants, in an antiabortion storm that helped lead to today's authoritarian right.[19] Bill Ryerson writes, "Recognizing that concern with population growth was one of the reasons many people supported legalized abortion, the Right to Life movement evolved a strategy to cast doubt on the existence of a population problem." It was their hold on Ronald Reagan that led him to end the international leadership of the United States on population stabilization at the 1984 UN population conference in Mexico City.[20] The old men of the Catholic hierarchy swore that those worried about overpopulation were anti-Catholic. Moreover, the Church set out "to disprove that rising population size had anything to do with deterioration of natural or human environments or the ability of poor countries with rapidly-growing populations to develop economically."[21] Unlike Nixon, at least on population, the Popes and Cardinals have been shortsighted old men, deaf to the whimpering of millions of hungry babies headed for slow deaths or crippled lives. Wrapping themselves in overproud blood-red they are answerable for untold woe and hurt.

18 Quoted in Donald VanDeVeer and Christine Pierce, editors, *The Environmental Ethics and Policy Book: Philosophy, Ecology, Economics* (Wadsworth Publishing Company, Belmont, California, 1994), 370. H. L. Mencken was far and away the wickedest and funniest pricker of swelled heads and bumpkins alike in America through the first half of the twentieth century. Lord, how empty we are without someone like him today. Pope Pius XI okayed the Rhythm Method in 1930 (*Casti Connubii).*

19 Theodore J. Lowi, *The End Of The Republican Era* (University of Oklahoma Press, Norman, 1995).

20 Ryerson, "Political Correctness," 102. The United Nations put on an international population conference in 1974 and every ten years thereafter. Each one further watered down the need to stabilize population.

21 Kolankiewicz and Beck, "Forsaking Fundamentals," 18-19.

The ugliness of the Catholic nobility's damnation of birth control was laid out by the head of Catholics for a Free Choice, Frances Kissling, in an op-ed for the *Baltimore Sun,* where she brought forth outlandish statements from Catholic leaders. An Ugandan Cardinal, Emmanuel Wamala, told Catholics in Africa that it would be better for women to get AIDS from their husbands than to use condoms. The president of the Pontifical Council of the Family, Cardinal Alfonso Lopez Trujillo, told BBC that HIV can go through a condom (it can't); and Kissling writes that a priest told her on CNN's *Crossfire* that "it was worse to lose your soul and go to hell because you used a condom to prevent AIDS than to die of AIDS."[22] Maybe the Catholic hierarchy would have gotten more upset with wayward priests had the priests used rubbers with young altar boys.

Even Islam, in so many ways mired in the Dark Ages, is not against contraception and can even abide some abortions. Abortion is legal in Turkey and Tunisia, both Muslim countries. Iran has strong and quite progressive family planning, where subsidies are cut after a third child and both men and women have to take a class about modern contraception practices before they can get a marriage license.[23] I wish the United States was that far ahead. (Alack, as *Man Swarm* was going to the printer, Iran's nutty president, Mahmoud Ahmadinejad, scorched birth control as a Western evil.)

Emergence of Women's Issues as Priority Concern of Population Groups

Some social activists became upset by population stabilization work in China and India, both of which were growing by leaps and bounds in the 1970s. By yelling about "coercion," such do-gooders killed family planning talk at the third UN population conference in Cairo in 1994. There, they flipped the goal from putting the brakes on growth

22 Frances Kissling, "Ban on Contraceptives Antiquated, Dangerous," *Baltimore Sun,* November 14, 2006.

23 Bruce Sundquist, "The Muslim World's Changing Views toward Family Planning and Contraception," August 2007, bsundquist1@alltel.net.

to the empowerment of women. Family planning experts, writing in the British medical journal *The Lancet,* say, "The recommendations of the Cairo Conference replaced the hitherto dominant demographic-economic rationale for family-planning programmes with a broader agenda of women's empowerment and reproductive health and rights." Funding for international family planning dropped. By 2000, the drafters of the U.N.'s Millennium Development Goals pretty much shit-canned worry about overpopulation and overlooked family planning.[24]

Feminist and human-rights groups were the big dogs in this shift. Outsiders from such outfits even were brought in to take over the population committee of the Sierra Club. Such folks had to quickly buy Sierra Club memberships after being asked to be on the committee. As a Sierra Club board member and member of the conservation governance committee then, I threw a hissy fit when the population committee's draft goal for the Sierra Club on population was written out as the empowerment of women.[25] No, I said, you are scrambling means and ends. The goal of the Sierra Club must be population stabilization and then reduction; empowering women may be a key path to that goal, but it is not the goal itself. I won for a while, but soon left the Sierra Club board because of the Club's back-off on population.

Kolankiewicz and Beck write, "Now centered in a feminist rather than environmental mission, many population, family planning, and women's groups would support no talk of stopping growth or reducing average family size because that implied restrictions on what they considered a universal right of women to choose their number of

24 John Cleland, Stan Bernstein, Alex Ezeh, Anibal Faundes, Anna Glasier, and Jolene Innis, "Family planning: the unfinished agenda," *The Lancet,* November 18, 2006.

25 In the Sierra Club's volunteer hierarchy, the conservation governance committee oversaw the population committee; any resolutions or draft policies from population and other committees had to first go through conservation governance before going to the board of directors.

children entirely free of the merest hint of official or informal pressure."[26] In this, what had been the family planning/population movement showed itself to be blind to limits to growth—and to the worth of other Earthlings. To say that women have the right to have as many children as they want is much the same as saying that men have the right to as many gas-guzzling, land-ripping SUVs as they want. Except it is worse. Either way, it says that it is okay for anyone to have selfish whims that ransack wild things. As in so many things, we scramble rights with irresponsibility. Freedom becomes a two-year-old's temper tantrum.[27]

Even the once-tough Zero Population Growth (ZPG) chickened out and swapped its name for the meaningless "Population Connection." Though its new acronym—PC—has a telling meaning.

Schism between the Conservationist and New-Left Roots of the Movement

Just as in other political ideologies, some on the left are at odds with conservation. Population is one of the flash spots. In the Earth-Day era, socialist environmentalists like Barry Commoner shunned the thought that population growth was behind any "environmental" plights. (Many anti-establishment bunches then, such as the Berkeley Ecology Center, were strong on the need to lower population, though.) Most environmental and conservation groups brushed aside the cornucopian lefties on overpopulation, but the class-struggle left bided its time. They believed that conservative conservationists "hi-jacked Earth Day" with population worrying and thereby weakened the environmental movement. In the 1998 Sierra Club election on immigration policy, the far-left cavalry rode to the rescue under the flag of a Bay Area Marxist outfit called the Political Ecology Group (PEG) to kill the immigration-lowering initiative.[28]

26 Kolankiewicz and Beck, "Forsaking Fundamentals," 21.

27 I'll go deeper into this in my forthcoming book *The Nature Haters.*

28 Dave Foreman, "Progressive Cornucopianism," *Wild Earth,* Winter 1997/98, 1-5 (posted at www.rewilding.org); Kolankiewicz and Beck, "Forsaking Fundamentals," 25-27.

Internationally, leftist environmentalists sidelined overpopulation early on—the 1972 United Nations Conference on the Human Environment in Stockholm, Sweden, did not deal with overpopulation. For one thing, social-justice leftists felt that talk about overpopulation blamed the world's poor for the "environmental" plight; instead, they said, we should target high living in wealthier countries. They were also upset by China's one-child policy and India's widespread sterilization as raids on freedom. Some of those writing on international overpopulation have underlined these so-called "human-rights wrongs" for why work on overpopulation was dropped by international agencies. China was able to keep its one-child policy going and slowed its population growth markedly. India, after the assassination of Indira Gandhi, shoved its program into a back room. The upshot now is that China has "sharply reduced child malnutrition" and only "7 percent of its children under 5 are underweight." Sad India, however, has an "epidemic" of childhood malnutrition, with 42.5 percent of its kids under five underweight.[29] There are other drivers behind deep hunger in India (a World Food Program report in 2009 said that India had 230 million hungry folks, or one-quarter of the world's whole), but bungled population work is a leading one. India is now set to become the world's most populous country. In doing so, it will gain a landslide of woe.

I am no lover of Chinese tyranny, mind you. Not only politically correct knee-jerkers, but some thoughtful population-freeze workers see that while China's one-child policy was a boon for it, it may have helped lead to shutting down family planning work elsewhere, leading to more births outside of China. Who knows? Now that China's per capita affluence is growing by leaps and bounds, though, I hope that it will stick to the one-child policy, lest it have even greater impact on the wild Earth.

29 Somini Sengupta, "As Indian Growth Soars, Child Hunger Persists," *New York Times*, March 13, 2009.

Immigration Became the Chief Cause of U.S. Growth

Recall that by the mid-1970s, TFR in the United States, as in Japan and many European countries, had come down below 2.1 children per woman. Our population was set to even out. We had clipped the wires on the population bomb—in the United States, at least. But then we threw our win away, without wilderness/wildlife keepers, including me, understanding what was happening.

Kolankiewicz and Beck write, "When most Americans began to focus on U.S. growth in the 1960s, immigration was an almost insignificant fraction of growth.... At the very time that American fertility fell to a level that would have allowed population stabilization within a matter of decades, immigration levels were rising rapidly.... By the end of the 1990s, immigrants and their offspring were contributing nearly 70 percent of U.S. population growth."[30] While Americans of breeding age were doing our share to stabilize growth, Congress cut us off at the knees by greatly raising immigration. Kolankiewicz and Beck further write, "If immigration and immigrant fertility had been at replacement level rates since 1972—as has native-born fertility—the United States would never have grown above 250 million. Instead, U.S. population passed 273 million before the turn of the century." Unless we do a quick U-turn, our population will shoot past 400 million before we know it. Former Colorado governor Richard Lamm, a Democrat and a liberal and conservationist, asks, "Given present realities, why do we want our children to face an America of 400 million people?"[31] Why, indeed?

In the forty years after 1925, immigration into the United States ran at about 200,000 a year. After immigration law "reforms" in 1965, yearly immigration leapt up to one million—or five times what it had been earlier. Since 1990, the immigration flood has swelled to

30 Kolankiewicz and Beck, "Forsaking Fundamentals," 28.

31 Richard D. Lamm, "The real bind is too many people everywhere," *High Country News*, September 5, 1994.

one and a half million every year, or more than seven times what it was when I was a child.[32] I can't help but think that only a year after the federal government passed the Wilderness Act in 1964, it opened the floodgates to a new threat to wilderness—exponential growth. What makes the 1965 immigration law so bitter is that the 1964 Wilderness Act put population growth at the forefront of threats to wilderness:

> *In order to assure that an increasing population, accompanied by expanding settlement and growing mechanization, does not occupy and modify all areas within the United States and its possessions, leaving no lands designated for preservation and protection in their natural condition, it is hereby declared to be the policy of the Congress to secure for the American people of present and future generations the benefits of an enduring resource of wilderness. Statement of Policy, Section 2(a), The Wilderness Act, PL 88-577.*

Here is where things get nasty. Because immigration is now the driver of population growth in the United States, the herd mindset of political correctness stops any unruffled, thoughtful talk about population in this country. Only acknowledging that immigration is behind population growth gets one keelhauled for racism. This only became so in the 1990s—in 1989 the Sierra Club's stand was that "immigration to the U.S. should be no greater than that which will permit achievement of population stabilization in the U.S."[33] Once-friends of mine in the Sierra Club drove me away when they hinted that backers of the 1998 immigration ballot initiative were anti-immigrant and therefore racist. No one called me racist to my face, but the hint was there. I laid out this sorry tale in "Progressive Cornucopianism" in

32 Philip Cafaro and Winthrop Staples III, "The Environmental Argument for Reducing Immigration to the United States," *Backgrounder,* Center for Immigration Studies, June 2009, 3.

33 Sierra Club Population Report, Spring 1989.

Wild Earth and won't dwell on it here (the article is at www.rewilding.org). In later chapters, I'll look at immigration more deeply.

By the way, my nieces, nephews, grandnieces, and grandnephews have last names of Pacheco, Serna, and Santillanes.

Kolankiewicz and Beck show how immigration stopped conservationists from working to freeze population in the United States. For one thing, the way environmental and conservation clubs see themselves as a wing of progressivism makes them fear to nettle leftist friends and leaders of racial-advocacy outfits by acknowledging what more immigration will lead to. Moreover, when some (most?) of the environmental and conservation funding community was taken over by social activists, foundations more and more ended funding to groups that spotlighted immigration and then overpopulation at all. Don Weeden, tough-nosed and fearless executive director of the Weeden Foundation, can't get the Environmental Grantmakers Association to even talk about population growth.[34]

Although the growthmongers of the *Wall Street Journal* bliss-out have helped elbow folks away from worrying about growth, it has been the politically correct leftist-Gestapo bludgeoning of Paul and Anne Ehrlich, the late Garret Hardin, Dick Lamm, and other population-freeze boosters that has undercut good population work among conservation and environmental clubs. Many true liberals like Wisconsin Secretary of State Doug LaFollette and former Senator Gaylord Nelson have long spoken out on the threat of overpopulation and worked for population stabilization, but the politically correct crowd has undercut freeze work. With Nelson's death in 2005, we lost anyone of his untouchable standing on our side of the wrangle in "The Environmental Movement." Without Nelson, leftist cornucopianism has become even stronger.

34 My book *Take Back Conservation* deals with how conservation is harmed by seeing it as a wing of progressivism.

Ehrlich vs. Simon. Simon Wins!

After the drop in American, European, and Japanese fertility rates, many believed that growth was no longer a worry. Thanks somewhat to *Population Bomb's* scenarios of widespread starvation leading to world war, which have not happened (yet), people reckon that growth is not something to fear. Now breathless warnings are coming from those who worry about falling populations—the birth dearthers. The fuzzy feeling that Ehrlich was wrong has shifted the minds not only of right-wing economists and fast-buck hustlers, it has swayed—to a height I didn't truly feel until now—the thinking of conservationists and environmentalists. Although these beliefs may bubble along just below mindfulness, they lead some environmentalists and conservationists to downplay population growth or to forget about it altogether. I took such beliefs behind the woodshed in Chapters 6 and 7.

Affluence Is Worse Than Population

Recall the Ehrlich/Holdren formula I=PAT, where Impact comes from Population x Affluence (Consumption) x Technology. Those who lean toward political correctness within the environmental and conservation crowds say that unbridled consumption among the wealthy has more to do with ecological Impacts than does the Population boom among the poor (or anyone). It's not how many Men there are so much as how much they have and how high on the hog they live. This is where we get matchups such as one American having as much Impact as seventy Nigerians or thirty-five Indians or whatever. This A versus P match is no small thing and I wrestle with it in the next chapter.

Human Nature

Now let's dig a little deeper to understand why we backed off on overpopulation. Maybe we are even asking the wrong thing, which has been, "Why have society at large and the environmental and conservation teams backed off from forthright work on population growth?" What we should ask instead may be: "Why did folks for a short while between the end of World War Two and the mid-1970s worry about population growth?" In other words, maybe the lackadaisical feeling of today is the everyday mood and the worried days of the population movement the oddity. I think Man's nature is where conservationists must look to understand the carefree way in which we think about growth today. In our evolutionary biology, we might learn why it is so hard to reckon well with growth.

First of all, we love babies. We can't help it. If we didn't love babies (or making babies) we wouldn't be here. Our burning yearning to have babies and to ward them from all harm comes from evolution. Not wanting offspring is odd. My wife Nancy Morton and I are evolutionary misfits and losers since we do not swoon over babies and children, and because we have steadfastly not made any. Were everyone like us, *Homo sapiens* would go *pffftt*. (I do think that it is widely agreed within my family that Nancy and I are a darned good aunt and uncle, though.)

Then there is that old devil, tribalism. Archaeologists and primatologists show how we humans and our forebears have worked to kill off nearby bands since at least our last shared forebear with chimpanzees five million or more years ago. In the age-old struggle for *lebensraum* and goodies, one's own band needed to be stronger than the neighboring bands. The quickest path for being mightier than your neighbors was to have a bigger gang of throwaway young-male spear-chuckers. We see this wanting of population overlordship playing out in the immigration wars today in Europe, North America, and Australia. Throughout the world, leaders of ethnic (tribal) immigration outfits flatly say that they want more immigration of their bunch for greater political might that will lead to takeover. Socio-political foes of wide-open immigration warn that the traditional American (or European) ethnic blend is being swamped by the ethnic makeup of immigrants.

This worry in the United States comes from blacks and non-Hispanic whites. I also hear it from native New Mexicans of Spanish and Native American backgrounds about those coming from Mexico and Central America. Moreover, we see the war club of more bodies being swung today in Israel-Palestine, in Sunni-Shia-Kurd Iraq, in Tibet, in Bolivia, in Ukraine, in Darfur, in Rwanda-Eastern Congo, in Fiji . . . .We also see it in the pin-striped-suit crowd of foggy bottom and other geopolitical lairs who believes that by keeping our population high, the United States can go on being *the* world power.[35]

Julian Simon further wins the day against Paul Ehrlich because he offered uplifting words against warnings, smiley faces against furrowed brows. Optimism may well be part of human nature. People want to believe that everything is going to be okay, that we are going to keep making headway in every way, that each generation will have a better life than mom and dad—even when all the warnings flash and screech "No!" The cornucopians shun carefulness as a social pathology. David Ehrenfeld sheds light on why this is so: "The motive for their constant insistence on being optimistic and 'positive' is simply the converse of this; optimism is necessary for those who are attempting the impossible; they could not continue to function without it."[36] Were they to face the dark pit before us, they would lose their will to live. They would have to come nose to nose with their madness. This they know. To keep the dread from their minds, they curse the truth tellers. Such is the root of the mean-spirited optimism of Dick Cheney and his button-down goons. They are snarling at us: "Do not pop our fantasy!"

I can almost understand conservationists and environmentalists who, after chewing on all this, feel that population stabilization is hopeless and think that their sweat is better spent on other work.

35 Are there pin-striped pantsuits? For those readers too young to recall, "foggy bottom" was the nickname given to the United States State Department thanks to its building being in a lowland bit of the District of Columbia given to fog. It fit on other grounds, too.

36 David Ehrenfeld, *The Arrogance of Humanism* (Oxford University Press, NY, 1978), 235.

Eugene Linden writes that "widespread optimism has always been a good indicator that disaster is around the corner."[37] His book, *The Future In Plain Sight,* is a careful, thoughtful look at likely tomorrows without believing in *wundorcraeft.*

Psychological experiments and watching others show that nearly all Men are shortsighted and cannot think for the long run. The dark tomorrows from Ehrlich and others did not happen by 1980 or 2000 (at least for Americans), so we think they were wrong.

37 Eugene Linden, *The Future In Plain Sight: Nine Clues To The Coming Instability* (Simon & Schuster, New York, 1998), 27.

Chapter 10

Population or Affluence—or Technology?

Take, for example, a hypothetical American woman who switches to a more fuel-efficient car, drives less, recycles, installs more efficient light bulbs, and replaces her refrigerator and windows with energy-saving models. If she has two children, the researchers found, her carbon legacy would eventually rise to nearly 40 times what she had saved by those actions."[1]

—*The New York Times*

In the camps of resourcism, environmentalism, and conservation, many of those who scoot overpopulation to the back burner or take it off the woodstove altogether yet believe that we must live within carrying capacity, that we must lower our Impact (I). But they believe that the way to do this is to lower Affluence (A) in the formula I=PAT. Others believe that technology (T), instead of heightening I, is how we can keep Impact down while we grow A and pay no mind to P. These technological optimists are cornucopians, but many resourcists

1 Kate Galbraith, "Having Children Brings High Carbon Impact," *New York Times*, August 7, 2009.

and even environmentalists think that Technology can do much of this wonderwork. To wit: the Sierra Club has earnestly deemed that Technology is a whopping big answer for our woes. The cover and leitmotif of the July/August 2005 issue of *Sierra* magazine was "Can Technology Save the Planet?" Carl Pope, at the time executive director of the Club, wrote in his opening column:

> *The planet cannot sustain 6 billion humans aspiring to better lives without 21st-century solutions. We need the services of science and technology, and the skills of engineers. We need to enlist human genius to solve problems, not merely to increase profits. Our role as environmentalists increasingly will be to make sure the appropriate rules and incentives are in place, and then stand back and let the engineers get to work.*[2]

I don't know about you, but standing back and letting the engineers get to work scares the daylights out of me.

What Technology Does to Impact

In truth, higher Technology can hike carrying capacity, letting both Population and Affluence rise. When we get down to it, this is the true saga of Man, going back not only through the 50,000-plus years of *Homo sapiens* but even further back to earlier *Homos*, as Steven LeBlanc shows so well in *Constant Battles*. However, while technology can stretch carrying capacity, it does not soften Impact. It shoots up Impact. Again, this is the true tale of Man. Better Technology lifts carrying capacity, lets Population and Affluence grow, and thus swells the Impact we have on wild things and on healthy lands and seas.

This straightforward tale notwithstanding, there are those resourcists and environmentalists so taken in by the sustainable-development cult that they think Technology can raise Affluence and cut Impact, and thus we don't need to give heed to Population. This is pretty much the sustainable-development path, though most

2 Carl Pope, "Let's Get Technical," *Sierra*, July/August 2005, 11.

"sustainables" would not like it put so baldly.[3] It's cockeyed, but that has never slowed Man before.

I have never quite understood how the Ehrlichs and Holdren thought Technology played in I=PAT. I may have forgotten or overlooked what they said about it somewhere. However, the way Technology works in I=PAT became sharp to me after reading Steven LeBlanc's *Constant Battles*.[4] A technological step "forward" raises the carrying capacity level for a band of our kind. Population and Affluence then grow until they come up against the new carrying capacity. Bad things happen until there is a new Technology breakthrough, which again raises carrying capacity. And so on. But a higher carrying capacity for Man means that we have a greater Impact on wild things. This cycle has been going on for longer than there have been *Homo sapiens*, at least back to *Homo heidelbergensis*, the forebear for both Neandertals and us (and likely for the newly unearthed hominin, the Denisovian, 30,000-year-old fossils of which have been found in the Altai Mountains of southern Siberia[5]). It may go back to *H. erectus* or *ergaster*. Let's see how it *might* have played out.[6]

For a long while, our forerunners' bunch was kept small by predation. We were cat food. Likely pretty darn easy cat food. With more skillful rock throwing, stone chipping, and then wielding of wooden spears and mastery of fire, however, we steadily became tougher prey, and our population slowly grew. When *Homo sapiens* as Cro-Magnons came to Europe, their better tool kit, which made them better big game hunters, raised their carrying capacity over what the

3 In my book *Where Man Is a Visitor,* I'll show how sustainable development is a phony god.

4 Steven A. LeBlanc with Katherine E. Register, *Constant Battles: The Myth of the Peaceful, Noble Savage* (St. Martin's Press, New York, 2003).

5 "Finger Points to New Type of Human," *Science* Vol 331, 7 January 2011, 19.

6 I draw a great deal from LeBlanc and *Constant Battles* here, but this is my take on the tale and is not meant to be an exact unfurling of LeBlanc's thinking. Please read his book; it is essential for knowing who we are.

Neandertals likely had. Better social organization; microliths, sewing awls, fish hooks; then atlatls, bows and arrows; bringing dogs into our bands; and other hunter-gatherer steps "forward" all drove the cycle: Technological breakthrough, raised carrying capacity, bigger Population, higher Affluence, greater Impact on wild things. The cycle jumped to a new, much higher plateau with settled life, grain storage, weaving, pottery, little cats volunteering to be security for stored grain, and domestication of wheat, beans, goats, sheep, pigs, and cattle. At this stage, we were no longer deors in an ecosystem. Niles Eldredge of the American Museum of Natural History is a top human paleontologist and sharp thinker about who we are. He writes, "The stunning growth of human population after the invention of agriculture can mean only one thing, namely, that the primordial limits to... growth were demolished. We did not simply get better at wresting a living from ecosystems: We actually stopped doing that... in favor of agriculture."[7] Then came copper, bronze, and iron; irrigation, wheels, and cities.

This tale plays out as: Higher Technology = higher Carrying Capacity = higher Population and Affluence = higher Impact on wild things. HT=HCC=HP+HA=HI. If I may be so bold as to tinker with the Ehrlichs and Holdren's equation.

Nearly everyone, even those in the population stabilization movement, seems to see the plight of population growth only as a modern problem or at most one that popped up with the rise of the first states. Archaeologist Stephen LeBlanc blows that Noble Savage wish out of the water with *Constant Battles*, his book with his wife, Katherine Register. In it, LeBlanc lays out the evidence from primatology, biological anthropology, human paleontology, archaeology, history, and ethnology that the unending bloodshed and war between and within human groups comes from population growth that leads to

7 Niles Eldredge, "Cretaceous Meteor Showers, the Human Ecological 'Niche,' and the Sixth Extinction," in Ross D. E. MacPhee, editor, *Extinctions in Near Time: Causes, Contexts, and Consequences* (Kluwer Academic/Plenum Publishers, New York, 1999), 13.

overshooting carrying capacity. LeBlanc puts to rest the myths of the Peaceful Savage and the Ecological Savage.

There have never been human bands that lived long in ecological harmony with their surroundings or that were sustainable. As their numbers grew, they overtaxed the land and wild resources around them, which led to scalping their habitat and to likelihood of hunger and starvation. When this happened, they began resource fights with their neighbors, waging war over many years to wipe out the others and to get rid of competition for resources in short supply.

At each step on the ladder of growing cultural complexity, new technologies boost carrying capacity of the land (and sea), leading to bigger populations and to deeper ecological wounds. Since the evolution of behaviorally modern Man some 50,000 years ago and our spread out of Africa into the rest of the world, this has been our history. No matter how cultures "progress" through the stages from foraging bands to tribes to chiefdoms to kingdoms to the modern state, we keep on overshooting carrying capacity even though technological advances at each step raise carrying capacity. We have now reached the end of that road. There are so many folks gobbling so much that our waste of carbon dioxide, methane, soot, and other greenhouse gases is shifting the make-up of the atmosphere, thereby leading to climatic weirdness, and acidification of the seas, which kills off coral reefs and other briny life. So, with seven billion people and still growing we have overshot the carrying capacity of the atmosphere and the oceans to take in and hold harmless our waste.

We may have at last reached the end of the cycle. A crash squats smugly ahead.

I believe that *Constant Battles* is a book next in importance to William Catton's *Overshoot* for understanding the overpopulation plight. Wild lovers need to read it.

The Ecological Footprint

Among those who work to cut Impact, however, there has long been a split between those who think the key is to freeze and then lower Population and those who think we need to cut back on wastefulness and highlife (Affluence) among the better-off. This is the clash we population-worried conservationists and environmentalists have with our conservation and environmental kith. In many ways, this cleavage shows the Weltanschauung of those taking either side, and often seems like an "Is so/Is not" kids' squabble. Forsooth, it isn't an either/or, but a both/and, as David Brower liked to say. We need to freeze and cut *both* Population and gobble-gobble consumption. However, in this chapter I want to show that without lowering population, cutting back on the highlife can't do the job.

A rather new and deft way to frame Impact is by means of one's Ecological Footprint. It has the same limitation and weakness as carrying capacity in that it weighs only our Impact on Earth's wherewithal to support Man in the manner to which we've become accustomed. In *From Big to Bigger,* a report for Progressives for Immigration Reform, Leon Kolankiewicz defines it this way:

> *The Ecological Footprint is a measure of aggregate human demands, or the human load, imposed on the biosphere, or "ecosphere." When all is said and done, the human economy, all production and consumption of goods and services, depends entirely on the Earth's natural capital—on arable soils, forests, croplands, pasturelands, fishing grounds, clean waters and air, the atmosphere, ozone layer, climate, fossil fuels, and minerals—to perform the ecological services and provide the materials and energy "sources" and waste "sinks" that sustain civilization.*[8]

8 Leon Kolankiewicz, "From Big to Bigger: How Mass Immigration and Population Growth Have Exacerbated America's Ecological Footprint," Policy Brief # 10-1, March 2010, Progressives for Immigration Reform, 1. This is a top-notch report. www/pfirdc.org

So, as an environmental reckoning, the Ecological Footprint is good. But for weighing how we wound other Earthlings, it falls short. We need to work out some kind of way to reckon our Wilderness Footprint. Nonetheless, for now, the Ecological Footprint may be the best way to weigh our Impact. *From Big to Bigger,* by the way, is the best short look at how the Ecological Footprint concept came into being.

Those who see Affluence/consumption as the key wield the Ecological Footprint as a yardstick for lowering their Impact through lifestyle shifts.[9] Among these shifts are:

- Drive less/Get a higher mileage car/Take the bus/Bicycle/Walk
- Buy food grown nearby/Eat organic/Grow your own/Eat lower on the food chain
- Make your house more energy efficient/Have a smaller house/Live with others

All of the above steps and like ones are good. We need to take them or some of them as much as we each can. There are some in the cut-Affluence/consumption clan, though, who take it to a sackcloth-and-ashes cult. Because they can live wonderfully thriftily, they think everyone can. They don't understand what outliers they are, that most folks are not going to give up a cozy life. Moreover, folks who live in mobile homes and have never bought a new car don't want to hear better-off folks talk about how we all need to cut back.

Americans can lower their footprints by trimming fat—but they aren't going to give up too much, as Colorado State philosophy professor Philip Cafaro and wildlife biologist Winthrop Staples III warn in their landmark paper, "The Environmental Argument for Reducing Immigration to the United States." Japanese and Western Europeans live well but one-on-one are thriftier with energy and otherwise have smaller footprints than do Americans and Australians. Cafaro and Staples say we should cut our consumption back to where Japanese and Europeans are, and doing so is even something we might

9 I'll shorten Ecological Footprint to footprint henceforth.

be willing to do. "Barring universal enlightenment or dire catastrophe," though, cutting back to how Mexicans live or—good heavens—Nigerians or Bangladeshis, "aren't live *political* options."[10] In other words, we can bring our per person footprint down, but not nearly enough for *generous sustainability*, which Cafaro and Staples frame as "(1) creating societies that leave sufficient natural resources for future human generations to live good lives; and (2) sharing the landscape generously with nonhuman beings."[11] It follows, then, that we have no choice but to freeze how many we are and begin to become fewer. Otherwise, we will lose more and more other kinds of Earthlings from our landscape. Those environmentalists, who think we can double or triple U.S. population without wiping out wildlife and scalping our last wildernesses, are living in a fool's paradise—not in the real world where we either will or will not keep the other Earthlings hale and hearty in our shared neighborhoods.

Much of the back-and-forth between goodhearted souls over Population or Affluence rests on feelings. I've at last dug up some good research and analysis that shows strongly that to make our footprint smaller, we must lower population along with hacking fat and sloppiness. I go into three of these studies below. We need more work like this that puts some objective heft behind the happy dreams of sustainability, and I would welcome hearing about any.

Sprawl

In Chapter 4, I looked at how overpopulation is the root of the Seven Ecological Wounds. One of those is the wrecking and withering of wildlands. Among the main ways we trample and snuff out wildlife neighborhoods in the United States is by urban and suburban sprawl. Sprawl may leap into our eyes more than do other wounds since it is

10 Philip Cafaro and Winthrop Staples III, "The Environmental Argument for Reducing Immigration to the United States," *Backgrounder*, Center for Immigration Studies, June 2009, 6-7.

11 Cafaro and Staples, "Environmental Argument," 7.

such a blight on the landscape and so easy to see, even for those without an "ecological education." In Chapter 4, I call for researchers and others to study how overpopulation leads to each of the ecological wounds. Sprawl is one where we already have careful research showing that population growth is a somewhat bigger driver than posh lifeways. In 2001, Leon Kolankiewicz and Roy Beck took a careful and thorough look at the 100 biggest-in-acreage cities in the United States to find out what was the key driver for each's sprawl—population growth or the trend to bigger houses and yards. Stock wisdom holds that high-flying, selfish lifeways are behind sprawl and that population growth plays small if at all. But Beck and Kolankiewicz found that growth was the big dog overall. Their study, *Weighing Sprawl Factors in Large U.S. Cities,* is a good path for other researchers to follow for finding how growth triggers the other wounds.

Over twenty years, from 1970-1990, new sprawl in the 100 biggest-in-acreage U.S. urban hubs paved or pimpled with homes more than nine million acres of wildland or cropland. It is widely believed that sprawl is driven by bigger homes and yards—*starter castles,* Nancy calls them. But Kolankiewicz and Beck found that there were *two* mainsprings: *per capita sprawl* and *population sprawl.* Per capita sprawl comes from bigger homes and lots, and is tweaked by tax, zoning, and transportation policies, while population sprawl comes from more bodies. Looked at overall, the two were nearly even for how much sprawl they drove, though population growth was somewhat higher. But newspapers, television news, and other mouths have mostly not looked at population and have instead played up bigger homes. Detroit and other rust-bucket cities that lost population yet sprawled out in acres spark this thinking, but our spurning of population growth as the driver of anything bad is also behind it.

The flip side, though, is Los Angeles. For years the mantra in the West has been "we don't want to be another Los Angeles." Even hell-bent for growth developers in Phoenix and like cancers have said "we don't want to be Los Angeles." I was floored, then, to learn that, well, maybe we do want to be like Los Angeles. For Kolankiewicz and Beck write about L.A., "No city in America may be a better model of attempting to restrain sprawl by channeling population growth into ever-denser settlements, both in the urban core and throughout the suburbs." Good heavens, I couldn't believe this when I read it. For all my life I had thought of Los Angeles as the king of sprawl. But since 1970, land-use restrictions have made the greater Los Angeles metropolitan area the most thickly settled landscape in the U.S., with only 0.11 acre per dweller. The suburbs of New York City are "only 60% as dense as those of Los Angeles." Nonetheless, Los Angeles has sprawled—from population growth.

Kolankiewicz and Beck delved into the 100 highest-sprawled cities in the United States from 1970 to 1990 and reckoned the percent rise or loss of population and the acreage for each dweller. Then they reckoned the growth of each city in square miles and then by percentage of the earlier land area. From that, they "apportioned" the percentage of sprawl to either population growth or per capita land consumption.

Detroit had the eighteenth most acres, a population loss of 6.9 percent, and a 37.9 percent growth in one-on-one land consumption. So in apportioning its sprawl, 0.0 percent is from population and 100 percent is from the jump in how much land each homeowner took.

Los Angeles has the sixth biggest acreage, a population gain of 36.5 percent, and an 8.4 percent *drop* in per capita land consumption. Apportioning its sprawl gives us 100 percent from population and 0.0 percent from growth in how much land each dweller took.

My hometown of Albuquerque is forty-fourth in the U.S. for land spread, a population gain of 67.1 percent, and an 18.1 percent bump in one-on-one land consumption. When apportioned, 75.5 percent of sprawl is from population growth and 24.5 percent from greater household land footprint.

Overall, Kolankiewicz and Beck find that from 1970 to 1990 50.9 percent of the sprawl is from population growth and 49.1 percent from per capita land consumption. What they find is sharp as broken glass: "smart growth," even when it does as well as it has in Los Angeles, cannot stop sprawl by itself. Only by also freezing population growth can sprawl of new suburbs onto rich cropland and wildlands be stopped.[12]

This is the kind of careful, thoughtful work that needs to be done on the drivers of all seven of the ecological wounds in Chapter 4. But what we can see from this kind of work is that none of the Seven Ecological Wounds can be healed without lowering population; none of the causes to which we conservationists and environmentalists give our lives can be won in a world with endlessly booming population.

We will not be able to lower greenhouse gas emissions.

We will not be able to gain clean air and clean water for our children to breathe and drink.

We will not be able to make sure that the other Earthlings who came into the twenty-first century with us will last until the twenty-second, as well.

Whatever your cause as a conservationist or environmentalist, it is a lost cause, without freezing and then lowering population.

Welcome to the Real World.

Jevons' Paradox

It's as plain as the nose on our mugs that if each of us (or just many of us) were to cut back on energy, water, food, appliances, cars, miles driven, and so forth, the overall weight of these things on Earth would ebb, and raw goods would last longer.

But it's been known for 150 years that it ain't so.

12 Leon Kolankiewicz and Roy Beck, *Weighing Sprawl Factors in Large U.S. Cities,* NumbersUSA, March 19, 2001.

At the end of the Civil War (1865), an economist named W. Stanley Jevons wrote a book about coal and how it was being used more efficiently in steam engines. In *The Coal Question* he wrote, "It is a confusion of ideas to suppose that economical use of fuel is equivalent to diminished consumption. The very contrary is the truth." Over a hundred years later, two economists, Daniel Khazzoom and Leonard Brookes, also wrestled with Jevons' Paradox. Jeff Dardozzi, in his fetching write-up *The Specter of Jevons' Paradox,* writes, "They argued that increased efficiency paradoxically leads to increased *overall* energy consumption." As more researchers have looked into the paradox, it has become more unforgiving. In 2008, Earthscan published a whole book, *Jevons' Paradox: The Myth of Resource Efficiency Improvements,* looking at the history of the puzzling truth and going through the latest studies showing it to be so.

The little troll that Jevons dug up does two things: spends the savings, and in so doing boosts consumption. When you sock away money by getting more for less, you then spend it in a way that does away with the savings. Dardozzi brings up that Americans have had higher energy-efficiency homes since the end of World War Two. But we now have much bigger homes than had mom and dad and their moms and dads and we have more energy-sucking gadgets and gizmos in them. We also see the same paradox with highway betterment and widening. Sure, it lowers crowding for a little while but then the roomier road draws more building along it and—bingo!—traffic goes up to become even worse than before the widening.

Dardozzi writes, "The second effect resulting from efficiency improvements is that when you save money you usually spend it somewhere else in the system of production, and that translates into increased energy and resource consumption." I think of my hometown of Albuquerque, where we in older neighborhoods are endlessly nagged to cut water use. But our cutting back on yard watering, baths, toilet flushes, or whatever doesn't mean Albuquerque sucks less water from the ground or the Rio Grande. Oh, no. It means that there is now "more" water for new home building on the growing West Side of town, or for new industrial plants. In other words, old folks who have lived in a house for fifty years should let their peach trees die from no watering so some fastbuck builder can put it one hundred new houses and have water for the home buyers being lured to Albuquerque. We need a new breed of dog that can sniff out what is truly behind all the "living-more-lightly" pleas from our city fathers and mothers.

Blake Alcott, an ecological economist, writes about this twist worldwide, "[G]iven global markets and marginal consumers, one person's doing without enables another to 'do with.'" We in the United States can cut way back on our driving, but what oil we don't burn will be gladly taken by all the new car owners in India and China.[13]

A Sandia Labs researcher in Albuquerque has found that Jevons' Paradox shoots down his once-hopeful prediction on lighting. In 1999, Jeff Tsao did a white paper that showed that if conventional light bulbs were swapped for solid-state bulbs, "The worldwide amount of electricity consumed by lighting would decrease by more than 50 percent and total worldwide consumption of electricity would decrease by more than 10 percent." Ten years later, though, Tsao has discovered Jevons' Paradox and how it plays with lighting. *Albuquerque Journal* science writer John Fleck, who is darned good, reports, "As lighting became more efficient—from candles and kerosene to gas and then electric lights—people wanted to have more light, rather than to use less energy."[14]

Jevons' Paradox looks more and more like the monkeywrench in the gears of energy efficiency.

As clever folks tinker with new ways to make energy (Carl Pope's engineers), I worry that the worst thing would be for someone

13 Jeff Dardozzi, "The Specter of Jevons' Paradox," *Synthesis/Regeneration* 47, Fall 2008. My ramble is drawn from this article.

14 John Fleck, "Energy Savings? No, More Light," *Albuquerque Journal*, September 21, 2010.

to come up with a straightforward, cheap, endless, clean wellspring of power. Among other things, it would let population zoom even higher. Nothing would wreck and tame the wild Earth quicker and more thoroughly than would clean energy too cheap to meter.

There is a way out of Jevons' Paradox. Freeze population. Bring it down. If it is hard to bring A down in I=PAT, we need all the more to bring down P.

CARBON LEGACIES

Many folks want to make their footprint smaller. Those of us who see Population behind big footprints, see Affluence heavy on our backs, too. Take Nancy and me. We do fly about some to scuba dive, birdwatch, and canoe back-of-beyond rivers. We eat meat and drink good red wine (but not as good as we'd like to). We buy lots of books, too. On the other hand, Nancy drives a Prius. I go to work by walking downstairs. Our home may seem a little big for the two of us and two cats, but The Rewilding Institute office is here, and, believe me, we more than fill it up. Moreover, our home is a passive-solar gem with a greenhouse, sunroom, and fifty-foot long clearstory, with brick floors, some adobe walls, and in the greenhouse black barrels full of water to soak up the sun. One morning last winter the temperature outside was eight degrees Fahrenheit and there was snow on the ground, but it was a sunny day. I never switched on the gas furnace nor did I kindle a fire in our low-smoke woodstove. The outside temperature never made it to 30 that day and yet I had to open two windows to cool the house down. To say that we have low gas and electric bills doesn't quite grasp it. We recycle, compost, and buy less; therefore we only put our garbage can out once every three or four weeks although we have weekly pickup. We've never owned a clothes drier other than the solar one that uses cord and clothes pins. Sometimes blue jeans freeze overnight on the line, but they dry out the next day. We also have a clothesline strung in the greenhouse.

I'll stop strutting our good works here, but I could go on. What I am getting at is that for suburbanites, we have a pretty small carbon footprint, yes; but the main thing that makes our footprint small is that we don't have children.

Don't think that this bit about no kids is over the top. New work out of Oregon State University strongly shows that children greatly swell the acreage of one's carbon footprint. *The New York Times* reports, "Take, for example, a hypothetical American woman who switches to a more fuel-efficient car, drives less, recycles, installs more efficient light bulbs, and replaces her refrigerator and windows with energy-saving models. If she has two children, the researchers found, her carbon legacy would eventually rise to nearly 40 times what she had saved by those actions."[15]

Forty times.

Paul Murtaugh, a statistics professor, and Michael Schlax, an oceanic and atmospheric science professor, both at OSU, published their research in the peer-reviewed journal *Global Environmental Change* in 2009.[16] To find the "carbon legacy of an individual," they looked at how many children, grandchildren, and so on one has and worked out a "weighting scheme" giving each offspring's Impact as a fraction of relatedness.

They also calculated how much one could cut one's carbon output with six lifeway shifts, and found it was about 486 metric tons of CO_2 in a run-of-the-mill American woman's lifetime. But the carbon legacies of each birth foregone under three emission scenarios (will they go up or down or stay the same) come out to between 9,441 and 12,730 tons. In other words, not having a child cuts a woman's carbon legacy twenty times more than six lifeway shifts. If you want any more of the math, you'll have to read the paper yourself. I'm already over

15 Galbraith, "Having Children Brings High Carbon Impact."

16 Paul A. Murtaugh and Michael G. Schlax, "Reproduction and the carbon legacies of individuals," *Global Environmental Change* 19 (2009), 14-20.

my head. What Murtaugh and Schlax have found, though, is that not having a kid dwarfs all the other "green" lifeway shifts put together.

Murtaugh and Schlax have shown well how overweight P is in I=PAT. Murtaugh "noted that their calculations are relevant to other environmental impacts beside carbon emissions—for example, the consumption of fresh water, which many feel is already in short supply."[17] I agree that their path could be followed for studies weighing P and A for the other ways we wound the living Earth. Their work is a true breakthrough and I thank them for leading the way.

These studies and analyses agree that we can't lower Impact only by lowering Affluence. We must also freeze and then lower Population. Not only that, but Population likely has a greater share of I=PAT than does Affluence. We who already know we must freeze and then lower Population need to wield the insights from the three studies outlined in this chapter to bring our wild-loving siblings over to seeing that Population is the big dog in I=PAT. After reviewing this chapter, Phil Cafaro wrote, "If you are not convinced that population is the big dog, you should at least accept it as one of the three heads of Cerberus busily tearing into the body of wild Nature." Cerberus is truly the metaphor for I=PAT.[18]

Now, even if this has not brought you over to acknowledge that Population has so much Impact that we can't brush it aside, and you still believe that Affluence is the key, think of this: Americans have the biggest Affluence Footprint per capita of any people in the world. Any population growth in the United States, then, is growth of these

17 Media Release, "Family planning: A major environmental emphasis," Oregon State University, July 31, 2009.

18 Cerberus, you will recall from Greek and Roman mythology, is the three-headed, dragon-tailed dog that keeps the dead from sneaking out of Hades.

big Affluence Footprints. Population growth in the United States is thus more harmful to the world than population growth anywhere else because of our over-big Affluence.

The world cannot afford more Americans.

CHAPTER 11

The Bugbear of Immigration

Immigration to the U.S. should be no greater than that which will permit achievement of population stabilization in the U.S.

—1989 Sierra Club population policy

IN CHAPTER 9, I went through a list of why conservationists, environmentalists, and others have backed off from working on overpopulation. Underlying all the reasons is the sweeping dearth of knowledge folks worldwide have about biological science. It's not just lack of learning; I believe we Men have a willful dislike for thinking that biology has anything to do with Mankind. We don't want to believe that the biology that hems in other Earthlings with carrying capacity works on us. Unfounded? Silly? For sure, but this feeling bores into even the best brains of Men.

Another big thing that has pulled the rug out from under worry about the Man swarm is that the scariest forecasts about overpopulation in the 1960s and 1970s did not happen. I've been rereading some of the overpopulation books and papers from that time, not only *The*

Population Bomb. As I've written earlier, more than a few of the scientists and others writing about too many births forty years or so ago saw awful things coming soon—soon as in before 1980. Now, the population boom has led to some truly gruesome things, such as down-and-out starvation all over the world, but we have not had the whole fireworks show and breakdown that was foretold. It is highly likely that some of these grim overpopulation forecasts will yet happen, but we still can't say when. Our minds, sharp as they may be, have some pretty dull edges to them. One of these is shortsightedness. Those making population explosion forecasts were tripped up by shortsightedness. They saw bad times coming, but they saw them coming too fast. The upshot is that today even some of those who once believed in the overpopulation bad news have backtracked—*it didn't happen soon enough.* (I showed in Chapter 7 how much of a misunderstanding it is that the population "doomsayers" were wrong.)

I think, worldwide, that these two things—biological benightedness and shortsightedness—are the main bugbears for why growth as the big threat is now flicked out of the way. But in the United States (and the few other wealthy countries that are still growing), another bugbear stands taller: immigration. I dealt with immigration some in Chapter 9, but I want to run after it a little more here. Conservationists and others won't work on growth in the United States until we forthrightly deal with immigration. We can't do that until we make a new playing field where we can talk about immigration without being damned to hell by erstwhile friends who say we are anti-immigrant. We need to think about how to do that. We can't just brush such qualms aside.

Above all else, I want you to learn one thing from this chapter: Without capping immigration to the United States, we cannot freeze our growth. Indeed, unless we cap immigration to the United States, we cannot keep from doubling or nearly tripling today's U.S. population by 2100. You might not like this hand, but it is the hand we are dealing ourselves.

Now, it is mathematically doable to bring down the fertility rate in the U.S. to where *some* net immigration would not lead to an overall gain in population. However, to bring our fertility rate down to where the 1.5 million net immigrants we now have coming in yearly do not shove up our population, we would need to cut back to one child per woman. Such a low fertility rate is unheard of and will not happen voluntarily. But we could bring our fertility rate down to that of many European countries where *some* net immigration could happen without raising our population. If we choose to be open to such immigration, however, it should be only after we bring our fertility rate down enough. I would much rather see, though, for us to bring our fertility rate to below replacement and still cap immigration at a no-net growth rung. Over the long haul, it's not enough to freeze the burly footprint of America; we must lighten it for the sake of wild things everywhere.

Immigration to the U.S. raises the overall world footprint

Keep in mind that folks come to the United States not to keep the standard of living they had in Mexico, the Philippines, or Somalia, but to get the standard of living of the everyday American. Because the American standard of living is built on the highest squandering of energy and other raw goods in the world (other than for a Gulf sheikdom or two or three), each American has a greater Impact than do others on the goodness of life for wild things.

The upshot is that the world cannot afford more Americans.

We in the United States cannot afford more Americans. Others in the world cannot afford more Americans. Above all, the wild things of the United States and the world cannot afford more Americans. This is key. Population growth in the United States does not only have a crushing Impact on wildlife and wilderness in the United States. Owing to our sky-high "standard of living," which is kept high by grubbing up wildlands all over Earth for raw goods, population growth in the United States has an overwhelming Impact on wild things worldwide. Indeed, population growth in the United States may have a more deadly Impact on wild things in many other countries than population growth in such countries themselves has. Immigration to the United States is not only a threat to the other Earthlings who dwell here, but to other Earthlings who dwell all over Earth.

Immigration from poor lands with lower footprints to the United States makes more folks with sky-high American footprints. This is one side of immigration that hasn't been closely looked at until lately. Philip Cafaro and Winthrop Staples finally looked at it in "The Environmental Argument for Reducing Immigration to the United States." See Table 11.1, adapted from their insightful article.[1] The goal of immigrants—lawful and unlawful—to the United States is to gain a U.S. standard of living as soon as they can. I can't blame them for wanting what I have. But let's not hoodwink ourselves into thinking that folks who come here from the Philippines, say, will keep the same footprint they had in the Philippines. Cafaro and Staples look at the ten countries that send the U.S. the most immigrants and then line up their *total ecological footprints.*

The United States has a total ecological footprint of 9.6 hectares (nearly 25 acres) per person. These global hectares are worked out with a mathematical formula crafted by John Holdren, co-creator of I=PAT, former president of the American Association for the Advancement of Science (AAAS), and now President Obama's chief science advisor. The 9.6 hectares each American needs are scattered all over the world. The total per capita ecological footprints for the ten countries that send us the most immigrants go from 7.6 for Canada to 0.8 for India. Mexico, which sends us about 30 percent of all our immigrants, has a 2.6 hectares (6.5 acres) per person footprint. So, when a Mexican immigrant or their child gains an every-day America life (not when they

1 Philip Cafaro and Winthrop Staples III, "The Environmental Argument for Reducing Immigration to the United States," *Backgrounder,* Center for Immigration Studies, June 2009.

Table 11.1. Average Ecological Footprint of U.S. Citizens and 10 Largest Immigration Source Countries, 2003 (global hectares per person)

Source Country	% of U.S. Immig. Pop. (2000)	Total Ecological Footprint
United States	---	9.6
Mexico	29.8	2.6
China/Taiwan/H.K.	4.5	1.6
Philippines	4.4	1.1
India	4.0	0.8
Cuba	2.8	1.5
El Salvador	2.7	1.4
Vietnam	2.5	0.9
Korea	2.3	4.1
Canada	2.2	7.6
Dominican Republic	2.0	1.6

Source: Condensed from Table 2, Philip Cafaro and Winthrop Staples III, "The Environmental Argument for Reducing Immigration to the United States," *Backgrounder,* Center for Immigration Studies, June 2009, 13.

first come to the U.S.), they will have goosed up their footprint by seven hectares. Leaving aside Canada, immigrants from the other nine of our top ten immigrant-sending countries will swell their total ecological footprint and the footprints of all of their offspring "by 100 percent to 1,000 percent or more." Mexicans will raise their footprint by 350 percent if they come to the United States and gain our fat life.[2] So, each immigrant to the U.S. raises their footprint and by doing so raises the worldwide footprint of Man.

2 Cafaro and Staples, "The Environmental Argument for Reducing Immigration."

IMMIGRATION'S UPSHOT

What it comes down to is this: If you don't back capping immigration to the United States, you back our population growing to between 700 million and 850 million by 2100.

What else do you back?

Cafaro and Staples put it this way. If you support continued mass immigration into the U.S.:

> *You don't just support drastically increasing America's human population. You also support more cars, more houses, more malls, more power lines, more concrete and asphalt. You support less habitat and resources for wildlife; fewer forests, prairies and wetlands; fewer wild birds and wild mammals....You support replacing these other species with human beings and our economic support systems.*[3]

If you don't believe in capping immigration to the United States, then you are for the United States growing from 307 million to over 700 million by 2100.

If the U.S. population grows to over 700 million in only ninety years, we will make it nigh on hopeless to keep wildlands and wild things on the landscape.

In 2007, *The New York Times* said, "Immigration over the past seven years was the highest for any seven-year period in American history, bringing 10.3 million new immigrants, more than half of them without legal status...." Moreover, 37.9 million folks—or one in eight—living in the U.S. was an immigrant.[4] In 1970, only 9.6 million immigrants lived in the United States. Even in what we think of as the great heyday of immigration to the U.S., from about 1920 to 1930, there were never more than 14.2 million immigrants in the U.S., says the U.S. Census Bureau. What you can take home from these figures is that we

3 Cafaro and Staples, "The Environmental Argument for Reducing Immigration," 7.

4 Julia Preston, "Immigration at Record Level, Analysis Finds," *New York Times*, November 29, 2007.

are wildly out of kilter today insofar as immigration goes. Lowering the immigration rate will in no way go against American tradition. And even if it did go against our tradition, so what? Not all of our traditions grant other Earthlings a home on the landscape. We don't slaughter buffalo anymore or dump DDT into our rivers. We bring back wild things—wolves, river otters, hawks—we once earnestly murdered. In the same light, we need to make a big shift in our immigration policies so as to keep and bring back the wildlife of North America.

Why is immigration so thorny?

In the next chapter, I outline some steps to cap immigration, lawful and unlawful, to the United States. First, though, let's look at why immigration is such a thorny little devil. Some on both sides of the U.S. immigration wrangle have shoved it into a dark, nasty, back parking lot behind a mean, grungy beer hall where we can't talk about it in a cool, thoughtful way, where otherwise good men and women become pigheaded and start yelling and swinging broken beer bottles and pool cues at each other. This is so because both sides talk too much about *immigrants* instead of *immigration*. Why?

Some who are pro-immigration say that those who want to slow or freeze immigration don't really care about immigration but care about who the immigrants are—darker-skinned, in want, and of other cultures and religions. In other words, most pro-immigrationists sketch those wanting less immigration as the bad guys of American history: nativists, racists, Ku Klux Klanners. Likewise, some who want to stop or slow immigration say immigrants from lifeways other than what are foremost in America are terrorists, welfare bums, and foreigners who mean to overthrow who Americans are. Both sides trot out economics, national security, and human rights to uphold their beliefs. Neither side talks about population growth, much less how growth in the United States is harmful to wild things worldwide.

In a short five or six years after the Sierra Club's thoughtful and fair 1989 immigration policy, most of the Club leadership flipped over to being against caps on immigration. I was on the national board of directors then, and I feared that some would go all out to not only ditch the 1989 policy but to come out for continued mass immigration. Moreover, I was scared it could go through the board. Why did this flip happen, and how did it happen so quickly? For one thing, recall that in 1994 California had a bloody political fight over ballot Proposition 187 that would have kept illegal immigrants from getting state-supplied social services. Whatever the arguments for or against 187 might have been, the election was deeply divisive in the state with outlandish charges and distortions being thrown back and forth. The California Sierra Club took a public position against the proposition. Some of us protested that whatever the feelings of individual Sierra Club members, the Club should have officially stayed out of the fight with no position on it. Prop 187 came only five years after the good Sierra Club immigration policy but it shifted the ground within the Club, markedly in California. It put many Sierra Club activists close to ethnic activists who led the fight against Prop 187. On the other side, *some* of those working for the proposition were hardcore nativists with a load of right-wing ties and baggage.

After the Prop 187 fight (it passed but was found unconstitutional by a federal court), the Sierra Club in California found itself in a new political landscape. So, the underlying shove against the 1989 Sierra Club Immigration Policy, I think, was that Club leaders did not want to be linked with the others calling for immigration caps after the nasty Prop 187 election. Also, seeing the Sierra Club more and more as a feather in the progressive wing of the Democratic Party, they felt at home with those against immigration caps. Moreover, leading Mexican-American politicians in California were good on Sierra Club issues in the state and Club leaders did not want to risk that backing by being thought of as anti-Mexican in any way. There was also a one-hundred-million-dollar ($100,000,000!) gift from a billionaire who told Carl Pope, Sierra Club Executive Director, that he would cut the Club off if it said anything against immigration.

Nonetheless, some old-time Sierrans put up an initiative in the 1998 Sierra Club election to go back to the 1989 policy. I won't go into the dirty fight some Sierra Club leaders waged against the initiative other than to knock down the lie that backers of the initiative were right-wing "outsiders" trying to take over the Club, as was loudly said by some against the initiative. Carl Pope and Board President Adam Werbach were among those slinging dirt against the worthy, mainstream Sierrans who wanted caps on immigration. See Table 11.2 for the names of some of the folks who backed the immigration initiative. This list shows that those backing the 1989 policy on immigration were anything but outsiders. Among the endorsers were well-known conservation leaders; moreover, there were folks from Hispanic, Asian, and African-American backgrounds. There were a few who had been Sierra Club leaders before Adam Werbach was born.

At this same time, however, The Wilderness Society took a fair, thoughtful stand on population policy, which dealt with "the consequences of population growth to our wild lands." It said, "As a priority, population policy should protect and sustain ecological systems for future generations." Among the policies "espoused" by The Wilderness Society was, "To bring population levels to ecologically sustainable levels, both birth rates and immigration rates need to be reduced."[5] With only slight updating, this 1996 policy should be taken by all conservation groups worthy of the name. The Wilderness Society didn't do anything to boost its policy, I'm sorry to say, but at the least, it undercuts the Sierra Club leadership's mudslinging at those backing immigration caps.

5 TWS Population Policy, The Wilderness Society, Washington, D.C., 2/22/96.

Table 11.2. Partial List of Endorsers of Sierra Club 1998 Immigration Initiative to Bring Back the 1989 Immigration Policy

Immigration to the U.S. should be no greater than that which will permit achievement of population stabilization in the U.S.

Anthony Beilenson, *U.S. Congress 1977-96, (D-CA)*

Lester Brown, *Worldwatch Institute*

Maria Shia Chang, *Political Science Professor, University of Nevada*

Herman Daly, *co-author,* For the Common Good

Elaine del Castillo, *founder, Save Our Earth*

Brock Evans, *former Associate Executive Director of Sierra Club*

Dave Foreman, *former Sierra Club Director, former SC Rio Grande Chapter VP*

Huey Johnson, *former California Secretary of Resources, former Western Dir. TNC*

Douglas La Follette, *Wisconsin Secretary of State (D)*

Martin Litton, *former Sierra Club Director, Grand Canyon Dories owner*

Dan Luten, *past President, Friends of the Earth*

Frank Morris, Sr., *former ED Congressional Black Caucus Foundation*

Farley Mowat, *author,* Never Cry Wolf, Sea of Slaughter, *other books*

Gaylord Nelson, *former Senator (D-WI), "Father of Earth Day," Counselor Wilderness Society*

Tim Palmer, *author of many river conservation books*

George Sessions, *author,* Deep Ecology for the 21st Century

Galen Rowell, *world-class mountaineer, author, and photographer*

Stewart Udall, *former Secretary of the Interior, U.S. Congress (D-AZ)*

Captain Paul Watson, *Sea Shepherd Conservation Society*

E.O. Wilson, *Harvard University, author,* The Diversity of Life, *other books*

This short list gives a feeling for the standing of some of the backers within the conservation team and the U.S. as a whole, as well as the ethnic spread of those backing immigration caps. These folks, many of whom had been in the Sierra Club for years and years, were among those tarred as right-wing outsiders trying to take over the Sierra Club.

Thanks to this fight, I came to understand that the main grounds for why conservationists and environmentalists no longer worked to cap immigration—even if it was the only way the United States could freeze its population—was that they did not want to be linked in any way with the right-wing, nativist, anti-immigrant crowd. The way the Sierra Club leadership and some others besmirched great conservationists for saying anything about immigration has only made it harder for conservationists, environmentalists, and progressives to stand up on immigration and on any population issue. I can understand why someone who loves wild things does not want to be tied to immigrant-bashers such as Tom Tancredo, former congressman from Colorado. Heck, I don't. The way to deal with this, however, is not to give up on working to cap immigration, but to take the framing of immigration policy into our hands as key for freezing growth in the United States. If we are to get most conservationists to back population stabilization—which, in the United States, is capping immigration—we have to show that cutting immigration is not anti-immigrant and is not tied to nativism or racism. We need to say that the question is *how many* not *who.* Until we in the overpopulation fight understand this and deal with it, we are not going to get a crowd of wilderness and wildlife lovers to back what needs to be done to freeze population growth. This is the bugbear we are up against.

HARD NUMBERS ON IMMIGRATION TO THE U.S.

So. I will have little to say about the economic, cultural, legal, or political smoke and shadows swirling about our immigration campfire.[6] Other thoughtful, fair folks have wrestled with the social side of immigration. I've drawn on the good paper from Philip Cafaro and Winthrop Staples already. Not only are they both conservationists:

6 This doesn't mean that economic, legal, or cultural grounds to cap immigration are wrong or without worth. Nor does it mean that they are nativist, racist, or discriminatory.

they also think of themselves as liberals. About half of their paper "The Environmental Argument for Reducing Immigration to the United States" deals with social justice, fairness, human rights, and such. Cafaro, who is a philosophy professor at Colorado State, is working on a book about immigration entitled *Bleeding Hearts and Empty Promises: A Liberal Rethinks Immigration.* There is also a new group called Progressives for Immigration Reform, which will campaign for lower immigration on liberal beliefs and values, including environmental and conservation good.[7] Moreover, Cafaro and Eileen Crist are editing an anthology that widely deals with overpopulation. I welcome their work. It will do much to show that wanting to cap immigration to the U.S. does not make one a heartless, racist right-winger.

But in this book I am dealing with population as a lover of wild things. So, what I will say is this:

> *Population growth in the United States, from any driver, be it too many births or more immigration than out-migration, and whatever the background, economic rung, or homeland of immigrants, is harmful to the quality of life in the United States, and to wild things in the United States and worldwide.*

We lovers of wild things who are worried about growth and therefore about immigration to the United States must take the talk back to *biodiversity carrying capacity* and how more men, women, and children mean fewer wild things.

Let's ask a few questions:

Is population in the United States growing?

Yes, it is. About 3 million is the yearly growth (the first census of the independent United States in 1790 found about 3 million Americans; we are now adding that every year). Math dolt though I am, I can even put our growth into a formula: $(B_c + I_m + B_i) - (D + M) = G$; or (Births to citizens + immigration + births to immigrants) – (deaths

7 www. pfirdc.org

+ out-migration) = Growth. By 2050, the Census Bureau forecasts that the U.S. population will be growing by some 3.5 million yearly. In other words, demographers think that, far from slowing down on the way to freezing, yearly U.S. growth itself will keep growing, as it has been doing for the last twenty-some years, with no end in sight. That is unless there is a true shift in immigration policy and a true downward shift in net migration. The Census Bureau shows "net international migration" at 1,338,000 in 2010 and 2,047,000 in 2050.[8] This is a 50 percent jump. Chew on that. Many of you who read this, unlike me, may be alive in 2050. Keep in mind that U.S. Census Bureau forecasts are nearly always low.

Where is the growth coming from?

Population growth in the United States flows out of three springs:

- Net immigration (lawful and unlawful)
- Net natural growth among U.S.-born (births to citizens)
- Net natural growth among foreign-born (births to immigrants)

Keep in mind that only Number 2 would be happening without net immigration. Numbers 1 and 3 must be wed to show the full net weight of immigration.

Over the next forty years, the best forecasts (see below) say that 82 percent of growth will be from immigration and births to immigrants. Only 18 percent will be from births to citizens. Now, there are those who say this is no big deal because bringing in immigrants to the United States *lowers* world population thanks to immigrant women having fewer kids than had they stayed home. Sorry, folks. You are dead wrong. The truth is that immigrant women to the U.S. *do not* have fewer births than their sisters back home. *They often have more.*

8 Referenced website: http://www.census.gov/population/www/projections/summarytables.html (Summary Table 1)

Women in Mexico today average 2.4 children, while Mexican women unlawfully in the U.S. have 3.5 on average—nearly 50 percent higher.[9] In other words, we are not only seeing births that would have happened anyway in Mexico instead of in the United States, we are seeing *more* births than would have happened in Mexico. Unlawful immigration to the U.S. from Mexico thus leads to more overall births worldwide.

Another way to look at it is that the U.S. TFR in the mid-1950s was about 3.7; it fell to 1.7 by 1975 (below replacement-level). But it then rose 24 percent due to higher fertility from immigrant women to 2.0 in 2002 and 2.1 in 2007.[10]

What is the up-to-date population of the United States?

The population clock at www.census.gov home page as of February 7, 2011 shows 310,771,156 as the population of the United States. You can go to this home page to see what the up-to-date population of the U.S. is when you read this. (World population is pegged at 6,898,339,328 on February 7, 2011.)

If the United States had adopted the Sierra Club 1989 proposal on immigration in 1989, what would be our population today? (The Sierra Club position was "Immigration to the U.S. should be no greater than that which will permit achievement of population stabilization in the U.S.")

The U.S. population in 1989 was roughly 250 million. Knowledgeable population watchdogs think our population would never have reached 300 million before it peaked and began a slow downhill slide. Keep this foremost in your head for weighing the numbers to come. Had the United States done something twenty years ago, our population may have never broken the 300-million wire. Recall also that demographers in the 1930s thought U.S. population would stabilize at 160 million (Chapter 8).

9 Steven Camarota, "Birth Rates Among Immigrants in America: Comparing Fertility in the U.S. and Home Countries," Center for Immigration Studies, Washington, D.C., 2005.

10 Stuart H. Hurlburt, LTE, *Front Ecol Environ,* 2009.

Under today's trends of legal and illegal immigration, what will be the population of the United States in 2050?

The mid-range or middle series U.S. Census Bureau forecast for 2050 is 439 million. This is also what the trusted Population Reference Bureau forecasts for the U.S. in their 2009 World Population Data Sheet. On its own, the Pew Hispanic Center has forecasted that 82 percent of this growth will be from immigration (immigrants and their U.S.-born descendants):

> *If current trends continue, the population of the United States will rise to 438 million in 2050, from 296 million in 2005, and 82% of the increase will be due to immigrants arriving from 2005 to 2050 and their U.S.-born descendants, according to 2008 projections developed by the Pew Research Center.*[11]

In other words, U.S. population in 2050 will be about 150 million more than it was in 2000—more than 50 percent more. The rise by 2050 will be the same as today's population of Canada and Mexico together. Another way to see it is that the growth from immigrants and their children alone will be the same as today's population of the United States west of the Mississippi River. The U.S. Census Bureau seems to always understate growth, so 439 million by 2050 could be too low a forecast; moreover, with ongoing immigration, we will still be in an upward swoop in 2050.

What would the United States 2050 population be if immigration were capped so that in and out migration matched? (The Sierra Club 1989 policy)

The Census Bureau zero-net migration projection for 2050 (grounded on 1990 reckoning) is 327,641,000—110 million fewer than the mainstream forecast of 438-439 million with immigration. The United States had about 110 million in 1925; thus, immigration

11 http://pewhispanic.org/files/reports/85.pdf

will raise the population of the United States in the next forty years by what the whole population of the United States was eight-five years ago.

What will the U.S. population be in 2100 if we don't at least slow immigration?

If net (not gross) immigration is kept at no more than 1.5 million bodies a year, U.S. population in 2100 will be over 700 million. However, some bills in Congress could goose lawful immigration to more than two million a year. Should such "reforms" become law, U.S. population could flood to over 850 million in 2100.[12] (Gross immigration is about two million a year now, but some 500,000 go back home for a net of 1.5 million.) This is why the immigration boosters of right or left never talk about numbers. The numbers are a mind-blowing nightmare.

12 Cafaro and Staples, "The Environmental Argument for Reducing Immigration."

Box 11.1. The United States in the Year 2100

IMMIGRATION WILL SET EVERYTHING

Today's Population:	310 million Americans
Today Yearly Net Immigration:	1.5 million
Yearly Net Immigration in 2006 Kennedy/Bush bill:	over 2 million
Population in 2100 with 1.5 million immigrants yearly:	over 700 million
Population in 2100 with 2 + million immigrants yearly:	over 850 million
Population in 2100 if we freeze immigration:	about 330 million

Which one do you want for your grandchildren?

Which one do you want for wild things?

(This holds true if today's fertility rates are not deeply cut.)

So. We can now ask what the outcomes of these sundry population figures will be. How many more tons of greenhouse gases churned out every year? Wild acres taken over by housing, highways, parking lots, shopping malls, farmland, coal strip mines and mountaintop removal, oil and gas drill pads and road/pipeline webs, and so on? Total energy use? New coal-burning power plants? New nuclear plants and nuclear waste with nowhere to put it? Total water use? More dams, irrigation, groundwater pumping? This is what we should be talking about when we talk about immigration. The bottom line is how many acres of homeland and foraging land for other Earthlings (wildlife) will be taken over by all the new men, women, and children in the United States. How much more water will Man suck up in this more crowded United States?

Conservationists worried by the upshot of immigration need to demand answers from the federal government on how immigration will make our footprint bigger and heavier—and deadlier. We must stand up loudly and call for a full environmental impact statement (EIS) on immigration policies. Conservationists need to file a lawsuit requiring such a study. We need to lobby members of Congress—Democrats and Republicans—to introduce a bill requiring such an environmental impact statement. Then we must bird-dog it to make sure it is thorough and farsighted. Such an EIS should be at the top of our to-do list. Who is going to get on board? Who will fund our campaign to demand an EIS? A thorough environmental impact statement on immigration to the United States might be the most important EIS ever done. It is the one way to bring all the facts—not emotions and sweet lies—into full public debate.

Before friends dug up the answers to my questions above, I did not know how truly bad population growth was in the United States. I didn't know the weight of immigration. It is much worse than I thought. Why, why are we doing this to our country? To the wild things living here? What do we gain? How are we better off to have more than one hundred million (100,000,000) more people in the United States in forty years? *Half a billion more people in ninety years?* Our head-in-the-sand madness and carelessness about population growth in the United States boggle my mind. And let me tell you, I am one world-weary, hardened, distrustful, cranky, old bastard. It takes a lot to boggle my mind.

However, shortly after having my mind boggled by immigration numbers, I chanced upon something that further boggled it. Digging around in my library, I came upon *The 1992 Information Please Almanac.* I thought that since it was a different brand of almanac, maybe it would have other figures on world population even though it was nearly twenty years old. I found one table called "World's 20 Most Populous Countries: 1991 and 2100." Knowing that the United States would still be the third most populous country in 2100, I glanced to see what the other nineteen would be. But the table listed the U.S. as *seventh,* with India, China, Nigeria, USSR, Indonesia, and Pakistan ahead. Okay, this was before the USSR broke up, but how did Nigeria, Indonesia, and Pakistan grow past us? My gosh, what were their populations projected to be? I looked at what the United States was forecast to be in 2100: 308,700,000. What? That was already the population of the U.S. in 2010. What was going on? The source for 2100 was the World Bank. Then it hit me: *As recently as 1991, the impact of immigration on population growth in the United States was not yet being seen.* Twenty years ago, even the World Bank couldn't forecast what immigration would do to our country.

The United States is not the only wealthy country looking at ecological wreckage thanks to immigration-driven growth. Tim Murray, from British Columbia, writes that 70 percent of Canadian growth comes from immigration. "Immigration in recent decades has generated sprawl over Canada's best farmland to the scale of 3-4 Torontos, 3-4 times larger than the tar sands, and has out-polluted the tar sands 3 or 4 to 1, accounting for 80% of our overshoot of Kyoto targets."[13] On the other side of the Atlantic, the Optimum Population Trust says, "Fertility levels in the UK have been below replacement level (2.1 children per woman) for around 30 years. Inward migration is currently the main driver of UK population growth, accounting for over 80 per cent of projected increase to 2074."[14] The Trust elsewhere reports on a UN warning that desertification would push 60 million people from sub-Saharan Africa to "northern Africa and Europe in the next 20 years."[15]

The ecological argument for immigration to the United States

I've heard only one argument from the pro-immigration side that rests on ecological grounds. Back when I was on the losing side in the fight over immigration policy in the Sierra Club in the mid-1990s, Carl Pope put it this way to me: For the sake of biodiversity, letting Guatemalans come to Los Angeles is better than them hunting wildlife and hacking out new *milpas* in the backwoods of Guatemala.

I think this is a clever argument and one that conservationists worried about immigration and population growth should weigh. I have weighed it and found it wanting. It seems to be grounded on the following beliefs:

Biodiversity has more worth in Guatemala than in Southern California.

The growing population in Guatemala will go to wildlands in Guatemala if they can't come to the U.S.

---

13 Tar sands may be the dirtiest and most harmful way to get petroleum. Hundreds of square miles of what was boreal-forest wilderness in northern Alberta are being clear-cut and then strip-mined to get so-called "tar sands" out of the ground for a highly polluting industrial process that yields a usable fossil fuel. But, says Murray, immigration-driven sprawl in Canada is even more harmful.

14 News Release, Optimum Population Trust, May 7, 2007.

15 "Desertification and migration: *An Optimum Population Trust Briefing*," Nov. 2006.

Someone in Guatemala will have a heavier footprint on wild things than someone in Southern California.

So, are these beliefs grounded on things as they are or do they come from clever argument?

First of all, let us acknowledge that here we are looking only at Guatemala and Southern California. Such thinking does not weigh the footprint gap between a Californian and a Guatemalan on the rest of the world (which we looked at earlier in this chapter). Moreover, it is akin to what I sometimes hear from those wanting more logging of the National Forests: Any less logging in the United States will only lead to more logging elsewhere in the world where logging is less regulated (if at all) and where biodiversity may be greater. I've heard the same song from nearly every other U.S. resource-extraction industry fighting checks on its plundering. It's all self-serving, ill-founded blather to rip off raw goods from the public lands. In truth, we in the United States take more care logging (though not enough) thanks to conservationists than do other countries; and by doing a better job here, we can show others how to do better. If we ransack our big woods, though, what trustworthiness do we have for showing other countries how to take better care of their forests? If we overfish within our exclusive economic zone, how can we tell others to not overfish their stocks? [16] And if we let our population boom to once-unthinkable crowds, how do we talk to other countries about cooling their growth?

But, insofar as Guatemala goes: what we in sooth are doing is being an overflow pond for reckless overbreeding in Central America and Mexico (and for the Philippines and Africa and…). So long as we offer that overflow pond, there is less need to lower birth rates in those countries (birth rates have come down but not enough for stabilization). Something like 10 percent of the adult population of

16 Countries with sea coasts have "exclusive economic zones" stretching out 200 miles from the coast where they have the rights to fishing, oil and gas drilling, seabed mining, and so on.

Guatemala already lives in the U.S. and most adults left in Guatemala would like to come as well, according to polls. Who can blame them? I can't. But the unhappy need is for them to stay in Guatemala and make it better. No one else will do it for them. The TFR for women in Guatemala is a whopping 4.6 children giving a yearly growth rate of 2.4 percent.[17] Family planning is not working in Guatemala, somewhat owing to the might of the Catholic Church. The main way it can keep having such a high and thoroughly unsustainable growth is by the U.S. being an overflow pond for the overmany births in Guatemala. If we quit being the relief valve for the steadily swelling baby spill in Guatemala, births would have to come down. The heavy breeding in Guatemala is also kept going by remittance checks sent from Guatemalans working in the U.S. to kin back home. Researchers need to look closely at how such remittances keep high births propped up in the third world.

Philip Cafaro writes me, "Opponents of immigration reduction often argue that overpopulation is a *global* problem, so we should pursue global solutions for it. But this overlooks the fact that solving the global problem depends on individual *nations* getting their own population houses in order. The U.S. can contribute to this by, first, getting our own house in order, by ending our own growth. And second, by taking away the safety valve that allows Mexicans, Guatemalans, Dominicans, and others to keep breeding irresponsibly. This *is* the main way we can contribute to a global solution to global overpopulation."

If we are an overflow pond for Meso-America, why not for the whole world? Where do we draw the line? *When* do we draw the line?

The least painful time to draw the line is now. Not when there are twice as many of us in the United States (or three times as many people in Guatemala). Truly, the best time to have drawn the line was in the 1980s before immigration to the United States boomed. We flopped and we flopped thoroughly. But that does not let us off the hook to do better today.

17 Cafaro and Staples, "Environmental Argument," 13.

Is there something wrong with thinking that wild things in the U.S. are less worthy than those in Guatemala? I think so. In temperate zones worldwide, the wildlands of Southern California are matchless as a tangled and manifold neighborhood of life and they are beset by the grinding and rending roll of building. Southern California has more threatened and endangered species than any landscape of like bigness in the U.S., but for Hawaii. Besides, *this is our home,* damnit, and we have a holy responsibility to love and keep its wildlife and wilderness. There is something deeply wrong and wickedly unpatriotic with thinking that the United States should be a sacrifice zone for the rest of the world.

Moreover, a go-getting newcomer to Southern California will have a much greater worldwide ecological footprint than someone living in Guatemala City. This is key. As I've said, those who come to the United States are not going to keep their old footprint. They are coming to the U.S. to have all the goodies and highlife folks in the U.S. have. Again, who can blame them? But it does jack up the harm from immigration-driven growth in the U.S., as we saw earlier in this chapter. Finally, research shows that those in the booming crowds in Latin American countries are not going to the backwoods to hack out new *milpas* but are pulling up stakes and heading to the cities.[18] So, when we come to the end of this little debate, it is not whether it's best for Guatemalans to come to Los Angeles or to cut down the rainforest, it's whether they go to Guatemala City or to Los Angeles. Thus the underlying question is bogus.

Again it shakes down to this: *Earth cannot afford more Americans.*

Put that bumpersticker on your car—or bicycle.

18 T. Mitchell Aide and H. Ricardo Grau, "Globalization, Migration, and Latin American Ecosystems," *Science,* Vol. 305, 24 September 2004, 1915-1916.

Why now is the time to take a stand on immigration

In the next chapter, I'll put political correctness aside whether left or right, and look at a whole sweep of ways to cap immigration, lawful and unlawful, to the United States. Now happens to be a good time for conservationists to make our case for capping immigration. A Fall 2009 Gallup Poll finds growing backing among Americans for cutting immigration. In 2008, 18 percent wanted immigration raised; 39 percent thought immigration was about right; and 39 percent wanted less immigration. In 2009, those wants had shifted to 14 percent more, 32 percent same, and 50 percent less. Backing for less immigration has gone up 11 percent in one year—likely owing to the recession and higher unemployment. Keep in mind that these thoughts come in full lack of knowledge about the upshot of ongoing immigration: from 310 million in the U.S. today to nearly 450 million in 2050 to likely 700-800 million in 2100. If those mind-blowing numbers were bandied about, how would thoughts on immigration shift?

Moreover, we need to keep in mind that it is a misunderstanding that liberals are overwhelmingly against immigration caps. That has been a clever ploy by high-immigration lobbyists to frighten conservationists and others away from backing caps on immigration. There is much more backing among progressives for lowering immigration than is believed. In the poll just mentioned, 46 percent of Democrats wanted immigration cut while only 15 percent wanted it bumped up. A year earlier, only 39 percent of Democrats wanted immigration lowered. "Thus," says the Gallup Poll, "As lawmakers consider when and how to pursue immigration reform, they should do so mindful that Americans of all political persuasions are generally more resistant to immigration in broad measure than they were a year ago." A stand for capping immigration that is grounded in carrying capacity and caring for wild things needs to be heard by all members of Congress. It will help show the broad sweep of Americans who want immigration lowered.[19]

19 Gallup Poll website, www.gallup.com. October 3, 2009.

In the middle of the immigration fight in the Sierra Club in 1998, *Mother Jones* magazine polled its readers on whether they backed a "reduction in net immigration." A majority—56 percent—wanted to lower immigration. *Mother Jones* is a leading leftist magazine in the United States.

Conservationists and environmentalists who want to stay away from immigration do so, we've seen, so as not to be tarred in any way with nearness to immigrant bashers. Another reason is to not queer growing political alliances with minorities, especially Hispanos in California. It is mistaken to take for granted that the beliefs of self-named leaders of ethnic advocacy outfits in the U.S. Hispano community (if there is such a thing, given its diversity) reflect the thoughts of most folks who happen to have some kind of Hispano background.[20]

In a November 2009 poll, Zogby International found that most Hispanos in the United States are not behind more immigration nor are they for some kind of "amnesty" for those here unlawfully. Fifty-six percent of Hispanos thought immigration was too high, with only seven percent saying it was too low. Moreover, 52 percent back "enforcement to encourage illegals to go home," while only "34 percent support conditional legalization." The authors of the poll say, "The overall findings of this poll show a significant divide between the perception that minority voters want legalization and increased legal immigration and the reality, which is that they want enforcement and less immigration."[21]

One way I weigh public opinion is by reading the letters-to-the-editor section in newspapers, bleak though that may be. I often see letters in New Mexico newspapers against more immigration and signed by folks with Spanish names. New Mexico's new Republican governor,

20 I write "Hispano" instead of "Hispanic" to make it consistent with "Anglo." I find it odd that Anglo has a Spanish spelling where Hispanic does not.

21 Center for Immigration Studies, "Minority Advocates, Constituents Differ on Immigration," Washington, DC, February 25, 2010.

Susana Martinez, is the former district attorney for Dona Ana County next to the border and is tough as nails on unlawful immigration (she is rather dreadful on conservation and environmental issues, though).

New Mexico is one of the few states in which Anglos are not the majority. Yet a public opinion poll in September 2010 showed that 72 percent of New Mexico voters opposed the state policy of granting driver's licenses to illegal immigrants (only 22 percent of Hispanics were for giving licenses to illegal immigrants).[22] Gov. Martinez is also against driver's licenses for those here unlawfully. Moreover, 53 percent backed the controversial Arizona law calling for state police to check immigrant status on those stopped for legitimate law enforcement reasons. Among New Mexico Hispanos, 39 percent backed the Arizona law. The city of Albuquerque has a new policy that everyone booked into jail be checked for immigration status. Eighty-four percent of all voters backed this policy, as did 79 percent of Hispanos.[23] Do not be tricked that immigration or unlawful immigration is a civil rights issue and that all those with Spanish backgrounds line up on one side. Pollster Brian Sanderoff, in explaining the poll's results, said, "Many native Hispanics [in New Mexico] resent people trying to lump them all into one category." He also pointed out that native New Mexican Hispanics whose families have been here for many generations aren't always sympathetic to immigrants.[24] Recall also that the hero of Hispanos in the United States, Cesar Chaves, spoke out against immigration as harming workers in the U.S.

Progressives for Immigration Reform is a new group for which I can only say, "Thank goodness; it's about time." Their website has a wealth of good information, including results from a national poll of

22 New Mexico's driver's license policy was not just helping unlawful immigrants from Mexico; folks in the U.S. unlawfully from Eastern Europe, the Middle East, Africa, and elsewhere were coming to New Mexico for driver's licenses.

23 Sean Olson, "Voters Support Strong Policy on Immigrants," *Albuquerque Journal,* September 5, 2010.

24 Olson, "Voters Support Strong Policy on Immigrants."

"self-identified liberals and progressives." Among the figures is that 58 percent feels that "current levels of immigration are harmful to the environment."[25]

Conservationists should not be browbeaten into thinking that only right-wingers back cutting immigration. Those who want wide-open immigration to the United States—many of which are reactionary business groups such as the U.S. Chamber of Commerce—have a well-greased, well-framed, strategically sharp campaign to scare progressives and other fair-minded Americans such as conservationists and environmentalists away from thinking about the true harm done by immigration.

Others shoving more immigration are outfits wanting ethnic power, such as *La Raza* activists. I would put some of them in the same boat as the white racists who are against immigration.

Don't let the immigration lobby get away with their lies. Be willing to open your eyes and think.

On top of these public attitudes in the United States is the surprising and welcome drop in immigration to the United States. "The number of illegal immigrants living in the United States has dropped for the first time in two decades—decreasing by 8 percent, a new study finds," reports the Associated Press in September 2010. The study from the Pew Hispanic Center finds that the downturn in the U.S. economy and tougher enforcement both play a role for why one million unlawful immigrants left the U.S. in the last year. The drop is even stronger among Central Americans than Mexicans.[26]

The upshot is that conservationists should not be cowed from taking an ecological stand on immigration reduction because of fears about harming possible political alliances.

---

25 www.progressivesforimmigrationreform.org

26 Hope Yen, The Associated Press, "Number of Illegal Immigrants Living in U.S. Drops 8%," *Albuquerque Journal,* September 2, 2010.

Chapter 12

How to Cap Immigration to the United States

This is not to excuse the fact that they either came to this country illegally, or overstayed a visa. As I've said many times, I think illegal immigrants, once detected, should be detained and deported. I just don't see the need to demonize them in the process.[1]

—Ruben Navarrette, Jr.

In the statement I quote above, I think Ruben Navarrette, Jr., an op-ed columnist for the *Albuquerque Journal* and other newspapers, gives those backing immigration caps and enforcement darn good political advice—and ethical guidance. It's the path I take in this chapter.

Understanding Immigration

To either slow or cap immigration to the United States (and other wealthy countries), we must take a keen look at the makeup of immigration. First, we need to ask how immigration today shakes out as

1 Ruben Navarrette, Jr., "Understand, Don't Demonize, Illegal Immigrants," *Albuquerque Journal*, March 3, 2010.

lawful and unlawful. Then unlawful immigration can be further shaken out into those who break the law sneaking over the border (*sneakers*) and those who come in lawfully on a timed visa and then tarry after the visa's time is up (*overstayers*). In both sneakers and overstayers are those already here and keeping out of sight (12 to 20 million) and the many more yet to slip in. However, we need to keep from only looking at the kinds of unlawful immigration. Unlawful immigration is a problem; but lawful immigration is way, way too high, too. If all the heed goes to unlawful immigration of either sneakers or overstayers, we never get around to asking about whether there is too much *lawful* immigration. Conservationists and environmentalists who care about the population explosion in the United States must sweep the border spotlight over to the flood of lawful immigration, too. And so, our job at the bottom is two-fold: (1) shift the talk away from immigrants themselves over to the ecological impact of population growth from immigration; and (2) look at lawful immigration as well as unlawful. Too much talk about unlawful immigration keeps us from talking about *lowering* lawful immigration, which we must do also if we are to stabilize population in the United States.

My lodestar for the need to cut immigration is footprint and carrying capacity as they harm wild things. I want to freeze how many men, women, and children there are in the United States and then see our crowd begin to ebb as it is doing in Japan and some lucky European countries. As we've seen, if the United States Congress had taken the Sierra Club stand in 1989, we would have already gained what Japan and Italy have. Let me say this again: *Had the United States taken up the Sierra Club immigration policy in 1989, the U.S. likely would have already stopped growing at below 300 million, or, at worst, been set to stop soon at no more than 325 million.* Because we did not, our population is flying to undreamed-of heights, shooting up to twice as many (600 million) or—good grief—even more (800 million) by 2100.

Why do folks want to come to the United States to live and work? For a better life: one that is more out of harm's way, one that has better likelihood of making enough to live well for oneself and one's offspring. Phil Cafaro brings up a key if touchy side of why folks immigrate: "Often, it is because they and their leaders have failed to create decent societies, where people treat one another with respect and where society's economic resources, however large or small, are shared out reasonably fairly." The flip side is why folks are held back from coming to the United States: dealing with the unknown, gambling one's life and happiness. One loses what is known back home: kith, kin, lifeway, and neighborhood.

Folks leave their homeland and trudge to another land mainly because they believe they will have better breaks in their new setting. The things that go into making up one's mind to leave home fall into three fields: how bad it is in their homeland, how easy it will be to get to the other land, and how much better they think the other land will be. If we want to slow or shut down immigration to the United States, we need to come at it in all three fields—and we need to give heed to lawful immigration as well as to unlawful in all three fields.

We might also look at schooling and income standing. The hungry, unskilled, untaught folks who risk life, limb, and freedom to work low-end jobs to send money home to hungry kin are unlike those who are physicians, engineers, and scientists, even if from third-world countries.[2] Homeland is key, too. Though many who come to the United States seek a better life, some who slip in from the south may be

2 However, these are not all lousy, low-paying, dangerous jobs that unskilled Americans won't do; the truth is more tangled, but such a discussion will only get in the way of my path. I'll leave this to folks like Phil Cafaro and his book.

in narco or youth gangs, and some coming in on educational, tourist, or other visas from Islamic and other countries might be terrorists or ripe to become terrorists.[3]

STEPS TO TAKE

I offer a sweep of steps to put the brakes on immigration to the United States. I'll deal them out in the three fields above in Table

3 Christmas Day 2009 brought this worry out into the light of day when U.S. security bungled and let a Nigerian, whose father had warned us about his son's new radical Islamism, on an airplane to the U.S. The good thing about his crotch bomb is that he won't be fathering any children.

Table 12.1. Steps to Cap Immigration to the United States

FIELD ONE: MAKE THE U.S. LESS BECKONING

- Make the 1989 Sierra Club Immigration Policy the law of the land and sharply cut lawful immigration to what it needs to be to halt population growth.
- Oppose any raise in immigration level.
- Oppose any kind of amnesty or "line jumping" for those here unlawfully.
- Send home all who are in the U.S. unlawfully and ban them from coming back.
- Take fingerprints or DNA samples of all people caught in the U.S. illegally, ban them from being allowed to become U.S. citizens in the future, and deport them.
- Let those here unlawfully turn themselves in to be sent home at no cost and with no future penalty.
- Better track all visitors to know whether they are here lawfully or not.
- Give employers a straightforward, quick, unerring way to check the lawful standing of all job seekers and workers and mandate that they use it.

- Make hiring unlawful immigrants a felony with jail time and high fines; enforce it.

Field Two: Make it harder to get into the United States

- Set up better checks at airports for those coming into the U.S.
- Do a better job checking those who apply for visas or other entry permits.
- Allow only accredited schools and universities to issue I-20 documents needed for a student visa.
- Be much more "choosy" about those seeking permanent residence or naturalization.
- Department of Homeland Security (DHS) border work must be hand-in-glove with federal land-stewarding agencies on their borderlands.
- Dept. of Homeland Security work must be in line with stewardship of the National Parks, Wilderness Areas, and other wild havens on the border.
- All border-barrier building, enforcement, and patrolling must follow all conservation laws, such as the Endangered Species Act.
- Border-barriers being built must be put on hold until an Environmental Impact Statement (EIS) is done.
- Already built border-barriers should be reworked to not block wandering by wildlife.

Field Three: Make homelands better than going to U.S.

- Help cut birth rates in lands sending immigrants, by funding family planning and contraception.
- Help job growth in lands sending immigrants.
- Target microloans to lands sending immigrants.
- Reform world agricultural trade and farm support to help farmers in hungry countries stay on their farms.
- Stop the "War on Drugs" folly.

Thanks to Dr. Philip Cafaro for additions to this list.

12.1. In the text, I'll go into each step more deeply. Though I want to give equal weight to cutting lawful and unlawful immigration, fewer steps are needed for cutting lawful immigration. Do not think I am downplaying the need to cut lawful immigration owing to there being more steps targeting unlawful immigration.

MAKE THE UNITED STATES LESS BECKONING

The following steps are meant to do three things: 1) put immigration into overall population policy; 2) end job hopes for sneakers and overstayers; and 3) encourage all here unlawfully to go home voluntarily.

Make the Sierra Club 1989 Immigration Policy the law of the land. Oppose any raise in immigration level. Oppose any kind of amnesty or "line jumping" for those here unlawfully.

The 1989 Sierra Club policy or something like it should become the law of the land for immigration. Cafaro and Staples argue that "*we should limit immigration into the United States to the extent needed to stop U.S. population growth.*" (Italics in original.) This is pretty much the same thing as in the Sierra Club policy. Cafaro and Staples say this will "eventually lead to zero population growth" since our TFR is 2.05 already and a 2.1 TFR is "replacement rate." (Recall that TFR is *Total Fertility Rate* and means how many births an average woman in a given nation will have in her lifetime.) Such legislation would likely bring lawful immigration down to 200,000 a year or less, much as it was before 1965 when we blew the lid off immigration numbers. With such a lower number, the United States can be much more choosy about who we allow to apply for entry. (Mind you, I am not saying that ethnicity or homeland should go into how we choose.) Just as we could have stopped growth by 1980, so can we do it today. Conservationists need to be in the lead. Progressives also need to be up front.

Send home all who are here unlawfully. Better track visitors. Give employers a way to check status of job seekers. Make hiring unlawful immigrants a felony.

If folks coming in on a timed visa know that they will be found and sent home if they overstay and that such law breaking will keep them from being let into the U.S. again, they will be less likely to linger. If it is straightforward, free, quick, and error-free for employers to check whether job seekers are here lawfully or not, and if they know they will be hit with heavy fines or jail time for hiring immigration outlaws, they will be less likely to hire those who are here unlawfully. We must make it not worth anyone's while to hire immigration outlaws for anything—from factory work to yard work. The only way we can do this is to make lawbreaking hurt.

If those who have slipped into the U.S. unlawfully or lingered past their lawful time know that they will have a nearly hopeless time finding work and that they will be caught, sent home, and banned from ever coming back, even as a tourist, they will be less likely to do so. Moreover, those already here can be encouraged to voluntarily leave by a free trip home and no future penalty of being banned from ever coming back.

The federal government already has built a workable, effective system called "E-verify." Phil Cafaro writes, "E-verify is now highly accurate and has proven its ability to cut back drastically in the numbers of illegal workers. Tens of thousands of employees used this system over the past year; we should make its use mandatory across the U.S. After all, we (U.S. taxpayers) have paid for it, and we (U.S. jobseekers and conservationists concerned about unending population growth) should get its benefits." Either by federal or state law, all employers should be required to use E-verify, which is jointly run by the Department of Homeland Security and the Social Security Administration. (I have heard from others, including a retired federal prosecutor, that there are some kinks in E-verify that need to be fixed. If so, making E-verify as accurate, workable, and effective as possible should be an urgent priority.)

Employers who don't use E-verify or who knowingly hire those here unlawfully must know they will get the book thrown at them in fines and jail time, and by being banned from government contracts in the future. Top executives and board members should be in the dock when their plants hire unlawfuls. All government agencies must share knowledge quickly and work together. Agencies should have good sweeteners to work together and get their butts in the wringer for not working together.

Now is a good time to push immigration caps because immigration from Mexico has taken a big drop thanks to the lack of jobs in the United States. *The New York Times* reports, "Census data from the Mexican government indicate an extraordinary decline in the number of Mexican immigrants going to the United States." The drop is 25 percent or 226,000 fewer people. Jeffrey Passel, a senior demographer at the Pew Hispanic Center, said, "If jobs are available, people come. If jobs are not available, people don't come."[4] Let's make it unerring, then, that "jobs are not available" to those here unlawfully.

Now is also a good time to limit immigration, since so many Americans are out of work. With unemployment officially just below 10 percent and unofficially even higher, with 25 million Americans out of work, many desperate for a job, it is folly to bring in more would-be workers. Americans are worried about their economic tomorrows, and would readily back cutting immigration at this time. Businesses from fast-food joints to slaughterhouses want to hire sneakers and overstayers even when American citizens are out of work because they can pay the sneakers and overstayers so much less and without benefits or job security. Unlawful immigration is a subsidy to unpatriotic and unethical American businesses.

4 Julia Preston, "Mexican Data Shows Migration to U.S. in Decline," *The New York Times,* May 15, 2009.

If you feel that any of the above is unfair, you might want to do a survey to find out how unfair it is. Without a passport, visa, driver's license, and such, sneak into Mexico, Guatemala, Philippines, China, Nigeria, Pakistan, India, or another country from which the United States gets immigrants. Try to get a driver's license. Try to get a job. When you are out of prison, come back and tell us how awful the U.S. is.

Moreover, as I wrote in the last chapter, a Zogby Poll from November 2009 shows little backing from U.S. Hispanos, Blacks, or Asians for amnesty for those here unlawfully or for greater immigration. Let's look at it again. Among Hispanos, 56 percent said immigration was too high (7 percent too low), and 52 percent backed enforcement to send those here unlawfully back home (only 34 percent wanted some kind of amnesty).[5] Surely, conservationists can take such stands without fear.

Make it harder to get into the United States

Have better checks at airports and for those seeking visas. Allow only accredited schools and universities to issue I-20 documents needed for a student visa.

I do not want it to be harder for tourists, students, scientists, researchers, meeting-goers and speakers, performers, and such to come to the U.S. Indeed, I would like it to be smoother for such guests to come to the U.S. I have helped bring in fellow conservationists from Canada, Mexico, and elsewhere to speak at meetings. We should be a welcoming land, open to meeting folks from all over the world and happy for them to see America.

I do, however, want to make it harder for anyone to get into the United States unlawfully or to be here unlawfully.

Those coming to the U.S. with a visa by air should have to show their return ticket. Use of that ticket should be tracked so that if it

5 "Minority Advocates, Constituents Differ on Immigration," Center for Immigration Studies, February 25, 2010.

isn't used by the expiration date of their visa, their return ticket will be forfeited and the visitor put on the list for known illegal aliens.

An ongoing loophole for shady immigrants is that unaccredited, even fly-by-night "schools" and "colleges" might be handing out I-20 documents to supposed "students" so they can get student visas. Some such schools then do not watch either attendance at classes or overstaying visas. This should be tightened up so that only accredited, honest-to-goodness schools can give I-20s.

The Department of Homeland Security and the Border Patrol must work better with land-managing agencies, follow management guidelines for Wilderness Areas and National Parks, and obey the Endangered Species Act and other conservation laws. An Environmental Impact Statement (EIS) must be done before more border barriers are built. Barriers in place must be modified to allow wildlife passage.

At first, I threw down enough words on the plight and woe of the U.S.-Mexico border for a whole chapter. However, I have cut nearly all of that. By spreading more ink about unlawful immigration over the Mexican border, I would only draw away heed that needs to be given to the other threats and plights of overpopulation, including the big picture of immigration in the United States. I stand by my recommendations above and encourage you to check the Defenders of Wildlife immigration policy report and website to learn about the plight of wildlife near the border.[6] Let me also say, though, that much of the harm done to the wildlands and wildlife of the U.S.-Mexico borderlands is done by those coming over as smugglers or would-be immigrants. Overall, I think the need to heavily patrol and fortify the border with Mexico will mostly fade if we take three other steps discussed elsewhere in this chapter: (1) Dash all hope of finding a job or

6 Brian P. Segee and Jenny L. Neeley, *On The Line: The Impacts of Immigration Policy on Wildlife and Habitat in the Arizona Borderlands,* Defenders of Wildlife, Washington, D.C., 2006. See also www.defenders.org

any other way of making a living by those here unlawfully; (2) Reform NAFTA and agricultural policies so that Mexican farmers, big and little, are not driven out of business by U.S. exports of cheap, subsidized corn, chicken, and other products to Mexico; and (3) End the War on Drugs so that Mexico has a better chance of building a safe, honest society, and to stop drug smuggling.

Make homelands better than going to the U.S.

Help cut birth rates in lands sending immigrants.

When the United States and other wealthy lands are overflow ponds for mushrooming Man swarms from hungry or jobless lands, they foster more births in the poor lands. If there were no overflow ponds for the growing throngs, births likely would fall in the homelands. Moreover, if the smarter, better-schooled, go-getting folks who now come to the United States and other wealthy lands had to stay home or go home after getting graduate degrees, they would use their skills to make things better at home.

In the next chapter, I'll deal with the need for birth-control help worldwide. Drying up the baby flood would do much to cut the need and want to emigrate. For the United States and Canada, we need to be strategic and target family-planning help to those countries now sending us the most immigrants, lawful and unlawful, such as Mexico, the Philippines, El Salvador, and Haiti. This is a key step to stem the flow of immigration. Europe and Australia need to do likewise. A top goal for the United States should be to help bring those countries down to replacement level fertility as soon as can be done. All kinds of carrots and sticks should be brought to bear to gain this. I don't know what all these carrots and sticks might be, but I hope to spur workable new ways not otherwise thought up yet.

Help job growth in lands sending immigrants. Make more microloans in lands sending immigrants.

Why do folks leave their homelands for big, loud Western cities where they may be treated badly? Life in the homeland seems to be without hope. Helping to make better-paying jobs in poorer lands would do more than tough border enforcement to keep likely immigrants home. The countries sending us the most souls should be at the top for help by the United States. Instead of hiring unlawful immigrants to work in chicken-processing plants in Arkansas, build a damn plant in Mexico that pays well. Had we spent the billion-plus dollars the border wall has cost instead on building jobs in Mexico and elsewhere, we would have done more to slow immigration—both lawful and unlawful. Money now spent for feckless border barriers would be better spent on making jobs in Mexico and Central America and for helping farmers stay on their lands and compete with crop sales at home and internationally. Microloans can help small business owners (especially women) lift themselves up. The founder of a leading microloan bank in Bangladesh was given the Nobel Peace Prize for his good work. Mexico, Philippines, and other lands sending us the most immigrants should be the main targets for the U.S. to help. Along with birth control and fair food trade, microloans would help keep folks home.

Reform NAFTA, world trade, and farm support to help hungry lands.

Wealthy countries unwisely and unfairly play hardball with third-world countries on agricultural trade, thanks to arm-twisting from their agribiz lobbies. Defenders of Wildlife says that "since the late 1990s, massive increases in exports of heavily subsidized U.S. corn to Mexico under the North American Free Trade Agreement have reportedly resulted in large displacements of Mexican farmers."[7] This is only one crushing upshot out of scores from the reckless, uncaring food

7 Segee and Neeley, *On The Line*, 37.

trade strategy of rich countries. Not only is world food trade unjust and unfair, it spawns throngs of poor farmers who cannot even feed their children anymore and who then struggle to get to the U.S., Europe, and Canada. By propping up their farmers and agribiz industries with unfair food trade, the United States and other wealthy countries do four things: (1) undercut and monkeywrench farmers in the third world; (2) keep poor lands in the mire of wretchedness; (3) add to overall hunger in the world; and (4) push immigration to North America and Europe. The unfair food trade we shove down the world's throat ends up doing us great harm since it drives mass immigration. Helping poor farmers in poor countries have a fair shake at their home market and the world market could do much to cap immigration—as well as lift up farmers in the third world and help poor countries better feed their own. Insofar as Mexico goes, we undercut Mexican farmers and others from earning a living at home, and then we spend untold dollars to keep them from coming north to find work. These policies not only backfire but they are mean and coldhearted, too. We need to help corn farmers in Mexico make a good living, not help agribiz in the United States wreck corn farming in Mexico. A thorough, wide-sweeping Environmental Impact Statement needs to be done on U.S. immigration policy that would weigh this tangled mess, among other things. And NAFTA needs to be thoroughly redone to help farmers in Mexico.

A 2007 article in the *Washington Post* went into depth about how NAFTA has screwed up things down on the farm in Mexico. Mexican farmers cannot compete with subsidized U.S. corn, chicken, whatever now being shipped to Mexico. This article helped me understand how much NAFTA has cheated and harmed farmers in Mexico and thereby driven a rush of out-of-work farmers north over the border. The article ends with a quote from Lorenzo Martin, president of the Tepatitlan Poultry Farmers Association and head of a big poultry farm. "If there are corn subsidies in the United States and none here, we're dead. If the U.S. starts selling things extra cheap outside the U.S., then it won't just be small farmers and individuals who will be leaving. It will be people like me." [8]

We could cut back immigration from Mexico more by reforming NAFTA and otherwise helping Mexican farmers be competitive than by walling the border. I find it harder and harder to blame folks for sneaking across the border when we are giving them the shaft economically. For crying out loud, can't we see what we are doing? Maybe if conservationists and progressives who want to cap immigration on ecological grounds were to howl more about NAFTA and other economic unfairness, we could get more conservationists and progressives to think about the harm immigration does.

Stop the bungled "War on Drugs" folly.

Were historian Barbara Tuchman still alive, she could write a follow-up to her *The March of Folly* book on the woodenheaded "War on Drugs." A big, big shove for heavy immigration from Mexico and some Central American countries to the United States is that the southern lands are becoming so-called "failing states" without public security or economic hope. The once-growing middle-class in Mexico is crumbling. Much (most?) of this woe comes from the War on Drugs. The winners in this folly are the drug lords in Mexico, Columbia, the U.S., and other countries.

The grounds for stopping the War on Drugs could fill a dump truck. Maybe the strongest is that Mexico and other countries cannot have fair, open, law-abiding, workable civil governments and safe streets and neighborhoods for their citizens so long as narcoanarchy wields its deadly might. The *Christian Science Monitor* reports that this fear of crime is behind the wish of many Mexicans—including the middle class and wealthy—to come to the United States. One-third

8 Peter S. Goodman, "In Mexico, 'People Do Really Want to Stay,' Chicken Farmers Fear U.S. Exports Will Send More Workers North for Jobs," *Washington Post*, January 7, 2007.

of all Mexicans, or 35 million folks, would like to leave for "el norte," says a Pew survey.[9] Stopping the War on Drugs and treating marijuana, cocaine, and other drugs the same as alcohol and tobacco are treated would slow immigration into the United States from Mexico and farther south more than any other one thing, I believe. The crooked, underhanded setup in Mexico could begin to clean itself up. Citizens would be safer in their homes and towns in Mexico. There would be more work in Mexico and thereby less need to go north for work. The power and wealth of the drug cartels and *Zetas* would go up in smoke. And more law enforcement in the United States would be freed up for immigration and making sure those unlawfully here can't get a job. Philip Cafaro has asked immigrants from Mexico why they came to the U.S. He writes, "Invariably, they spoke of 'corruption' and the fact that a poor man or woman cannot make a good life in their countries."[10]

One of the nastiest things happening in California National Forests, Parks, and other public lands are marijuana plantations. No longer in little plots gardened by back-to-the-land hippies, backwoods dope growing is now big, sophisticated, deadly, and harmful to wildlands and wild things. Many of the plantations are farms for big narco gangs from Mexico with fulltime farmers from Mexico on them, well-laid-out irrigation networks, heavy fertilizer and pesticide spreading and dumping, poaching wildlife for food and as "pests," deadly booby traps, threats to hikers, and so on. So, narcoanarchy is a rumbling storm not only in the backwoods of Mexico and Columbia, but also in California. Moreover, such "farms" have started some of California's worst forest

9 Sara Miller Llana, "For Mexicans Seeking to Cross the US Border, It's not Just About Jobs Anymore," *Christian Science Monitor,* September 27, 2009.

10 Philip Cafaro and Winthrop Staples III, "The Environmental Argument for Reducing Immigration to the United States," *Backgrounder,* Center for Immigration Studies, June 2009. 15.

fires lately.[11] A great ecological good of ending the War on Drugs would be the end of these wounds on our public lands.

A full, thorough environmental impact statement on the War on Drugs would show what a mistake U.S. drug policy is, and would peg scores of woes and harms done by it.[12]

I call for three big steps to be taken as soon as can be done:

1. Mexico should legalize marijuana and cocaine, and regulate and tax them as it does alcohol.
2. The U.S. Federal government should decriminalize marijuana and cocaine, and allow their regulated import.
3. States in the U.S. should regulate and tax marijuana and cocaine as they do alcohol and tobacco. Growing marijuana should be treated like growing tobacco or the ingredients for alcoholic drinks.

I know a few things about drug abuse. My brother started selling lids of marijuana in his college dormitory and went on to importing hundreds of pounds from Mexico. He died of a heroin overdose when he was thirty-three after more than a decade of burglary and ripping off his family (our mother, cousins, aunts and uncles, and me) to support his habit. Had we a wiser policy on drugs then, I think he would have done much better. Indeed, I think fewer young folks in the U.S. would abuse marijuana and cocaine if they were legal as is alcohol. Moreover, without the highly dollar-wasteful "War on Drugs," there would be much more money to treat addicts and abusers.

Let me be straight about helping to make life better in Mexico and other woebegone lands now sending immigrants to the U.S. I think the steps I've outlined above could help make things better and give

11 Jesse McKinley, "In California Forests, Marijuana Growers Thrive," *New York Times*, August 22, 2009, is a good look at the plight.

12 Likewise, if we want "victory" in Afghanistan, we should tell farmers there to grow all the opium poppies they want and the United States will pay them top dollar for everything they harvest.

some folks more hope and better lives. But I do not share the unreal dreams of the poverty-ending crowd that poor, overpopulated countries can be flipped into wealthy countries. Nor am I going to blame the United States for all the world's problems nor wealthy countries only for the poverty and corruption of third-world countries. The people, educated classes, and leaders of other nations have to take responsibility for making their own lands better. They need to take the responsibility to balance their population with the natural ability of their land to produce food and a decent living for all. There are fields, such as world agriculture trade, where I think wealthy countries are in the wrong and need to change things so that farmers in third-world lands can stay on their farms and compete to produce food in their country and on the world market. But in other areas, the need for responsibility lies with citizens of each country. Highly educated people from third-world countries now working in the West need to go home to India, Pakistan, Africa, or wherever and make their homelands better.

Overpopulation is at the bottom of why folks immigrate, and why wretchedness holds sway over much of the world. Recall that Mexico had about 20 million people when I was born in 1946. It has about 110 million today. Mexico's population has grown more than five times in sixty years. Moreover, forecasts are for Mexico to have about 148 million in forty more years. Honduras? In the 1940s, it had about 1.2 million. Today it has nearly 7.5 million. In 2050, it is forecast to have 12.6 million—or ten times what it had in 1950.

That is the plight. And the sorrow.

The United States boosts more population growth when we serve as an overflow pond for Mexico and Honduras. Instead, the U.S. would do far better to lift Mexico and Central America—our neighbors—to the top of our foreign policy work and to do everything we can to work with them to stabilize their populations.

What we do or don't do today will build the world of tomorrow. No other thing than capping or not capping immigration will have such far-reaching and overwhelming consequences for the United States and the world. If we do something now, we can make a United States that will never have more than 325 million people. But if we do nothing, then we build a United States that within the lifetime of a child born today will have twice the population of today—over 600 million—or even nearly three times the population of today—over 800 million. What kind of U.S. do you want? You choose with what you do today what kind of America the living Earth has to bear in 2100.

You can act by letting your members of Congress and the President know about the consequences of the immigration flood and what you think about it. These last chapters have given you the knowledge you need to teach our leaders. Teach them well.

Chapter 13

What Do We Do?

How do we get the general body politic to accept the truth?"
—Garret Hardin (1972)

So. More of our kind is bad for all living things.[1] What do we do about it? First off, we need to understand that much of what we need to do is not hard. In both the technical and public health worlds, we know what to do. We have the tools. We have the skills. We have the worldly background. We have steeply cut the birth rate in many lands, climes, and times, and have seen wins in slowing, freezing, and nudging back population growth. See Box 13.1. We need to keep doing what we have done with family planning and population education, but do more of it in more lands, and give it a new thrust of burning need. It is not hard; it only needs will. Will, however, is missing now, both in the United States and worldwide. And therein lies our woe. When will is not forthcoming but is shy, doing is unlikely. Finding the will is what is hard.

1 But for a few weedy kinds such as German cockroach, Norway rat, cheatgrass, and feral goats.

Box 13.1. Family Planning Success

Thailand

By the late 1980s, Thailand's TFR (Total Fertility Rate—the average number of children per woman) had dropped below replacement-level to fewer than two births per woman (compared with about seven births per woman just two decades earlier) and currently remains low at 1.7. Cost-benefit analysis estimates that Thailand's program will have prevented 16.1 million births between 1972 and 2010, saving the government $11.8 billion in social service costs, or $16 for every dollar invested in the program.

Iran

Iran restored its family planning program in 1989. Between 1976 and 1997, the proportion of married women of reproductive age using contraception increased from 37 percent to 73 percent. After reaching 6.8 in 1984, the TFR dropped from 5.5 in 1988 to 2.8 in 1996 and is currently at the replacement-level of 2.1 births per woman.

Joseph J. Speidel, et al., "Family Planning and Reproductive Health: The Link to Environmental Preservation," Bixby Center for Reproductive Health Research and Policy, University of California San Francisco, 2007. (3333 California St., Suite 335, Box 0744, San Francisco, CA 94143-0744.)

Garret Hardin saw this well forty years ago when he wrote, "[H]ow do we get the general body politic to accept the truth?"[2]

But when he asked that in 1972, doing something about growth wasn't as tough, for then there were only *half* as many of us.

2 Garrett Hardin, "We Live on a Spaceship," *Bulletin of the Atomic Scientists,* XXIII (1972), 23-25, reprinted in Roderick Frazier Nash, ed., *American Environmentalism: Readings In Conservation History* Third Edition (McGraw-Hill, New York, 1990), 238.

Since dousing the population bomb came to be near the top of the worldwide to-do list, population has doubled. Since I began talking and writing about overpopulation, population in the United States has shot up by half, from 200 million to over 300 million.[3] Moreover, without the good work done in the 1970s and since, today's population likely would have tripled or worse worldwide.

When Hardin asked his question, the way was smoothed by the many folks—and nearly all conservationists, environmentalists, and resourcists—who saw the frightening clouds of the too-many billowing up. Now, our way is rocky and potholed owing to how few of us have eyes. Notwithstanding how sharply some of us see the manifold ways our growing swarm withers and kills wild things, most conservation and environmental clubs, as we have seen, now look away from the building storm clouds of the Man swarm. Too many wilderness lovers gainsay that our growing throng kills what we love—or it doesn't cross their minds. And this after the ghastly snowballing of the Man swarm worldwide and in the U.S. over the last forty years.

That overpopulation has been dropped as a worldwide care—nay, has been made taboo, as the Optimum Population Trust says, owing to its "sensitivity" for some in our politically correct whiny new world—has had outcomes. For one, we see in Africa's most populous country, Nigeria, that women still want nearly seven offspring each.[4]

---

3 Overpopulation has never been my main work, but I have steadily nipped at its heels since 1970. In 1972, I had a column, "Closing Pandora's Box," in the University of New Mexico *Daily Lobo.* Some were about overpopulation. Our bunch, Students for Environmental Action, handed out scores of copies of *The Population Bomb* at Earth Day 1972 and otherwise. *The Earth First! Journal* in the 1980s, which I edited and published, ran many articles on overpopulation, a bunch by me; in the 1990s, *Wild Earth,* of which I was publisher and author of the "Around the Campfire" column, was the one conservation magazine that ran tough articles on overpopulation.

4 Elizabeth Leahy, "Demographic Development: Reversing Course?" *Research Commentary* Volume 1, Issue 10, November 2006, Population Action International.

The Optimum Population Trust furthermore reports that only four percent of Nigerian women is willing to stop at two. No wonder Nigeria is growing by 2.4 percent a year and will likely have 299 million in 2050. Nigeria is not alone among its neighbors just south of the Sahara Desert. All will double their populations in thirty years and "fewer than 15% of married women use any type of contraception."[5] These pitiful, hungry countries torn between Muslims and Christians who hate each other—ahh, can anyone believe they will make it to 2050 without bloodbaths and starvation? If you do, my friend Tinkerbelle has a bridge to sell you.

Down on the ground, there are two humps for us to get over—"us" being the lovers of wild things who see population growth as the big driver behind ecological wounds. First, the population-freeze fellowship today in the United States and other wealthy countries is small and has been sidelined by the conservation/environmental establishment, mainly over the need to cap immigration.[6] More than a few folks who want to cut immigration are old-time conservationists upset by population growth and the harm it does to wild things. But like the late Alan Kuper, a mensch of our time, they have been told to get lost by the Sierra Club and most other conservation/environmental outfits. This lets the news media, led by *The New York Times,* overlook those of us who want to stabilize population growth in the United States and worldwide. As we've seen, immigration is why population in the United States is still growing. With the population-stabilization movement kicked into the shadows, the immigration donnybrook is played by the media as being about Mexican immigrants. Population growth does not come into it.

5 Rosamund McDougall, "Desertification and migration: An Optimum Trust Briefing," November 2006.

6 It's truly more than "sidelined"; many conservation foundations and donors will cut off and blacklist clubs that stand up on how overshoot drives the scalping and killing of wild things.

Here is where we run into the thickest brick wall on our path to build up a population-freeze campaign among U.S. wilderness and wildlife lovers: most folks—even other conservationists and environmentalists—don't understand the gap between those of us who want to cap immigration to stop growth in the United States and those who want to keep foreigners out owing to who they are. Thus they turn a cold shoulder to working on population growth. I delved into this in the last two chapters.

The other hump is that much of the limits-to-growth team today, such as it is, comes in two hues. One is the "sustainability movement," mostly made up of those worried about shrinking fossil fuels, those searching for new ways to crank out energy without wrecking the air and sea, and those who target highlife and wastefulness. If they worry about I=PAT, it is A and T about which they worry. Too few are willing to acknowledge that the ongoing landslide of babies is behind all these woes of overshoot, that babies are the land mines in the road to sustainability. Nor do they worry about the true losers from our gobble-gobble—wild things.

The other bunch clusters around "ecological footprints," which is good as far as it goes, as I wrote in Chapter 10. But this worry is mostly environmental—how does our heavy footprint squash ecosystem services and other goods Earth gives Man? From what I've read, the footprint gang doesn't see wild things as the "footkill" left in our lumbering wake.

Those who do understand how the growth of our throng overshoots carrying capacity and how it harms all Earthlings are often scientists, naturalists, and old-time conservationists, but they are not gathered together as a visible web within the wildlife-wildlands clan and they don't throw their weight about.[7] Gladly, a shift is beginning: this

7 Old-time conservationists are not just old farts like my even-older mentors and me—youngsters can be old-time conservationists, too. It's the mood, not the years.

book, the Conservation Leaders' Forum, the Apply the Brakes website, and Progressives for Immigration Reform are marks of this shift, as is the Optimum Population Trust in the United Kingdom. I hope that we soon will have a bustling, growing flock of population-freeze workers within the conservation-environmental world.

In earlier chapters, I've gone through the historical, psychological, and even evolutionary grounds for this head-in-the-sand outlook on population. It now seems to me that the thirty-some years after World War Two, when there was acknowledgment that the baby boom was a threat, may have been an odd time for Man. Maybe the everyday zeitgeist, back into which we've sunk, is one of blithe blindness to the threat of too many. Worrying about and holding back our growth may be unnatural for us; the years of warning about growth after World War Two may have been thanks to something in the mood of the time. Archaeologist Steven LeBlanc teaches that no bunch of us from band to empire for 50,000 years has fettered its population growth, and that this rising tide of mouths has always led to hunger, overshooting carrying capacity, and endless bloodletting.[8]

Eileen Crist is dead-on when she writes that the dusty old stack of arguments slung about to show that population growth is a threat is no longer acknowledged by most folks. Because the dazzling, breathtaking, continent-sweeping starvation and out-and-out resource wars still have not happened, old warnings from *The Population Bomb* and other books and articles of that time are shrugged off. Never mind that today many, if not most, of the blood-fights within and between nations are tied to overpopulation and resource shortages, as Michael

8 Steven A. LeBlanc with Katherine E. Register, *Constant Battles: The Myth of the Peaceful, Noble Savage* (St. Martin's Press, NY, 2003). Within anthropology and the other liberal arts, it is still widely believed that pre-civilized cultures had means to keep population growth down. LeBlanc buries this myth along with others. Those who think that hunting and gathering bands had the skill and knowledge to keep births down so as to stay within carrying capacity need to read *Constant Battles.*

Klare shows well in his books.[9] Moreover, tens of millions have starved and are starving, but the linkage of resource wars and starvation to overpopulation is dim at best to most folks. Since Hardin's "body politic" sees neither wars nor killing hunger over the last forty years as coming from the booming Man swarm, they don't see any of this as the understandable outcome of overbreeding. We in wealthy lands today are still cozy, notwithstanding 2008's bank crash, and we see fast growth in wealth—not starvation—in the poster-child countries of overpopulation awfulness: China and India (though yearly millions yet die of hunger in India). In wealthy countries some little towns and the hinterlands have lost bodies. Shops and diners have closed doors. Therefore folks in such hamlets think there is no growth elsewhere or envy the growth elsewhere. Owing to the shortsightedness with which our minds are cursed, if bad tidings do not happen right away, if they don't happen nearby, or if they do not hit us hard enough to break our nose, we shrug them off and think they will never happen.

Crist is right, then, that the best beacons for the harm done by population growth are right before our noses: wholesale extinction, scalped and plowed wildlands, and climate weirdness. But too many who are worried about such things do not see—or want to see—that it is the flood of new mouths that makes them happen, or if they see they are afraid on political grounds to say so or they do not have enough like-minded friends to do anything about it.

And when we get right down to it, freezing world and U.S. population is not nearly enough. Stout-hearted, free-thinking J. Kenneth Smail, an anthropology professor at Kenyon College in Ohio, has shown that there is truly no choice but to sharply lower the population of Man over the next one or two hundred years.

---

9 Michael T. Klare, *Resource Wars: The New Landscape Of Global Conflict* (Henry Holt and Company, New York, 2002).

In two articles in European academic journals around the turn of the century, Smail lays out what I think is a sound, watertight framework that we must work to bring the population of Man down to about two billion else we face utter ruin. I came upon his articles and the responses they sparked in *Politics and the Life Sciences,* a UK journal, late in writing *Man Swarm* and can't do them justice now, lest this damn book never be done. However, I think we who love wild things and who know that the population explosion is killing them and their wildworld now need to grab Smail's work and build on it. For the sake of wild things we must bring our population down to no more than two billion. For those of us now on Earth, we can begin to lay the groundwork for such a campaign. There is nothing better we can do. I hope that Apply the Brakes, Progressives for Immigration Reform, and others in our crowd will study and promote Smail's work. We need to make it widely available first off. His seminal articles are "Beyond Population Stabilization: The Case for Dramatically Reducing Global Human Numbers" in *Politics and the Life Sciences,* September 1997, and "Confronting a Surfeit of People: Reducing Global Human Numbers to Sustainable Levels" in *Environment, Development and Sustainability,* July 2002. Smail's article in *Politics and the Life Sciences* drew "Roundtable Commentaries" in the same issue from a sweep of scholars, some with their heads in the sand and others backing him with worthwhile thinking and knowledge.[10]

So. I build my To-do List for Freezing and Lowering Population on these tangled and sundry thoughts. Foremost on the To-Do List is for more of us to boldly say and show how, when, where, and why

10 J. Kenneth Smail, "Beyond Population Stabilization: The Case for Dramatically Reducing Global Human Numbers," *Politics and the Life Sciences,* Vol. 16, No. 2, September 1997, Beech Tree Publishing, Surrey, UK, 183-192; and "Confronting a Surfeit of People: Reducing Global Human Numbers to Sustainable Levels," *Environment, Development and Sustainability,* 4, July 2002, Kluwer, the Netherlands, 21-50.

population growth (overshoot) is the main driver of climate weirdness, wholesale extinction, and scalping of wildlands. We then need to build a new population-freeze team within the kith and kin of those who love

Table 13.1. Conservation Leaders Calling to "Apply the Brakes" on U.S. Population Growth

Lester Brown, *Earth Policy Institute, author of many books*

Philip Cafaro, *philosophy professor, Colorado State University*

John Davis, *founding editor,* Wild Earth

Veronica Egan, *executive director, Great Old Broads for Wilderness*

Brock Evans, *former staff of Sierra Club, Audubon, Endangered Species Coalition*

Dave Foreman, *The Rewilding Institute, author,* Rewilding North America

Amy Gulick, *conservation photographer*

Andy Kerr, *former ED Oregon Nat. Res. Coalition, free-ranging conservationist*

Katie Lee, *actress, singer, songwriter, author, river runner, icon*

Susan Morgan, *The Rewilding Institute, former staff for many conservation groups*

Roderick Nash, *history prof. UC Santa Barbara, author,* Wilderness & the American Mind

Tim Palmer, *author of many river conservation books*

Douglas Tompkins, *founder, North Face & Esprit, Foundation For Deep Ecology*

Don Weeden, *executive director, Weeden Foundation*

George Wuerthner, *author, photographer, free-ranging conservationist*

David Brower*, *founder, Friends of the Earth, Earth Island Inst., former ED Sierra Club*

Gaylord Nelson*, *former U.S. Senator Wisconsin, "Father" of Earth Day*

**Now deceased*

Organizations for identification purposes only; bios are greatly condensed

www.applythebrakes.org

wild things. To further this, we need to gather case studies worldwide of how population growth worsens the harm we do to wildlife and wildlands. Conservationists, Nature writers, and scientists have a landslide of facts and tales of how we are ransacking and slaughtering life on Earth. But we have not carefully linked this killing and harming of wild things to population growth. I don't think it will be hard to do this, but we must begin to *thoughtfully* do it. When we study, write about, or talk about any of the Seven Ecological Wounds and their outcomes, we need to show how our population growth drives them. We also need to wield the rock-hard numbers of the population explosion. Mild,

Box 13.2. Apply the Brakes website

www.applythebrakes.org

This website is the result of a meeting of long-time conservationists held in western Oregon in the spring of 2006. The purpose was to discuss the decades-long retreat of U.S. conservation and environmental organizations from addressing domestic population growth as a key issue in both domestic and global sustainability.

The group decided the gap left by traditional conservation and environmental organizations should be filled, starting with a website forum in which individual leaders in the conservation movement would be able to present their own positions on a comprehensive approach to sustainability and also invite the general public and members of conservation and environmental organizations to endorse and forward their views to their Congressional representatives.

Each of the conservation leaders who appears on the home page—and those who will join them over time—has an established track record and reputation in the American and/or regional conservation movement. Visitors are encouraged to review their biographies and positions they advocate through the links on the home page. Please address questions about this website to Bill Elder at Bill.Elder@ApplyTheBrakes.org who coordinates it on behalf of the leaders group.

fuzzy talking about growth is like stroking with a feather; wielding hard numbers is like smashing with Thor's Hammer.

By no means should we cut back on our work to shield wilderness and wildlife from the harmful work of Man. We must keep at the job of setting up and stewarding wild havens throughout the world. The shift we need to make, though, is to link the bubbling-over crowd of men, women, and children to the plight of wild things and to make it clean and sharp that the best way to shield and keep wild things for the long run is to stop our population growth.

And so, I call for lovers of wild things to band together in the work to link overpopulation to the slaughter of what we love. I am far from alone in this call. On the Conservation Leaders' Forum at the Apply the Brakes website (www.applythebrakes.org) are thoughts from leading conservationists about the linkage between our growing throng and the death of wild things. See Table 13.1 for a list of the conservation leaders on this site. By signing a short, sweet statement (Box 13.3), you can help us show that this is a mainstream flood of caring folks in all conservation groups.

We do not yet know whether this gathering of like minds will lead to a new conservation-population group or whether it will keep on as a loose network. For now, we are gathering more conservation leaders and their statements on overpopulation for the Apply The Brakes website. It is the best link to the ongoing work to make overpopulation a conservation keystone again. See Box 13.2 for more about the Conservation Leaders' Forum and Apply the Brakes.

Table 13.2. What You Can Do

Conservation

- Sign on to the short statement "Conservationists' Overpopulation Pledge" and send it in to The Rewilding Institute, POB 13768, Albuquerque, NM 87192.
- Go to the Apply the Brakes website (www.applythebrakes.org), The Rewilding Website Population Page (www.rewilding.org), the Progressives for Immigration Reform website (www.progressivesforimmigrationreform.org), and the Optimum Population Trust website (www.optimumpopulation.org) to keep updated.
- Gather knowledge, news, and research showing how population growth worldwide and at home leads to a heavier footprint and greater ecological wounds—send such studies and news of how growth drives the loss of wild things and lowers our quality of life to The Rewilding Institute, POB 13768, Albuquerque, NM 87192, or to TRI@rewilding.org.
- Publicize such news and research in your local newspaper, conservation club newsletter, talk radio show, and so on.
- Help develop a "Wilderness Footprint" reckoning.
- Speak out on what drives population growth and how population growth drives ecological wounds, such as extinction, greenhouse overshoot, and wrecking wildlands.
- Write op-eds and letters to the editor for your local newspaper about the costs of population growth.
- Give this book and the "Man Swarm" brochure to members of your conservation club, university department, church, and so on.
- Bring a speaker on overpopulation and biodiversity loss to your group.
- Back conservation and environmental clubs that take strong stands on freezing and lowering population.
- When a group to which you belong starts an activist campaign on sprawl, open space, or threatened wildlife, join the campaign—and work to make sure it highlights how population is behind the plight.

- In the U.S., join Progressives for Immigration Reform (www.progressivesforimmigrationreform.org) and back their work to cap U.S. population growth to protect wild things.
- Call for tough, meaningful stands on overpopulation from conservation and environmental clubs to which you belong, and urge them to make common ground with family planning advocates and groups.
- Gather around a strong, hopeful vision, such as Lester Brown's Plan B, along with continental-scale Rewilding as Dave Foreman outlined in *Rewilding North America.*
- Work for new National Parks and other strong wild havens as cores within wildlands networks, keeping and restoring wildlife, and tough enforcement.

You and Kin

- Have no children or one, or, at most, two.
- Coax kin and friends to lessen baby making.
- Cut your household's ecological footprint.

Political and Economic

- Set a goal of zero population growth by the earliest doable date.
- Set a population ceiling for the U.S. that we will not go beyond (325 million?).
- Call for a steady lowering of world population to about two billion, or less.
- Tell governments and international agencies to stop welfare that fosters more births and to take strong steps toward freezing population.
- Call for an end to government tax breaks and subsidies for those who have more than two children.
- Tell your government to set a population cap for your country.
- Back free, widespread, convenient family planning help of all kinds worldwide.
- Ask public health foundations and public health agencies to fold family planning into all of their third-world health work.
- Back women's equality and learning and work opportunities worldwide.

- Back organizations such as the Population Media Center (www.populationmedia.org) that work to strengthen family planning in other countries.
- Ask your city council to set an optimal population for your city or town—or run for the council and do it yourself.
- Back tax, zoning, and transportation policies that will put a damper on growth in your town and region.
- Help your society shift from an endless-growth economy to a steady-state economy—learn more from the Center for the Advancement of the Steady State Economy (www.steadystate.org).
- Call for Capping the Grid in your country.
- Work to lower consumption and to embolden "voluntary simplicity."
- Back limits on immigration.
- At the next community meeting for your member of Congress or Senators, ask that they co-sponsor bills that would cut immigration into the United States, as well as bills that would raise funding for family planning here and worldwide.
- Ask your governor, state representative, and state senator to introduce and sponsor a bill that mandates use of E-verify by all employers in your state.
- Ask your representatives to back a legislative ban on all immigration from countries that do not allow legal abortions or that hinder family planning.
- Ask your representatives to oppose any forgiveness for unlawful immigration.

Thanks to Dr. Philip Cafaro for many suggestions for items on this list.

What You Can Do To Freeze Population Growth

In Table 13.2 is a short list of what we can do about overpopulation. In the rest of this chapter, I'll go through each step. Much of it is being done in one way or another already, but it is helpful to bring it all together in one list. Some, however, is new insofar as I know. I won't go into the technology, since, as I wrote earlier, most of it is old hat. I've already gone through some of the steps we could take to cap immigration into the United States in the last two chapters and I won't recap them here. As you read the steps in this list, please mull them over and think of other things to do. We need to be clever, eye-catching, and even outrageous to wake folks up. To wit: The Center for Biological Diversity has started an overpopulation campaign highlighted by "endangered species condoms," with packaging that will "feature endangered species art along with witty slogans and information on the extinction crisis, designed to generate media buzz and change perspectives on reproduction."[11] Don't be caught with your pants down without one.

Each of us has to choose where we can best work to help freeze population. All of us who love wild things need to pitch in, whether near to home, nationally, or worldwide.

CONSERVATION

Sign on to the Conservationists' Overpopulation Pledge

We need to show that many, many conservationists understand that population growth is the main driver of extinction, habitat destruction, and the greenhouse threat. The Conservationists' Overpopulation Pledge is a straightforward acknowledgement of this. You can sign it yourself, hand it out for others to sign, and get conservation groups to which you belong to back it. The statement is in Box 13.3 here, in the Man Swarm brochure, and on The Rewilding Website. It is also on a tear-out sheet at the back of this book.

11 "Overpopulation outreach: from social justice to safe sex," *Endangered Earth,* Fall 2009, Center for Biological Diversity.

Box 13.3. The Conservationist's Overpopulation Pledge

I understand that the human population explosion is still happening and that it is the main driver of mass species extinction, wildland destruction and development, and global weirdness (greenhouse gas pollution).
I support stabilizing population worldwide and in the United States (or your country:______________________________),
and I ask conservation groups to once again make population stabilization a priority.

Name ____
Address ______________________________________
City _________________ State ______ Zip ________
Country ______________________________________
Email ____
Organization ___________________________________

GO TO THE APPLY THE BRAKES WEBSITE (www.applythebrakes.org)

The Conservation Leaders Forum highlights words from some of North America's top conservationists and scientists on why population growth and immigration are threats with which we must deal. It is meant to embolden wilderness and wildlife lovers to stand up for freezing population worldwide and in the U.S., and for capping immigration to the U.S. Seeing the sweep of leading folks behind population freeze work should underline how this is a mainstream campaign. Reading their thoughtful and uplifting words for halting more growth of our kind will help you think out your own stand and make you stronger as you talk about overpopulation.

The Rewilding Website (www.rewilding.org) also has much on how overpopulation harms wild things and will steadily update its list of resources (books, websites, groups, reports, etc.) for working on overpopulation.

Get the scoop on how population growth leads to ecological wounds

We need to gather both targeted and general news and knowledge of how overpopulation leads to the Seven Ecological Wounds, such as threatened species and extinction, wildland loss, and the greenhouse threat. Chapter 4 "Overpopulation and Ecological Wounds" shows the kind of information we need. Write-ups of any kind are helpful, but scientific studies are most needed. Researchers who can tie ecological wounds to population growth are needed. Please send such information, with references to The Rewilding Institute, POB 13768, Albuquerque, NM 87192 or to TRI@rewilding.org.

Help develop a Wilderness Footprint reckoning

Scientists and conservationists need to take the Ecological Footprint path and develop an alternative Wilderness Footprint that will quantify one's impact on wild things, instead of on only the goods Nature gives Man.

Speak out on and write about what drives population growth and how population growth drives ecological wounds

Work to hold back the Man swarm has lessened owing to how few folks are making a fuss about it. Even when something is truly bad, it can be overlooked or brushed aside if too few are talking about it. We wild lovers need to talk about how the growing Man swarm is the underlying threat to life on Earth, but without becoming cranks or being shrill, which will lead others to shut their ears to us. Use the news and research our campaign gathers to give solid grounds for the Man swarm plight.

Write about the cause of growth and the problems caused by growth in letters and op-eds to newspapers, magazines, blogs, and so on.

If you are a graduate student, think about doing your thesis or dissertation on how population growth drives species extinction, other ecological wounds, and other problems.

If you are a journalist, university professor, talk show host, or anyone else with a platform, write and talk about population growth and how it drives conservation and other problems.

Wield the knowledge in this book, the Rewilding Website, the Apply the Brakes website, and elsewhere to talk about the need for freezing population. Hand out the brochure.

BRING A SPEAKER ON OVERPOPULATION AND BIODIVERSITY LOSS TO YOUR GROUP

You can also set up a talk and book signing by me in your college, town, or for your conservation group. Email TRI@rewilding.org or go to the Rewilding Website www.rewilding.net. Other CLF leaders also give talks. Ask the Conservation Leaders Forum for a speaker who can talk about overpopulation and what to do.

GIVE THIS BOOK AND THE "MAN SWARM" BROCHURE TO OTHERS

Man Swarm has a low cover price to spur getting it out. Bulk orders can be had cheap from TRI. Hand them out to your wilderness or wildlife group, university department, church, and what-have-you. Buy them at wholesale and sell them at retail as a fundraiser for your wildlife or wilderness club. An order form is in the back of this book. The Man Swarm brochure is free from TRI for handing out.

BACK ORGANIZATIONS THAT DO TOUGH WORK ON FREEZING POPULATION GROWTH

Hail wilderness and wildlife outfits and others who take a strong stand on freezing population. Send them money, and let them know you are backing them thanks to their work on overpopulation. Drop groups that are weak on overpopulation and tell them why you are leaving. We'll have updated click-on links to good groups on the Rewilding Website. The Rewilding Institute needs support for its overpopulation work, too. Tax-deductible contributions can be mailed to POB 13768, Albuquerque, NM 87192 or made through the website www.rewilding.org. Contact TRI@rewilding.org for information on tax status and federal ID number, or for any other questions.

IN THE U.S., JOIN PROGRESSIVES FOR IMMIGRATION REFORM

Philip Cafaro and others have started Progressives for Immigration Reform (www.progressivesforimmigrationreform.org) to make the progressive case for lowering immigration. Use their information and arguments to talk to your liberal or progressive friends about the need to cut immigration so as to stabilize population in the U.S. Back their work to cap U.S. population growth to protect wild things.

CALL FOR STRONG STANDS AND BOLD WORK FROM CONSERVATION CLUBS ON FREEZING POPULATION, AND URGE THEM TO MAKE COMMON GROUND WITH FAMILY PLANNING ADVOCATES AND GROUPS

Conservation club leaders and board members need to hear from their members and staffers that overpopulation should be acknowledged as the root of ecological wounds. Groups should not drop the work they are already doing, but at least they should talk about overpopulation and the need for freezing. Embolden those clubs with which you work. Get them on board with the Conservationists'

Overpopulation Pledge. As more outfits set up population campaigns, it shouldn't be as hard to get others to do so. When a group to which you belong starts an activist campaign on sprawl, open space, or other issues, join the campaign—and work to make sure it highlights how population is behind the plight.

Dr. Joseph Speidel and his associates at the Bixby Center for Reproductive Health at the University of California San Francisco called for environmentalists and conservationists to work together with family planning advocates in their short, top-notch 2007 paper "Family Planning and Reproductive Health: The Link to Environmental Preservation."[12] Conservationists and environmentalists should download this report from http://crhrp.ucsf.edu/publications/files/Speidel_FamilyPlanning_2007.pdf. The report shows what better-funded family planning assistance around the world and in the United States could do for slowing growth. Later in this chapter, I'll bring out some recommendations from the report. For now, though, conservationists need to work with family planning advocates such as Dr. Speidel and the Bixby Center.

Gather around a strong, hopeful vision, such as Lester Brown's Plan B

The tireless, visionary, human encyclopedia Lester Brown and his Earth Policy Institute have an eye-catching campaign with their Plan B to save Earth. (Plan A is doing what we've been doing—the doom-dealing path we are on.) Among the four slices of Plan B is "the stabilization of the world's population at eight billion by 2040."[13] Other conservation and environmental groups should get on board with this.

12 Joseph J. Speidel, et al., "Family Planning and Reproductive Health: The Link to Environmental Preservation," Bixby Center for Reproductive Health Research and Policy, University of California San Francisco, 2007. (3333 California St., Suite 335, Box 0744, San Francisco, CA 94143-0744.)

13 Lester Brown, "Could Food Shortages Bring Down Civilization?" *Scientific American*, April 22, 2009.

Work for National Parks and other strong wild havens in Wildlands Networks worldwide, keeping and restoring wildlife, and tough enforcement

We need to freeze population, but at the same time we need to keep working to keep wildlands from being overrun by Man, and we need to shield wildlife, foremost threatened and endangered wildeors, from further harm. The Rewilding Website has click-on links to more than 100 such conservation outfits. Read *Rewilding North America* to learn what to do. Here, too, we need to be guided by hopeful visions, such as the North American Wildlands Network I outlined in *Rewilding North America.*

YOU AND KIN

Have no children or, at most, two

There are many things you can do to make both your ecological and wilderness footprints smaller. The good grows with each step up. To wit: Drive less. Trade in your gas-guzzler for a higher-mileage car or hybrid. Ride a bicycle, walk, or take the bus or subway. Cut back on things and recycle, make your home more thrifty with energy or make it solar, eat lower on the food chain, don't eat ocean fish, and so on. We are awash in tips for what to do.

However, there is nothing better you can do to lower your footprint than to have no children. If you don't have a burning yearning to be a mommy or daddy, then choose childlessness. It is a good life, as Nancy and I can say. If your life will not be whole without children, then have one or at most two. You could also adopt or become a godparent or aunt/uncle to the children of your sibs or dear friends. But if you *must* hand your own genes down the line, have only one. If you think your one child needs a sibling, rear it with a cousin or child of a friend. If you must have a full house, then adopt after making one or at most two of your own.

Unless you must, do not have children. Today's medicine gives us everything we need to oversee our ovaries or testicles. I have lived with a vasectomy for many years without any woe. It does not put a crimp in your sex life in any way except to take away worry. I have a crowd of friends who are childless. Those of us who have chosen to be childless should not be shy in talking about it; we should be proud of it. We need to talk about how one can have a full, rich life without being a mother or father. As for Nancy and me, we have a little sticker on our refrigerator that says, "If I ever need to hear the pitter-patter of little feet, I'll put shoes on my cats." (By the way, our nieces, nephews, grandnephews, and grandnieces like us. And we like them. We take them on river float trips, among other things.)

Likewise, if you have one or two offspring and want no more, feel free to brag about that. If no one had more than two, our swarm would not only freeze, but would begin to lower.

So, if you know you do not want to bring children or any more children into the world, get a vasectomy or have your tubes tied now. There will never be a better time. And you do not have to jump through hoops to get the okay today for being "fixed" as I did in the 1970s.

Coax kin and friends to lessen baby-making

When my niece became pregnant with her second child, she told me not to worry: it would be the last one. Now, I've never been a nagging scold telling kin and friends to not have babies, but I've let them know what it means to Earth and wild things. You need to be a counterweight to moms and dads who keep hassling their kids to give them grandchildren. And for Earth's sake, if you have kids don't hassle them about giving you grandkids.

Cut your household's footprint

Population is the big deal in I=PAT, but we still need to lower our ecological and wilderness footprints by using less energy and buying fewer things. While we must underline that freezing and lowering population is tops, we should not shrug off greedy consumption as a driver of ecological wounds.

POLITICAL AND ECONOMIC

Set a goal of zero population growth by the earliest doable date. Set a population ceiling for the U.S. that we will not go beyond (325 million?). The same needs to be done for other countries by their citizens.

Setting goals comes first. This is run-of-the-mill planning. Making up our minds to stop population growth by a set time at a set number leads to the need to cap immigration. For the sake of some kind of target, I'll call for a population of the United States of no more than 325 million, with zero population growth gained by 2025. It would be better if it could be lower than this. And we should work to lower it after 2025. How about a goal for a U.S. population of no more than 200 million by 2100? With such goals, we can better reckon what we need to do to gain them.

Call on your government to set a cap on population

National commissions should be set up in every country to set what the highest population should be, and Earth lovers need to watchdog them to keep the population cap low. Rosamund McDougall of the Optimum Population Trust writes, "At the end of 2008, Britain became the first country in the EU to set a cap on population growth, with a ministerial pledge not to allow it to grow beyond 70 million." The United Kingdom now has 61 million inhabitants and is growing by 400,000 a year thanks to immigration and a too-high birth rate. McDougall warns that the pro-growth policies of British governments "look like a catastrophic environmental error. It is hard to see how the country will be able to sustain 70 million people in 2050." The Optimum Population Trust is calling for "numerically balanced immigration" and "stopping at two children." They believe such a path could cut population to 55 million by 2050.[14] The United States and other countries need to follow the lead of the Trust.

Call for long-term lowering of world population to no more than two billion

Outrageous and outlandish though it will seem to many, some of us need to begin calling for lowering Man's population and gathering the facts behind such a need. I highlighted Kenneth Smail's work earlier in the chapter.

Tell governments and international agencies to take strong steps to freeze population and to stop programs that foster births

Write your leaders (president, prime minister; members of congress or parliament) asking them to take a stand on population stabilization. Bring up the policies below, along with those in the earlier chapters dealing with immigration.

Take every chance to talk to your representatives and to their staffers to let them know how you feel about population growth and immigration.

Call for no subsidies or tax cuts for two or more children

Some governments now goad or wheedle women to overbreed with tax write-offs, cash payments, and other prods. Work in your country to end such birth boosting. Stand up against the Birth Dearth madness that shoves governments into spurring overbreeding. See Chapter 6 for more about the so-called Birth Dearth and how to undercut its misbeliefs.

---

14 Rosamund McDougall, "Defusing the population time bomb," *The National,* May 8, 2009.

Back free, widespread, convenient family planning help

Today's health science lets any woman have no more children than she wants. Throughout the world, women say that they want fewer children. Two big hitches are cost and accessibility. Our goal should be to make all safe means to deal with births widely, easily, and freely at hand for every woman and man on Earth. By *freely,* I mean at no cost for those who can't afford it. Back private organizations that offer such help. Call on your government to link all foreign aid to *working* birth control programs. No foreign aid of any kind, including military, should be given to nations that do not offer family planning help to their citizens or that criminalize abortion.

The third big hitch in family planning is the heartless bullying (and worse) of women by men in much of the world that keeps women from using birth control or makes them afraid to use it. Birth control availability needs to be such that women can get it whether their big bruiser of a man wants it or not.

Sao Paulo, Brazil, took steps in 2007 that will get birth control to those in need. The city "is offering 'morning after' contraceptive pills at metro stops and 90 percent off contraceptive pills at pharmacies," reports *The Christian Science Monitor.* Moreover, men are offered free vasectomies by the Health Ministry, which is also working with teachers to teach sex education and give condoms to students. Since one-in-three pregnancies in Sao Paulo is unwanted, these bold steps will lower unwanted births and sharply cut abortions.[15] Steps like these are needed in countries throughout the world—even in the United States and Great Britain.

In 2006, a team of family-planning experts wrote "Family planning: the unfinished agenda" for the British medical journal *The Lancet.* After highlighting how well international family planning once worked, they show how it has slacked off owing to loss of "commitment"

15 Andrew Downie, "Brazil Doles Out 'Morning After' Pills," *The Christian Science Monitor,* November 20, 2007.

Box 13.4. How Conservationists Can Help International Family Planning

- Country-level advocacy to reduce restrictions on access to family planning information and services, including for young people and the unmarried;
- Advocacy for the financial and human resources necessary to strengthen family planning and related reproductive health services, including programs that address the HIV/AIDS epidemic;
- Supporting access to all methods of family planning including safe abortion services that are essential to reproductive health and childbearing choices; and
- Advocacy for international development efforts such as education (especially for girls) that encourage slower population growth.

In the United States, steps should include:

- Outreach and education about how population growth affects the environment and quality of life;
- Advocacy and other efforts to help ensure universal access to sexuality information, education, and services, especially for young people;
- Advocacy to ensure that all reproductive health policies and programs are based on scientific evidence, rather than ideological beliefs;
- Advocacy in support of universal access to affordable family practice programs, especially for those that serve low-income populations and youth;
- Advocacy in support of universal and affordable access to safe abortion;
- Outreach and advocacy in support of an open and rational dialogue around U.S. immigration policies and programs.

Quoted from Dr. Joseph Speidel and the Bixby Center at the University of California San Francisco. Speidel, et al., "Family Planning and Reproductive Health," 14. Reprinted with permission of Dr. Speidel.

and since "international funding and promotion of family planning has waned in the past decade." They warn, "What is currently missing is political willingness to incorporate family planning into the development arena."[16] They show that family planning and lowering the birth rate can greatly improve health and reduce poverty in the third world. Getting the development community to understand the need for more funding of family planning programs will lead to fewer hungry mouths and to population stabilization worldwide. Conservationists need to work with family planning stalwarts to build international will and funding so as to bring birth control to every woman and couple in the world.

Dr. Joseph Speidel and the Bixby Center at UCSF call for conservationists to work for family planning: "Environmental organizations can make an important contribution by educating their membership, policy makers, and the public about the need for global action to improve access to family planning both in the United States and worldwide." See Box 13.4 for the steps conservationists and environmentalists should back internationally.

Right now, there is a great, unmet need for family planning in the world. Speidel and others call for "$15.9 billion in annual spending for family planning and basic research, $15 billion for reproductive health, and $14.9 billion for the full range of HIV/AIDS prevention, treatment, care, and support." This would total $45.8 billion.[17] Given the sweeping long-term benefits and the billions now wasted, such funding is small potatoes.

16 John Cleland, Stan Bernstein, Alex Ezeh, Anibal Faundes, Anna Glasier, and Jolene Innis, "Family planning: the unfinished agenda," *The Lancet*, November 18, 2006.

17 Speidel, et al., "Family Planning and Reproductive Health," 11.

ASK PUBLIC HEALTH FOUNDATIONS, SUCH AS THE BILL AND MELINDA GATES FOUNDATION AND WELLCOME TRUST, AND PUBLIC HEALTH AGENCIES TO FOLD FAMILY PLANNING INTO ALL OF THEIR THIRD-WORLD HEALTH WORK

Ask private foundations working on world health to put family planning in all their work. Since some governments, such as that of the United States, sometimes bend to the Dark Ages mindset of the Vatican and fundamentalist Protestants and won't fund birth control, private groups are needed to fill the gap. The many private groups spending hundreds of millions of dollars a year on childhood diarrhea, malaria, AIDS, tuberculosis, childhood malnutrition, and other health woes in the third world would take more suffering out of the world by far if they made sure that birth control was in the hands of every woman in the world who wants it. Recall what Lyndon Johnson said: "Five dollars invested in population control is worth one hundred dollars invested in economic growth."[18] In many ways, nongovernmental organizations (NGOs) are better and quicker at bringing family planning help to the third world than are governments and the United Nations.

BACK WOMEN'S EQUALITY AND EDUCATION WORLDWIDE

This, of course, has become almost hackneyed for progressives and the poverty-lessening crowd. Often it has elbowed population stabilization out of the way, as I showed in Chapter 9. Nonetheless, helping women to raise their standing in benighted lands will do much to bring down birth rates. It is also the right thing to do for the welfare and freedom of women everywhere.

18 Quoted in Paul R. Ehrlich and Anne H. Ehrlich, *Population Resources Environment: Issues in Human Ecology* (W. H. Freeman and Company, San Francisco, 1970), 259, 295.

Back organizations such as the Population Media Center that work to strengthen family planning in other countries

Bill Ryerson and the Public Media Center do amazing work by producing birth-control themed soap operas on television in many third-world countries. See what they do at www.populationmedia.org and back them. I don't have room to trumpet how good Ryerson and PMC are, but I think their work is tops.

Work locally to control growth

Ask your city council to set an optimal population for your city or town—or run for the council and do it yourself. Even towns that talk about "smart growth" do nothing to think about how big they want to get. By setting an optimal population ceiling, your community has a strong handle on growth.

Back tax, zoning, and transportation policies that will put a damper on growth in your town and region.

Work to help your society shift from an endless-growth economy to a steady-state economy—learn more from the Center for the Advancement of the Steady State Economy (www.steadystate.org)

Call for Capping the Grid in your country

Capping the Grid means that a country will not produce or consume more energy than what it is doing now. (It is a term coined by conservationist and micro-hydro engineer Bob King and has nothing to do with cap-and-trade scams, by the way). As new kinds of energy that are greenhouse-friendly come on line, the worse kinds—coal-fired power plants and hydroelectric dams—come down.

Back lower consumption and "voluntary simplicity"

Lowering births is the key to lowering the ecological and wilderness footprints of Mankind on Earth. Nonetheless, at the same time we need to lower how high on the hog we live. Americans, Australians, and Canadians foremost, folks in wealthy lands can lower the *quantity* of their lives without lowering the *quality* of their lives. People in Western European nations and Japan live as well as Americans, Australians, and Canadians, and sometimes better, but with lesser footprints. At the least, the three fat countries need to cut back to where Japan and Sweden are. However, some of the ecological footprint standouts such as Japan and Norway are at the bottom of the barrel for wilderness footprint. Slaughtering great whales is only one of their many sins against wild things at home and worldwide. This is why putting together a wilderness footprint is needed soon. Conservationists need to harp on how Japan, Norway, and others with middling ecological footprints but dreadful wilderness footprints are hypocrites and even international outlaws. Shaming them in such a way could help shove them away from whale murdering, overfishing, and other crimes against wild things.

Back workable, fair, enforceable caps on immigration

In the United States, Canada, Australia, Europe, and other wealthy countries, immigration is the main driver behind population growth. In the last two chapters I looked at how we might deal with this thorny woe. To repeat: The best path is the one put forward by the Sierra Club in the United States twenty years ago:

1989 Sierra Club population policy
Immigration to the U.S. should be no greater than that
which will permit achievement of population
stabilization in the U.S.

Such a policy is needed in all countries growing from immigration.

Ask your members of Congress to help cap immigration

At the next community meeting for your member of Congress or Senators, ask that they co-sponsor bills that would cut immigration into the United States, as well as bills that would raise funding for family planning here and around the world. Ask your representatives to back a legislative ban on all immigration from countries that do not allow legal abortions or that hinder family planning. Insist that they do not back amnesty for those here unlawfully. Sadly, some of the otherwise best conservationists in Congress are awful on immigration. Conservationists need to show how the two are linked. Likewise, most who are tough on immigration are rotten on family planning and conservation.

Get your state to mandate the use of E-Verify by all employers

Ask your governor, state representative, and state senator to introduce and sponsor a bill that mandates use of E-verify by all employers in your state. As we saw in the last chapter, E-verify is an easy-to-use, almost foolproof program developed by the federal government for employers to use to make sure all applicants are in the United States lawfully and eligible for employment. Getting your state to require its use by all employers might do more than anything else to halt unlawful immigration. (If there are glitches in E-verify, they need to be found and worked out straightaway so that E-verify can be put to work everywhere it is needed.)

E-verify or something like it needs to be used for all those applying for driver licenses, business licenses, post office box rentals, and so on. My state, New Mexico, lets those here unlawfully get state driver licenses, which they then use as legal identification. Unfair to legal residents though it may be, the federal government and other states should not honor such compromised driver licenses. Indeed, the New Mexico driver license should not be accepted identification for boarding an airplane. It seems like a terrorist's dream come true. I'll happily use my passport for domestic flights if it makes flights safer. (I've been a strong backer of New Mexico Governor Bill Richardson on most issues—he's been a great friend on conservation, but on driver licenses he's wrong as can be.) With a new governor against driver's licenses for unlawful immigrants, it is likely this mistake will be repealed in New Mexico.

There is such a dearth of leadership and work on the threat of overpopulation that there is a great responsibility and need for some of us to take the lead and to bring population stabilization back to the core cares of conservation and environmental groups. It is up to us. We cannot count on any of the existing "leaders" of our movement to lead on it.

Epilogue

Whither Life?

Do not let us be blamed by our descendants for not trying.[1]

—Sir Charles Galton Darwin

I've nailed together a bunch of steps into a ladder we can take that would help end population growth in the United States and worldwide. I'm sure there are many other steps, too. There are two key steps, however, without which the others won't work. They are the bottom ones.

One, we must make population stabilization a conservation care again.

Two, within conservation we must build a strong body of population stabilization workers.

I hope that with this book I have found the bedrock on which these two can stand. I am not asking for anything new; I'm only asking for those of us who love wild things to get back to talking about and

1 William L. Thomas Jr., ed., *Man's Role In Changing The Face Of The Earth* (The University of Chicago Press, 1956), 1117.

working on population stabilization as the way for keeping and restoring wild Earth.

I know well that the numbers of Men on Earth will go down. But I don't know if our swarm will become smaller thanks to our work—birth control—or owing to our overshooting carrying capacity—death control. In 1968, Paul Ehrlich knew that those were the only two paths for us in the long run.

So, I won't tell you that we will win this fight. I will tell you, though, that we can't win this fight if we don't take it on; and that for the world's wild ones, everywhere spared the onslaught of Man is a win for life. Do we have the wisdom and the will to at long last brake our mad run? Here we can only follow the wise words of Charles Darwin's grandson, Sir Charles Galton Darwin, quoted above. Let us not be blamed by those who come after us—of any kind of life—for not trying to bring ourselves down to within a carrying capacity that has room for everyone else.

Paddle forward.

—Dave Foreman
Sandia Mountains Foothills

Glossary

This glossary is for those words and phrases that might be little known to the reader of any of the five books in the *For the Wild Things* series.[1] They are of two kinds. First are those of a set, technical meaning; glossaries are most often for such words and phrases.

The second kind is for some archaic English words with which I write. Today's English is an odd and tangled tongue. Although English is within the Germanic (Deutsch) Family of Indo-European Languages, and has evolved from an unwritten Proto-Germanic, most of the words in it now are from the Romance Language Family, mostly French and Latin, also in the bigger family of Indo-European.

With the Norman Conquest of Great Britain one thousand years ago, French became widely spoken, as it was the tongue of the new overlords and landowners. Many French words made their way into English over the next few hundred years and thereby shoved aside widely spoken and written English words meaning the same thing. Latin words, through the Roman (Catholic) Church and then as the

1 A version of this glossary will be in each book.

way for European intellectuals to talk and write amongst themselves, later came into everyday speech and writing in English, shoving out yet more good English words. Although some linguists say that one cannot write anything but doltish English without using mostly French and Latin-rooted words, I do my best to show them wrong—though I have to sling about a few Romance words on every leaf if I don't want my writing overtangled or even daft. Some of my good Anglo-Saxon (A-S) or Old English (OE) words are still widely spoken; others are yet in the dictionary but tagged as "archaic." I am also working to bring back some even older A-S words no longer found in dictionaries—*wildeor,* for one. Such words are given meaning in this glossary. If there are other words you don't know, look in a dictionary—that's what such wonderful books are for.

Now—you may ask—why am I so queer for Anglo-Saxon English? In some odd way, I'm drawn to Old English by mood quirks that also draw me to wilderness, though I do not want to muddle language and wild things. I guess my love for Old English comes somewhat from my anti-modernist bent. I'm a stodgy, mossback, old conservative in mood (but not in the ideology of today's phony "conservatives"). When we get down to it, I like the way A-S words sound and feel in my mouth and look on the leaf. Indeed, Strunk & White and other word-crafters of their ilk tell us to write with true English words instead of French and Latin gatecrashers for a stronger, pithier style. Nonetheless, sometimes I have no choice but to write with Latin-rooted words—such as "style"—since there is no good Deutsch-rooted word with that meaning left in our tongue. So, to get down to it, I write and speak as much as I can with Anglo-Saxon words on the grounds that I like to do so.

For each of the words or phrases in this glossary, I give which books in the *For the Wild Things* series they are mostly to be found.

Amateur Tradition: In his insightful book *The American Conservation Movement: John Muir and His Legacy,* historian Stephen Fox clove the conservation of the late 19th and early 20th centuries into *amateurs* and *professionals.* Fox sees citizen conservation groups as within the Amateur Tradition (to wit: John Muir and the Sierra Club) and government agencies and professional societies (Gifford Pinchot and the US Forest Service) as within the Professional Tradition. One needs to understand that amateur and professional in this meaning are not about whether one has a job or is paid for conservation work, but *why* one does conservation work: out of love for wild things (amateur) or owing to a career in resource management (professionals). Moreover, some professionals working for the Forest Service and other government agencies are themselves within the Amateur Tradition and some who work for nongovernmental conservation groups may be very much in the Professional Tradition. *Take Back Conservation* and *Conservation vs. Conservation* both look at the amateur and professional traditions.

Cannot: Aldo Leopold wrote, "There are some who can live without wild things, and some who cannot." Those who need and love wild things, then, might be called *Cannots.* Such Nature lovers or Cannots are the conservationists who work to keep and rebuild wilderness and wildlife. In the *For the Wild Things* books, then, I sometimes write *Cannot* as a name for believers in the good of wild things for their own sakes. However, John Davis warns me that *Cannot* is too negative a name for wildlovers. On the other hand, that jarring may be what grabs one's heed.

Carrying Capacity: A key yardstick in ecology is the carrying capacity of the ecosystem (neighborhood) for each species. How many mule deer can the Kaibab Plateau in Arizona "carry" without harm to the ecosystem or starvation of the deer? Today, population writers look at carrying capacity for Man, too, either for standalone islands or neighborhoods or for the whole Earth. There are bumps here, though. For one, most Men, whether thoughtful or not, bristle at biology having meaning for ourselves. This dislike is toasted in all cultural, political, economic, and religious clubhouses. Two, those who weigh carrying capacity for Man mostly do so in a narrow way, overlooking the needs of all other Earthlings. Man's carrying capacity too often means only whether Earth can give Mankind what it needs; wild things do not play in this reckoning. It is past time for Man's carrying capacity to be reckoned by its impact on wild things and on evolutionary processes, not only on the flow of raw goods into our industrial web. I look at carrying capacity in *Man Swarm* and in my earlier book, *Rewilding North America.*

C.E.: *C.E.* means *Current Era,* and is written instead of *A.D.;* likewise *B.C.E.* means *Before Current Era,* and is written instead of *B.C.* So, 1800 C.E is the same year as 1800 A.D. Other abbreviations are *B.P.* for *Before Present* and *mya* for *million years ago* (*kya* for *thousand years ago*). So, five mya or 5 mya means "five million years ago."

Club (Cannot Club): A threat undercutting the work of those who need wild things is the shove toward corporatization, institutionalization, and professionalization in nongovernmental conservation outfits (what a load of Latinisms to be up against!). Wilderness and wildlife keeping should be a grassroots, folk undertaking of kith and kin instead of nine-to-five work in posh offices where there are sharper eyes for institutional growth than for the hallowed call to keep wild things wild. Words such as *corporation, organization,* and *group* bring with them the whiff of institutionalization. I would rather think of the Sierra Club, New Mexico Wilderness Alliance, and others as *clubs* instead of *organizations* so as to underline the high worth of putting the amateur tradition at the fore. We can see each conservation organization, then, as a Cannot Club, and the conservation movement as a kinship of such Cannot Clubs. Likewise, the words *network* and *web* are better for the overall gathering than is *movement.* I go into these cares in *Take Back Conservation.* (I know, I know that some will see me as an overfussy schoolmarm, but I make up for it by being sloppy in other ways.)

Conservation: Since their beginnings in the late 19th century, there have truly been two conservation movements or networks—Nature conservation, caring about keeping wild things wild, and resource conservation, given to taming and squeezing wild things for the short-time good of Man. I rather call resource conservation *resourcism* and keeping and bringing back wild things *conservation* (although lately I've had a growing dislike for the word *conservation,* therefore you'll see other words for what we Cannots do, such as *wilderness and wildlife keeping*). Moreover, the wild kind of conservation is not the same as *environmentalism,* which is not about wild things at all but about the health, safety, and quality of life of children, women, and men, nor is it the same as *animal rights* or *animal welfare,* both of which care more for the wellbeing of individual animals than about wild things. Therefore, I put resourcism, conservation, environmentalism, and animal rights/welfare in their own camps and not in one, broad network. However, there are not high, hard walls between these, and one can have leanings for more than one of them. It is good when they can work together, but there will always be times when one network wrangles with another.

Ecological Wounds: Aldo Leopold wrote, "The penalty of an ecological education is that one lives... in a world of wounds." In our wildlands network plans for the Southwest U.S., Bob Howard, MD, and I, both then with The Wildlands Project, took Leopold's thought to deal out the kinds of harm Man has done to wild things. We finally settled on Seven Ecological Wounds, which I then fleshed out in *Rewilding North America. Man Swarm* also delves into the Seven Ecological Wounds.

Folk Conservation: Clif Merritt, the great field director of The Wilderness Society after the 1964 Wilderness Act, called the grassroots wilderness lovers fighting agency logging, road building, and other land-taming *citizen conservationists.* I call them *folk conservationists* or *grassroots conservationists.*

CORNUCOPIAN: The *cornucopia* from classical Greek mythology is a ram's horn overflowing with fruit, grain, vegetables, and other good things, which never run out. Those who do not believe that Earth has limits, then, are widely known as *cornucopians* and are the foes of those worried about overpopulation and overconsumption. Cornucopians are always uber-optimistic, so they can also be called *Eco-Pollyannas*. *Man Swarm* and *The Nature Haters* both look at cornucopians.

DEOR: The Anglo-Saxon word for animal was *deor,* which now is given to only one kind—*deer*. The Normans switched deor to *beast,* which was later switched to the Latin *animal.* Other Deustcher (Germanic) tongues, however, kept their early words, so Deutsch (German) has *tier* for animal and Swedish has *djur.* I'd like to bring back deor in English as the everyday word for animal and *wildeor* for wild, untamed animals, and so I often write or speak deor and wildeor for animal and wild animal.

EARTHLING: One of Charles Darwin's great breakthroughs was to understand that all Earthly life kinds are kindred, that we all come down from one forebear (the Last Common Ancestor or LCA, biologists say now). Thus, all living things from microbes to fungi to plants to animals are Earthlings as much as we (Men) are, and we should see all of them as kin.

ENVIRONMENTALISM: Environmentalism and conservation are not the same thing. Environmentalists and conservationists have their own drives, folk heroes, goods, and lore, although there is overlap: most conservationists are also environmentalists and many (but not all) environmentalists are conservationists, too. *Take Back Conservation* looks at how conservation and environmentalism are not the same.

"THE ENVIRONMENTAL MOVEMENT": I put "The Environmental Movement" in quotation marks to show that there is truly no such thing, but that conservation (wild things) and environmentalism (human health) are each their own network, though they sometimes overlap and are akin. This is a key thrust in *Take Back Conservation.*

ENVIRONMENTALIST STEREOTYPE: The "Environmentalist Stereotype" is wielded by foes of conservation and environmentalism to make a leftist caricature of "environmentalists" out of step with "real people." The "Environmentalist Stereotype," which some environmentalists and conservationists fit and a few even boost, is that pollution fighters and wilderness shielders are leftists or progressives within the Democratic Party, and that they are therefore anti-gun ownership, antihunting, vegetarian, urban, intellectual elitists. *Take Back Conservation* and *The Nature Haters* deal with the Environmentalist Stereotype hurdle.

ENVIRO-RESOURCISM: *Enviro-resourcism* is my rather clumsy word for the foundation staffers, media and other consultants, board members, political operatives, executive directors and other staffers of conservation clubs who likely can live without wild things, and who are slowly taking over our clubs and the whole conservation network. They undercut tough stands and weaken or shove aside the lore, grassroots/amateur tradition, and outspoken belief in wild things for their own sake, and bring in their stead such Man-saked mush as "ecosystem services," economic worth, political pragmatism, anthropocentric values, organizational might, and leadership by paid "expert" staff and outside consultants. Enviro-resourcists are a blend of environmentalists and resourcists, not lovers of wild things foremost. Enviro-resourcist is a broad sweep and some may not fit the whole bill but only in one or two ways. *Take Back Conservation* is a call to take back wilderness and wildlife clubs and their network from the enviro-resourcists.

FOOTPRINT: The "Ecological Footprint" is a new, helpful yardstick for the population and consumption impact on the world for each of us, for chosen bands, and for nations. It is weak in that it mostly looks at impact on raw goods and "ecological services" for Man's good instead of on wild things. Cannots need to craft a "Wilderness Footprint" to weigh the impact of population growth and consumption on wild things. I deal with footprints in *Man Swarm.*

GLOBAL WEIRDING: Pollution by carbon dioxide and other "greenhouse gases" is leading to much more than overall warming. The upshot is tangled beyond anyone's ken, hence the need to use "global weirding" instead of "global warming."

GROWTH: "Growth for the sake of growth is the ideology of the cancer cell," wrote Edward Abbey. Since at least Gilgamesh's great-great-great granddaddies, growth has also been the ideology of Mankind. Whether population, economic, infrastructure, or whatever, the ideology of growth is why we cannot deal meaningfully with global weirding, extinction, rainforest scalping, and manifold other ills. Founders of the Wilderness Area idea were driven by fear over growth in the United States after World War I; conservationists and environmentalists today should likewise see growth as the big, bad foe of true "sustainability."

KIND: *Kind* is an Anglo-Saxon word for *species* in long use, even by Charles Darwin.

LAND: Aldo Leopold wrote, "The land ethic simply enlarges the boundaries of the community to include soils, waters, plants, and animals, or collectively: the land." *Land,* then, is a much better word than the dreadful *environment.* I rail about this in *Take Back Conservation.*

MAN, MEN, MANKIND: I use *Man* or *Men* capitalized as the overall ungendered word for the species *Homo sapiens, woman* for the female of the species, and *man* uncapitalized for the male. This is more in keeping with Anglo-Saxon English, which had another word for male *Homo sapiens*: *wer,* which lives on today as werewolf. *Wiv* or *cwen* was the word for a female *Homo sapiens*. Today's English is odd for not having a straightforward word for our kind that is also not the gendered word for the male. Deutsch and other Germanic tongues still have an ungendered old word for the species that is not the same as the gendered word for the male. Later English tangled things by doing away with a standalone word for males and using man for both male humans and humans of both genders. To have to call ourselves by a Latin word, *human,* is cumbersome and abstract. I do not write Man in a sexist way but for the goodness of the English tongue.

Neighborhood: The science of ecology often writes *community* to mean *ecosystem*. Aldo Leopold wisely wrote that Man had to stop being the conqueror of the land community and become a plain citizen and member of it. I like the Anglo-Saxon word *neighborhood* better for its cozier feeling than community. Wild neighborhoods, then, are ecosystems, and their members—whether plants, animals, fungi, or microbes—are our neighbors when we stop by or wander through. The goal of natural history is to meet and know your wild neighbors.

Noble Savage Myth: Jean Jacques Rousseau is the best-known flag-waver for the Myth of the Noble Savage, which holds that Man in a natural state was noble, peaceful, and ecologically sweet before being besmirched by civilization. Anthropology, archaeology, paleontology, history, field biology, conservation biology, and so on have shown this belief to have no ground on which to stand. It in no way puts down living tribal folks to acknowledge that Man has long been anything but peaceful or that Man is not an inborn conservationist nor ecologically minded. In *True Wilderness,* I show that the Myth of the Noble or Ecological Savage is mistaken, unfair to tribal folks, and sometimes gets in the way of keeping wild things.

Raw Goods: *Raw goods* are natural resources such as metal ores, coal, tar sands, petroleum, timber, grass and other forage, groundwater, stream water, and such that are still in the ground, not yet exploited and refined for use by Man.

Resourcism: Beginning with Paul Shepard, academic conservationists have called resource conservation *resourcism* instead of *conservation,* so as to underline the overweening drive of wildland and wildlife managing agencies worldwide to tame wild things, to lift resource extraction above other "multiple-uses," and to wink at whatever wounds such "management" brings on. I delve into resourcism and what is wrong with it in *Conservation vs. Conservation.*

Stewardship (also Caretaking, Keeping, Warding): *Management* is what resourcism does and it carries within it the meaning of stamping Man's will over self-willed things, be they forests, rivers, or wildlife. Conservationists have long been unhappy with management as the word for what we do with wild things. Instead, many of us write and say *stewardship* or *caretaking. Keep* and *ward* are other verbs that can work instead of manage. *Steward,* however, comes from *sty-ward,* or the one who takes care of the pigpen. Still, stewardship is a better word than management.

They, Their, Them: Today's overseers of the English tongue have worked to hack out so-called "sexist language." Among their key targets is how the male-gender, third-person, singular pronoun (*he, him, his*) has been used when the gender of the person is unknown. Some rather cumbersome wording has been offered instead of *he, him, his*—such as *his/her*—or even, good heavens, *hiser* or *shhe.* We've shut our eyes to the good pronoun *it,* which is used for a gender-neutral, third-person, singular pronoun for everything but Man. *It* and *its* would be my choice instead of *he, his, him,* but most English speakers would gag on it. Even when I call a baby *Homo sapiens* "it," I'm slapped down. It's quite funny that we are so unsure about our proud "human exceptionalism" that we can't take the most likely and wieldy choice for a gender-neutral, singular, third-person pronoun.

The next best choice is for the plural third-person pronoun *they, them, their* to become the gender-neutral singular third-person also. We are told this is bad grammar even though many of us unthinkingly say or write it in this way. In sooth, I was wrong to use "become" at the beginning of this paragraph since *they, them, their* was the run-of-the-mill sexless, single, third-person pronoun from Chaucer and likely earlier until Anne Fisher wrote *A New Grammar* in 1745 (the first English grammar, by the way). Fisher, though an early feminist, was the school mistress "first to say that the pronoun he should apply to both sexes," write Patricia O'Connor and Stewart Kellerman in the *New York Times Sunday Magazine* column "On Language" (July 26, 2009). Therefore, I write *they, them, their* instead of the clumsy *he/she, his/her, her/him*. And, should you wish to wield good grammar in your writing and speaking, I encourage you to do so as well.

WIGHT: In Old English and as an "archaic" word in today's English, *wight* means "creature" or "living being." In Old English, a wight could be a deor or a Man. I use it for both.

WILDEOR: In Old English, *wildeor* or *wildedeor* meant wild animal, or more literally a self-willed animal instead of a tamed or domesticated animal. *Deor* meant animal. *Deor* is in today's English as *deer*. I write *wildeor* widely in its early meaning as an undomesticated animal, one who is not under the will of Man. *Wildlife* means the same.

WILDERNESS DECONSTRUCTION: Some humanities and social science academics within the cult of postmodern deconstructionism have questioned how biologists, naturalists, and conservationists see "Nature," some going so far as to say we create Nature in our minds. Some postmodern deconstructionists have gotten their bowels in an uproar about ideas of wilderness and have even questioned whether Wilderness Areas should be set aside. Some link themselves to those calling for so-called "sustainable development" instead of protected areas (wild havens), and with followers of the Noble Savage Myth in its put-down of Western science. I call this intellectual giddy gilding *wilderness deconstruction* and such naysayers of wildlife and wilderness conservation *wilderness deconstructionists.* In *True Wilderness,* I deconstruct wilderness deconstructionism, sustainable development, and the Myth of the Ecological Savage.

WILD HAVENS: Throughout the world and Man-time there have been and are many kinds of protected areas set aside and stewarded for wildlife, wilderness, natural scenery, nonmotorized outdoor recreation, and biodiversity. National Parks and Wilderness Areas are among such lands. *Protected areas* is the catchall term for such set-asides; I like *wild havens* instead.

WILDLAND: The word *wildland* is slung about in many clumsy and tangled ways. Some think it means the same as *wilderness.* But wildland has a wider meaning than wilderness. In other words, all wilderness is wildland, but not all wildland is wilderness. Wildland is pretty much land that is not cropped or urbanized. It has native vegetation although sometimes in a beat-up state. A National Forest clearcut still is wildland, but I would not call a tree plantation wildland. Wildlands may have scattered settlements as well, whereas wilderness should be kept as the name for lands without year-around dwelling by Men.

WILDLIFE: Not until the 1870s in the United States did hunters and conservationists come up with *wild life,* then *wild-life,* and at last *wildlife* for wild animals. I call all wild beings, whether animals, plants, fungi, or microorganisms *wildlife.*

Wild Things: Living beings that are not under the will of Man are wild things. Geological processes (earthquakes), weather (hurricanes), atmospheric phenomena (sunsets, rainbows), landforms (mountains, oceans), and so on are also wild things if they are not made by or under the will of Man.

Wort: In Old English *wort* was a plant or vegetable. It is still in play for the names of plants such lousewort, St. Johns wort, and so on. I often write *wort* instead of *plant*.

About The Rewilding Institute

The Rewilding Institute is a small nonprofit working for the network of those who love wild things. We offer guidance on how to stay true to the wild by means of the "Five Feathers": grassroots leadership, far-reaching vision, toughness on policy, doggedness over the long haul, and a straightforward biocentric ethic (wild things for their own sake).

We do this by means of:

- A meaty, thoughtful website (www.rewilding.org) with a blog;
- An Internet conservation column on policy, ethics, and lore—*Around the Campfire* by Dave Foreman (to subscribe—free—contact Susan Morgan: rewilding@earthlink.net);
- A forthcoming series of five books *For the Wild Things* by Dave Foreman with help from Institute Fellows;
- Public lectures and seminars by Dave Foreman for colleges, nonprofit groups, conservation conferences, zoos and

museums, and such (to set up a talk, contact Christianne Hinks: christianne@rewilding.org);

- A series of widely distributed "Wildeor" brochures offering visionary protection and recovery plans for key wildlife in North America; and
- Working through sundry means for a meaningful, sound, and strong North American Wildlands Network with at least four Continental Wildways and bringing back native wildlife to suitable habitat.

The bedrock work of The Rewilding Institute is to fight the extinction crisis. The 6th Great Extinction now ongoing and driven wholly by one species—*Homo sapiens*—comes from what TRI calls the "Seven Ecological Wounds": Overkill, Habitat Destruction, Habitat Fragmentation, Loss and Upsetting of Evolutionary and Ecological Processes, Invasion of Harmful Exotic Species, Biocide Pollution, and Greenhouse Gas Pollution. The underlying drivers are the human population explosion and our overblown and wasteful consumption.

For the Wild Things

A series of five books from

The Rewilding Institute and Raven's Eye Press

By Dave Foreman

There are those who can live without wild things,
and those who cannot.

—Aldo Leopold

For the Wild Things is a much-needed gathering of five new books from one of Earth's leading wilderness thinkers and shielders. The five books are thoughtful, hard-hitting, and targeted.

Man Swarm and the Killing of Wildlife

The population blowup thunders through the world and the United States. It is the underlying driver of how Man wounds Earth and wild things by killing wildlife, taming and scalping wildlands, and belching out greenhouse gases. Here are the hard truths about population growth and how our growth is the overwhelming threat to wild things and a healthy Earth. A wide sweep of answers to the plight of too many is offered.

CONSERVATION VS. CONSERVATION: The 20th Century Fight Between Wilderness Lovers and Land Managing Agencies Over America's Last Wilderness*

Here is the lore and understanding every wilderness keeper needs. The first half of the book looks at how European settlers killed wildlife and scalped wilderness, and then at how public lands came to be in the United States. The last half goes into depth on the 20th Century fight over America's last wilderness and wildlife, highlighting the struggle between Resourcism (the Forest Service, Park Service, and state wildlife agencies) and Wildlands Conservation (the Sierra Club, Wilderness Society, and many other citizen clubs).

TAKE BACK CONSERVATION: Why Lovers of Wild Things Need to Take Back the Wilderness and Wildlife Conservation Network*

The grassroots conservation network, made up of defenders of wild things and of conservation biologists, has been undercut and taken over. Instead of tough grassroots clubs that fight for wild things for their own sake, bureaucrats, environmental careerists, funding professionals, consultants, political party operatives, and others want to make over grassroots wilderness and wildlife clubs and the scientific fellowship of conservation biology into middle-of-the-road, compromising, resource management institutions that talk about "ecosystem services" and other goods wild things give Mankind. True conservationists—those who love wild things for their own sake—need to take their clubs and their science back. Foreman lays out the whole threat to hamstring the holy work to keep wild things wild.

TRUE WILDERNESS: Why Wilderness Areas and other Strong Protected Areas Are Still the Best Tool for Keeping Wild Things*

Wilderness Areas, National Parks, and strongly held and policed wildlife havens have long been the backbone of wildland and wildlife protection in North America and worldwide, and they have been acknowledged as the best tool conservation has. For twenty-five years, though, such wild havens and traditional conservation have been under fire from postmodern deconstructionist academics; the sustainable-development scam of international financial institutions, consultants, and anticolonial ideologues; and the well-meaning but fuzzy belief in the "Myth of the Ecological Savage." Foreman deconstructs these "wilderness deconstructionists" and shows that strongly enforced protected areas for wildlife must always be the heart of the work to stop mass extinction and the scalping of Earth's last wild havens.

The Nature Haters: and How to Stop Them*

While conservationists love wild things, there are those who hate wild things out of fear, selfishness, narrow-minded but tightly held beliefs, and greed. Who are they, what are their backgrounds, what are their arguments against keeping wild things, and how do wildlovers answer them? Foreman has a matchless background for understanding and thwarting the Nature Haters.

**Titles may change.*

These books, written by Dave Foreman in the *For the Wild Things* series, will be published by The Rewilding Institute and Raven's Eye Press from 2011 to 2012. Fliers will go out as each is released. Series Editors are John Davis and Susan Morgan. Foreman has a matchless 40-year background of fighting for wild things and of thorough scholarship and research in the history of both grassroots and institutional conservation.

To order books, get further information, and to learn when titles are printed, go to The Rewilding Institute (www.rewilding.org or POB 13768, Albuquerque, NM 87192). Discounts are available for bulk purchase by wilderness and wildlife clubs for fundraising.

Index

AAAS (American Association for the Advancement of Science), 50, 160
Abbey, Edward, xii, xxi, 103, 118, 244
Abortion, 94, 123, 125-27, 214, 225-26, 231
Affluence (Consumption), viii, 5, 6, 19, 41-42, 48, 50, 60, 62, 64-65, 123, 130, 134, 139-55, 214, 223, 230, 242-44, 252
Afghanistan, 67, 98, 198f
Africa, 7, 14, 32, 46, 54, 65, 93, 99, 105-6, 120, 127, 143, 165, 175-76, 181f, 199, 203
African Wild Cat, 8
Agricultural Subsidies, 187, 193-97, 199, 213, 224
Agriculture, xvi, 14f, 21, 24, 25f, 26, 32-35, 47, 53-4, 74, 78, 94, 106, 116, 142, 173-74, 187, 198f, 199
AIDS, 101, 127, 226-28
Alaska, 27, 55, 262
Albuquerque, 148, 150-51, 181, 260
Albuquerque Journal, 151, 183
Alcott, Blake, 151
Altai Mountains, 141
Amazon, 20, 26, 60
American Economic Association, 77
American Environmentalism, 108
American Geophysical Union, 25
American Museum of Natural History, 142
Americas, 7, 32
Anarchy (Social Chaos from Overpopulation), 6, 21, 42, 45, 103, 116-18
Anglos (U.S.), 181
Antarctica, 7
Apply the Brakes, xii, 206, 208-12, 216, 218, 263
Arctic, 63
Arctic National Wildlife Refuge, 24, 44
Arizona, xxii, 19, 56, 181, 192, 239
Arizona 2010 Immigration Law, 181-82
Arkansas, 194
Around the Campfire, 203f, 251
Arrogance of Humanism, The, 71-72, 110
Asia, 7, 32, 55, 65, 93, 99, 165, 191
Associated Press, 182
Atlanta, 54

Atlantic Ocean, 175
Australia, xx, xxii, 7, 32, 114, 135, 145, 193, 230
Aztec Empire, 115

Baby Boom, 19, 86, 123, 206
Baltimore Sun, The, 127
Bangladesh, 48, 55, 82, 146, 194
Bartlett, Al, xii, 79-81
Bates, Marston, 109
BBC, 127
Beauty, Health, and Permanence, 121
Beavers, 52f, 57
Beck, Roy, xii, 18, 122-23, 125, 128, 131, 133, 147-49
Bering Sea, 27
Berkeley Ecology Center, 113f, 129
Betrayal of Science and Reason, 94, 100-101
"Beyond Population Stabilization: The Case for Dramatically Reducing Global Human Numbers," 208
Beyond the Limits, 112
Big Stumble of Limits-to-Growth, vii, 22
Bill and Melinda Gates Foundation, 228
Biocides (also see Pollution), 47, 58-59
Biodiversity, 1, 22-23, 49, 51, 55, 67, 93, 168, 175-76, 212, 218, 248
Birth Control, 16, 18, 45, 94, 96-97, 111, 122, 127, 193-94, 225, 227-29
Birth Dearth, vii, 13, 85-91, 134, 224
Birth Subsidies, 85-91, 127, 213, 224
Bixby Center at University of California, 3, 10, 16, 202, 220, 226-27
Blair, Tony, 61
Bleeding Hearts and Empty Promises: A Liberal Rethinks Immigration, 168
Bolivia, 67, 136
Bonobos, 7, 9, 67
Books of the Big Outside, 114
Border Barriers (with Mexico), 187, 192, 194
Border Patrol, 187, 192
Borders, International, xx, 56, 181, 184, 187, 192, 194-97
Borgstrom, Georg, 33-34
Borlaug, Norman, 97
Boulding, Kenneth, 77
Brand, Stewart, 86
Brazil, 26, 58, 60, 67, 225
Bristlecone Pines, 5
British Columbia, 174
Brookes, Leonard, 150
Brower, David, xii, 111-12, 144, 209
Brown, Lester, 26, 44-45, 97-98, 117, 166, 209, 213, 220
Buffon, George Louis, 105
Bureau of Reclamation, U.S., 74

Cabeza Prieta National Wildlife Refuge, 56
Cafaro, Philip, xiii, 53, 64, 76, 82, 88, 145-46, 154, 160-62, 167-68, 177, 185, 187-89, 197, 209, 214, 219
Cairo, 127-28
Calhoun, John, 43
California, xxii, 16, 19, 53-54, 164, 166, 175-76, 178, 180, 197, 220
Camarota, Steve, 89
Canada, xx, xxii, 57, 160-61, 171, 174, 175f, 191, 193, 195, 230
Cancer, population as, 11-12, 53, 66, 103, 118, 147, 244
"Can Technology Save the Planet?" 140
Cape Buffalo, 49
Cap the Grid, 214, 229
Carbon Legacy, 139, 153-54
Carolina Parakeet, 54
Carrying Capacity, vii, viii, xviii, 17, 19, 26-39, 45, 73, 83, 87, 90-91, 99-100, 110, 113, 116, 139-44, 157, 168, 179, 184, 205-6, 234, 239-40
Carson, Johnny, 111
Carter, Vernon Gill, 109
Catholic Church, 123, 125-27, 177, 237
Catholics for a Free Choice, 127
Catton, William Jr., vii, xii, 27, 29-38, 74, 114, 143
Center for Biological Diversity, 20, 42, 215
Center for Immigration Studies, 89, 161
Center for the Advancement of the Steady State Economy, 214, 229

Central America, 136, 176, 182, 194, 196, 199
Chamber of Commerce, U.S., 71, 182
Chaves, Cesar, 181
Cheney, Dick, 136
Childlessness, 51, 123-25, 152-55, 213, 221-22
Chimpanzees, 7-9, 67, 78, 135
China, 59-61, 66-67, 95, 97-98, 115, 127, 130, 151, 161, 174, 191, 207
Christian Science Monitor, 196, 225
Civilization Breakdown, 6, 22, 29, 37, 43-45, 72, 97, 105-7, 109-10, 220
Civil War, The, 150
Clark Air Force Base, 65
Clash of Civilizations, The, 117
Closing Pandora's Box, 203f
Club of Rome, The, 112
CNN, 127
Coal Question, The, 150
Cochiti Dam, 105f
Coercion, 127-30
Cold War, 71, 122
Collapse, 109
Colorado, xiii, 57, 131, 167
Colorado State University, xiii, 76, 145, 168, 209
Columbia, 196-97
Columbus, Christopher, 31
Comintern, 71
Commoner, Barry, 69-70, 129
Condoms, 62, 86, 127, 215, 225
"Confronting a Surfeit of People: Reducing Global Human Numbers to Sustainable Levels," 14f, 208
Congo, 67, 136
Congress, U.S., 131-32, 166, 172-73, 179, 184, 200, 210, 214, 224, 231
Conquest of the Land Through 7,000 Years, 106, 107f
Conservation (and Conservationists), xviii, xix, xxi, xxii, 2, 6, 13, 17-21, 24-25, 36, 48-50, 54-55, 70, 72-73, 83, 86-88, 93-94, 100, 105, 107-8, 110, 112-13, 116, 118-23, 125, 129, 131, 133-36, 139, 144, 149, 157-58, 165-68, 173, 175-76, 179-82, 184, 187-89, 191, 196, 203-6, 209-13, 215-21, 226-27, 230-33, 239-48, 251, 254-55, 263
Conservation Foundation, 107
Conservation in Practice, 87
Conservationist's Overpopulation Pledge, ix, 212, 215-16, 220, 223, 263
Conservation Leaders' Forum (CLF), xii, 20, 206, 210-11, 218
Constant Battles, 31, 118, 140-43, 206f
Cornucopianism, xix, 12, 22-23, 28, 33, 38, 60, 69-83, 85, 94-95, 98, 104, 107, 117, 129, 132-33, 136, 139, 242
Cougars (Pumas, Mt. Lions), 55, 57
Counterculture, 86
Coyotes, 55
Crash, Population, xvii, 22, 27, 37-38, 109, 143
Crist, Eileen, vii, xii, xiii, 6, 17, 22-23, 25, 28-29, 36, 43, 93, 101, 168, 206-7
Critias, 104
Cro-Magnons, 141
Crossfire, 127

Daily Lobo, 203f
Dale, Tom, 109
Dams, 19, 24, 44, 46-47, 57, 94, 105f, 173, 229
Dardozzi, Jeff, 150-51
Darfur, 136
Darwin, Charles, xviiif, 7f, 30, 110, 234, 242, 244
Darwin, Sir Charles Galton, 110, 233-34
Deevey, Jr., Edward, 75
Defenders of Wildlife, 192, 194
Democratic Party, 164, 173, 179, 243
Denisovians, 141
Denver, 57
Department of Homeland Security, U.S. (USDHS), 187, 189, 192
Desertification, 103-5, 110, 175, 204
Deserts on the March, 18, 105
Detritovore. Man as, 37-38
Detroit, 147-48
Diamond, Jared, 28, 109
Disease, 32f, 33, 47, 58, 98, 115, 119
Disney, Walt, 4, 81
Domesticated Earth, xvi, 23-26

Dominican Republic, 161, 177
Dona Ana County, 181
Drawdown, 33, 35, 37
Driven Wild, 72
Driver's Licenses, 181, 191, 231-32
Dust Bowl, 31, 105
Dutch East Indies (Indonesia), 30

Earth Day 1970, xi, xx, 19, 112-3, 129
Earth First! Journal, 203
Earthlings (other species), vii, xi, xii, xviii, xx, 2 6, 22, 26, 28-29, 35-36, 39, 43-44, 48, 58, 64, 76, 88, 91, 96, 129, 145-46, 149, 157, 160, 163, 173, 205, 240, 242
Earth Policy Institute, 117, 209, 220
Earthscan, 150
Easterbrook, Gregg, 78
Ecological and Evolutionary Processes, Loss of, 46-47, 57, 240
Ecological Wounds (see also Overkill, Landscalping, Fragmentation, Invasive Species, Ecological Process Loss, Biocide, and Global Weirding), vii, xi, 6, 20, 41-42, 46-49, 51-53, 61, 63-65, 103, 108, 143, 146-47, 149, 198, 204, 210, 212, 217-19, 223, 241, 246, 252, 253
Ecosystem (Wildland) Loss, 3, 17, 22-23, 26, 28, 43, 46-47, 57
Ecosystem Services, 24-25, 36, 205, 243, 254
Education Visas, 186-87, 191-92
Efficiency, 139, 145-46, 149-54
Egypt, 105
Ehrenfeld, David, 71, 110, 136
Ehrlich, Anne, xii, 5, 18-19, 37, 79, 94, 100, 114, 133
Ehrlich, Paul, vii, xii, 5, 16, 18-19, 37, 43, 60, 69, 75-77, 79, 83, 93-101, 108, 111, 114, 133-34, 136-37, 141-42, 234
Eisenhower, Dwight D., 121
Eldredge, Niles, 142
Elephants, 7, 49, 52, 54-55, 57, 67-68
El Salvador, 161, 193
Employment of Illegal Immigrants, 184-96, 214, 231
Endangered Species Act, 187, 192
Energy Demand, 24, 34, 50-51, 65, 78, 144, 150, 159, 229
Environ/Mental, 108
"Environmental Argument for Reducing Immigration to the United States, The," 145, 160-61, 168
"Environmental Consequences of Having a Baby in the United States," 51
Environmental Defense Fund, 120
Environmental Grantmakers Association, 133
Environmental Handbook, The, 112-13
Environmental Impact Statement (EIS), 173-74, 187, 192, 195, 198
Environmentalism (Environmentalists), xxi, 17-19, 21, 24, 74, 83, 86, 94, 100, 113, 116, 120-21, 129-130, 134, 139-40, 144, 146, 149, 157, 167, 180, 182, 184, 203, 204, 220, 227, 241-44,
"Environmental Movement's Retreat From Advocating U.S. Population Stabilization," 122-23
Environment, Development, and Sustainability, 208
"Essay on the Principle of Population," 29-30, 104
Essex County, New York, 59
Ethiopia, 14-15, 67-68, 82, 98
Europe, 7, 23, 28, 31-32, 59, 66, 73, 85-86, 90, 95, 97, 104, 106, 115, 125, 131, 134-35, 141, 145, 159, 175, 181f, 184, 193, 195, 208, 230, 237-38, 254
E-Verify, 189-90, 214, 231
Evolution, 5, 30, 36, 42-43, 46-49, 57, 135, 143, 206, 240, 252
Exclusive Economic Zones, 176
Extinction, vii, xi, xix, xx, 2, 15, 20, 22-23, 25, 28, 36-37, 46, 48-49, 51-52, 54, 89, 101, 207, 209, 212, 215, 217-18, 244
Extinction—6th Great, 2, 8, 23, 41,49, 55, 89, 113, 142f, 215-16, 252, 255, 263
Exuberance, Age of, 31-32, 34-36

Family Planning, 61, 94, 97, 126-30, 154, 177, 187, 193, 201-2, 213-14, 219-20, 225-29, 231
"Family Planning and Reproductive Health: The Link to Environmental Preservation," 202, 220
"Family Planning: the unfinished agenda," 225
Famine (Hunger, Starvation), xi, 6, 14, 21, 31, 42-45, 74, 93-99, 103, 111, 120, 134, 143, 158, 204, 206-7
Fantasia, 4
Feminism, 122-23, 127-29, 228
Fertility Drop, 123-25, 131, 134, 175, 202
Fiji, 136
Fire, Use of, 141
Fleck, John, 151
Flores Island, 7
Footprint, Ecological, xviii, 36, 39, 49, 85, 144-46, 148, 152-55, 159-61, 173, 176, 178, 184, 205, 212-13, 221-22, 230, 243
Footprint, Wilderness, 145, 184, 205, 212, 217, 221-22, 230, 244
Foreign Affairs, 85, 87
Forest Cutting/Clearing, Logging, 19, 26, 46-47, 53, 56, 60, 73, 104, 162, 175f, 176, 178, 241, 244, 248
"Forsaking Fundamentals," 122
Fossil Acreage, 34-35
Fossil Fuels, 31, 33-35, 37, 50, 94, 97, 99, 117, 144, 175f, 205
Fowler, Charles, 64-65
Fragmentation of Habitat, 43, 46, 56-57, 252
Franklin, Benjamin, 9, 26
Friends of the Earth, 112, 166, 209
From Big to Bigger, 144-45
Fundamentalist Protestants, 126, 228
Future in Plain Sight, The, 73

Gallup Poll, 122, 179
Gandhi, Indira, 130
Generous Sustainability, 146
Ghost Acreage, 33-35
Gilder, George, 76-77
Global Environmental Change, 153
Global Weirding (Greenhouse Effect), xix, 7, 13f, 36, 46-48, 60-65, 76, 79f, 87, 89f, 89-90, 101, 114, 143, 149, 173, 212, 215-17, 229, 244, 252-53, 263
Gorillas, 7-9, 67
Great Bet Myth, The, 100-1
"Great Denial, The," 81-82
Great Old Broads for Wilderness, 209
Great Plains, 35, 125
Greece, 70, 86, 104-5, 242
Green Hate, xxi, xxii, 129, 132-33, 163-67
Green Revolution, 94, 97-99
Guatemala, 82, 175-78, 191
Guatemala City, 178
Gulf of Mexico, 44

Habitat (Wildland) Destruction, 17, 23, 26, 28, 38, 43, 46, 49, 89, 162, 215, 252
Haiti, 193
Hall, Charles, 51
Hardin, Garret, 13, 16, 21, 43, 81-82, 108, 113, 133, 201-3, 207
Harris, Marvin, 71, 93, 99
Harvard University, 114, 166
Hawaii, 7f, 178
Hays, Samuel, 121-22
Heinberg, Richard, 115-16
Henderson Island, 28
Hern, Warren, 10-12
Herodotus, 103-4
Himalaya Mountains, 5, 63
Hispanos (Spanish), U.S., 180-81, 191
Hobbits (*Homo floresiensis*), 7
Hobbs, Larry, 64-65
Holdren, John, 5, 60, 134, 141-42, 160
Holland, 33-34
Homo erectus, 7-8, 32, 32f, 140-41
Homo ergaster, 140
Homo floresiensis, 32f
Homo heidelbergensis, 141
Homo sapiens, Evolution of, 7-8, 141
Honduras, 67, 82, 199
Hubbert, M. King, 110

Human Exceptionalism, 27, 246
Humanism, 71-72
Human Nature, 73, 123, 135-36
Human Web, The, 9, 114-15
Humboldt, Alexander von, 105
Huntington, Samuel, 117

I-20 Document, 187, 191-92
IPCC (Intergovernmental Panel on Climate Change), 62-63
Iltis, Hugh, v, xi, xii, xx, 113,
Immigration, xx, xxi, xxii, 53, 55, 82, 86, 89, 113, 120, 123, 125, 129, 131-33, 135, 145, 157-200, 204-6, 214-16, 219, 223-24, 226, 230
Immigration EIS, 173-74, 195
Immigration, Illegal, 55-56, 163-64, 170-71, 181-94, 197, 214, 231-32
Immigration, Legal, 163, 172, 184-86, 188
Immigration Numbers, 120, 131-32, 161-62, 167-175, 223-24
India, 8-9, 45, 54-55, 58-59, 63, 67, 115, 127, 130, 134, 151, 160-61, 174, 191, 199, 207
Indonesia, 67, 174
Information Please Almanac, The, 1992, 174
Invasive (Exotic) Species, 46-47, 58, 252
I=PAT, 5-6, 42, 48, 134, 139, 141, 152, 154, 160, 205, 222
Iran, 67, 127, 202
Iraq, 67, 136
Iron Law of Traven, 81
Irvine, Sandy, 70, 81
Islam, 117, 127, 186
Israel, 136
Italy, 14, 86, 105, 184

Jaguars, xxii, 8, 52f, 67
Japan, 14, 66, 85-86, 90, 95, 97, 125, 131, 134, 145, 184, 230
Jerusalem, 106
Jevons' Paradox, 149-52
Jevons' Paradox: The Myth of Resource Efficiency Improvements, 150
Jevons, W. Stanley, 150
Johnson, Lyndon, 122, 228

Kahn, Herman, 76
Kapoor, Coomi, 54-55
Kentucky, 49
Kenya, 49-51, 57, 67
Kenyon College, 207
Khazzoom, Daniel, 150
King, Bob, 229
King, Jr., Dr. Martin Luther, 119
King, Sir David, 1
Kissling, Frances, 127
Klare, Michael, 96, 116, 207
Kneese, Allen, 77
Kolankiewicz, Leon, xii, 18, 18f, 122-26, 128-29, 131, 133, 144, 147-49
Korea, 86, 95, 161
Kotok, Chief, 20-21
Ku Klux Klan, 163
Kuper, Alan, xii, 204
Kyoto, 174

LaFollette, Doug, 133, 166
Lagos, 59
Lamm, Richard, 131, 133
Lancet, The, 61, 128, 225
Landscalping, 21, 25, 42-43, 47, 103-4, 109-10, 143
Latin America, 65, 178
LeBlanc, Stephen, xvii, 30, 83, 118, 140-43, 206, 206f
Leftist Opposition to Population Movement, 129, 132-33, 163-67, 182, 204-5
Leopards, 49, 67-68
Leopold, Aldo, xviii, xx, 22f, 41, 48, 72, 108, 110, 239, 241, 244-45, 253
Leopold, Luna, 110
Liebig's Law of the Minimum, 36
Life Expectancy, 15, 33
Limits to Growth, 17-18, 21-23, 29-30, 70, 71-72, 74, 80, 103-4, 112, 118, 120, 129, 142, 205, 242
"Limits to Growth and the Biodiversity Crisis," 22-23
Limits to Growth, The, 112
Limits to Growth, The: The 30-Year-Update, 112

Lincoln, Abraham, 26, 105
Linden, Eugene, 73, 137
Lions, 49
Living Within Limits, 113
London, 62
Longman, Phillip, 85-87
Los Angeles, 147-49, 175, 178
Los Angeles Times, 78
Lowdermilk, W. C., 106, 107f, 109
Lynx, 34, 57

MacKaye, Benton, 72
Mali, 82
Malthus, Thomas, 29-30, 81, 98, 104-5, 110
Man and Nature, 105
Man's Role in Changing the Face of the Earth, 109-10
"Man Swarm Brochure," 212, 215, 218
March of Folly, The, 196
Margaret Sanger Award in Human Rights, 119f
Margulis, Lynn, 114
Marsh, George Perkins, 105
Marshall, Bob, 72
Martin, Lorenzo, 195
Martinez, Susana, 181
Massachusetts Institute of Technology (MIT), 112
Mayr, Ernst, 30f
McDougall, Rosamund, 223-24
McKinley, Daniel, 58, 108
McNeill, J. R., 9, 35, 115
McNeill, William, 9, 32f, 35, 115
Meadows, Donella, 112
Mediterranean Sea, 105
Mencken, H. L., 125, 126f
Merritt, Clif, 241
Merry, Robert, 73
Meso-America, 177
Metropolitan Webs, 9
Mexico, xx, xxi, xxii, 56, 67, 136, 159-61, 170-71, 176, 181f, 190-99
Mexico City, 126
Michigan State University, 33
Middle East, 105-6, 181f
Millennium Development Goals, 128
Mills College, 124
Mills, Stephanie, xii, 124
Milpas (Slash-and-Burn Agriculture), 56, 175, 178
Mississippi River, 171
Moose, 37
Morgan, Susan, xii, xiii, 85, 89, 209, 251, 255, 261-62
Morrison, Reg, 38, 114
Morton, Nancy, xiv, xxi, 74, 135, 147, 152, 221-22, 260
Morton, Robert, 11
Mother Jones, 180
Mouse, Mickey, 4
Mumford, Lewis, 109
Murray, Keith, 113f
Murray, Tim, 174
Murtaugh, Paul, 153-54
Myers, Norman, 55

NAFTA, 193-96
NASCAR, 118
Nash, Roderick F., 108, 202, 209
National Forests, 19, 176, 197
National Geographic, 86
National Parks, 7, 45, 52, 187, 192, 197, 213, 221, 248, 254
National Wildlife Federation, 109
Natural Selection, 30, 48
Navarette, Jr., Ruben, 183
Neandertals, 7, 32f, 140-42
Nelson, Gaylord, 19, 133, 166, 209
New Jersey, 109
New Mexico, xiii, xxi, xxii, 18-19, 105f, 180-81, 231-32, 360, 262
New Mexico Wilderness Alliance, 240, 259
New Society Publishers, 116
New York, 59, 261
New York City, 62, 148
New York Times, 20, 63, 90, 153, 162, 190, 204, 247
New Zealand, 7f, 32
Niger, 82, 120
Nigeria, 67-68, 134, 146, 174, 186, 191, 203-4
Nixon, Richard, 95, 123-24, 126

Nobel Peace Prize, 76, 194
North America, 32, 35, 97, 105, 122, 135, 163, 195, 216, 252, 254
North American Wildlands Network, 221, 252
North Korea, 98
Norway, 230
Noss, Reed, 26
NPP (Net Primary Productivity), 4, 37-39

Obama, Barack, 160
Oceania, 32
Ohio, 207
Olson, Storrs, 28
One-child Policy, 60-61, 130
On the Line: The Impacts of Immigration Policy on Wildlife and Habitat on the Arizona Borderlands, 192f
Optimism, 35, 70-78, 97, 117, 136-37
Optimum Population Trust, 61-62, 123, 175, 203-4, 206, 212, 223
Orangutans, 7-9
Oregon, 209-10
Oregon State University, 153
Osborn, Fairfield, 107-9
Ostrich Factor, The, 113
Our Plundered Planet, 107
Outgrowing the Earth, 26, 98, 117
Overkill, 46, 52, 210-11, 252
Overshoot, 29-30, 37-38, 114, 143
Overshoot, xx, 19, 22, 28-30, 37-38, 45, 87, 99-100, 103-4, 114, 143, 204f, 205-6, 209, 212, 234
Ozymandias, 83

Pakistan, 174, 191, 199
Palestine, 136
Party's Over, The, 115-16
Passel, Jeffrey, 190
Peak Oil, 24, 110
Peccei, Aurelio, 111
Pension (Retirement) Worries (from slowing births), 86-91
Pew Hispanic Center, 171, 182, 190
Pew Polling, 171, 197
Phantom Carrying Capacity, 34
Philippines, 65, 67, 159-61, 176, 191, 193-94
Phoenix, 54, 147
Pimm, Stuart, 4, 37-39
Plagues and Peoples, 115
Plato, 104
Polar Bears, 7
Political Correctness, 122, 132, 134, 179
Political Ecology Group (PEG), 129
Politics and Life Sciences, 208
Pollution (also see Biocides), xix, 18, 18f, 46-47, 59, 61, 63-64, 69, 99, 112, 216, 243-44, 252
Polynesians, 28
Pontifical Council for the Family, 127
Pope, Carl, 140, 151, 165, 175
Population Bomb, The, 18-19, 75, 93-98, 100-101, 111, 134, 158, 203f, 206
Population Bomb, 12, 16, 18-19, 65, 114, 123, 131, 203
Population Connection, 129
Population Explosion, v, xi, xix, 1, 6-7, 12, 49, 54, 61, 68, 88, 103, 112, 122, 158, 184, 208, 210, 216, 252
Population Explosion, The, 4-5, 114
Population Growth Numbers, 1-4, 7-16, 45, 50-51, 54-55, 67-68, 104-8, 120-21, 131-32, 168-74
Population Media Center, 122, 214, 229
Population Momentum, 124
Population Reduction (Lowering), xviii, xix, 1, 14, 20, 42, 49-50, 61, 113, 128-29, 144, 146, 149, 154, 207-8, 212-13, 222-24
Population Reference Bureau, 171
Population Resources Environment, 18
Population Stabilization (Freeze), xviii, xix, xx, 6, 14, 17-18, 20, 22, 43, 49, 61, 64, 82, 87, 99, 106, 113, 117, 120-23, 125-28, 130-33, 136, 142, 144, 146, 152, 154, 157-59, 163, 166-67, 169-70, 172, 176, 184, 199, 201, 204-9, 212-16, 218-24, 227-28, 230, 232-34, 263
Predation on Early Man, 141-42
Princeton University, 109
Proceedings of the Royal Society, 64

Progress, Idea of, 70-73
"Progressive Cornucopianism," 70-72, 81-83, 129, 132-33, 139-40
Progressives for Immigration Reform, xiii, 82, 144, 168, 181, 206, 208, 212-13, 219
Progressive Takeover of Environmentalism, 132-33
Proposition 187, 64
Protected Areas (see Wild Havens), 52, 247-48, 254-55

Rand Corporation, 74
Ravens, 2
Reagan, Ronald, 123, 126
Register, Katherine, 142
Reindeer (Caribou), 27
Replacement Birth Rate, 14, 85, 124-25, 131, 159, 170, 175, 188, 193, 202
"Reproduction and the carbon legacies of individuals," 152-53
Republican War on Science, The, 89f
Resource Depletion, xi, 21, 24, 28, 34-37, 42-44, 60, 70, 76-77, 103, 106, 109-10, 112-13, 116, 143, 162, 206
Resource Wars, 9, 30-31, 45, 95-96, 116, 118, 143, 206-7
Resourcism, 17, 18f, 119, 139, 239, 241, 243, 246, 254
Retreat from Population Work by Conservationists, 18, 119-37, 210
Rewilding, 90
Rewilding Institute, The, xiii, 20, 51f, 118f, 122f, 133, 152, 209, 212-13, 215, 217-19, 221, 251-53, 255
Rewilding North America, 2f, 32, 46-47, 52f, 57f, 209, 213, 221, 240-41
Rhinoceros, 8, 48-49, 50, 67-68
Rhythm Method, 125, 126f
Richardson, Bill, 232
Right to Life Movement, 126
Rio Grande, 105f, 151
Rise of the West, The, 115
Roads, 19, 56-57
Road to Survival, 107
Rockefeller Panel, 74
Roe vs. Wade, 126
"Round River," 108
Russia, 14
Rwanda, 45, 82, 136
Ryerson, William, 122-23, 126, 229

Sahara Desert, 175, 204
Sand County Almanac, A, xviii
Sanderoff, Brian, 181
Sandia Labs, 151
Sands of Empire, 73
San Francisco, 25, 124
San Francisco Chronicle, 101
Sao Paulo, 225
Sauer, Carl, 31, 106, 109
Schneider, Steve, 101
Schlax, Michael, 153-54
Science, 5, 50
Scientific American, 75
Scientific Medicine (Germ Theory, Antibiotics, Public Health), 33
Sears, Paul, 18, 105, 105f, 106, 109
Seeger, Pete, 19
Sessions, George, 22
Shell Oil Company, 110
Shepard, Paul, 108, 246
Shortsightedness, 24, 77, 86-87, 91, 96, 126, 137, 158, 207
Sierra Club, 19, 75, 111-12, 128f, 128-29, 132, 140, 154, 164-67, 170-71, 175, 180, 184, 186, 188, 204, 209, 230, 239-40, 254, 259
Sierra Club Immigration Policy, 128-29, 132, 157, 164-66, 170-71, 175, 180, 184, 186, 188, 230
Sierra Magazine, 140
Simon, Julian, vii, 23-25, 69-70, 78-80, 83, 86, 100-1, 134, 136
Smail, J. Kenneth, 207-8, 224
Social Security Administration, 189
Social Unrest (see Anarchy)
Society for Conservation Biology, 87
Soil Conservation Service (SCS), 106, 107f, 109
Solow, Robert, 76
Somalia, 98, 159
Something New under the Sun, 115
Sonora, 56

Sonoran Pronghorn, 56
"Sorcerer's Apprentice," 4
Soulé, Michael, 24
South Korea, 86
Specter of Jevons' Paradox, The, 150
Speidel, Joseph, 16, 202, 220, 226-27
Spirit in the Gene, The, 38, 114
Sprawl (Urban), 46, 53-56, 73, 120, 146-49, 174, 175f, 212, 220
Spread of Man, 3, 7-8, 32, 46, 54, 141
Stanford University, 5
Staples, Winthrop, 53, 64, 145-46, 160-62, 167, 188
Steadman, David, 28
St. Matthew Island, 27
Subsidies for Births, 85-87, 127, 213, 224
Subversive Science, The, 108
Sudan, 67, 82
Sumatra, 55
Sumer, 9, 9f
SUNY College of Environmental Science and Forestry Syracuse, 51
Superabundance, Myth of, 32, 73
Supreme Court, 126
Sustainability, 29, 36, 39, 64, 65, 77, 81, 121, 140-41, 141f, 143, 146, 165, 177, 205, 208, 210, 244, 247-48, 255
Sutter, Paul, 72
Sweden, 130, 230
Syria, 21

Takeover, xxii, 32-33, 56, 115, 135
Tancredo, Tom, 167
Technology, 5, 6, 19, 34, 41-42, 48, 60, 64, 69, 71-72, 74, 78, 86, 99, 104, 134, 139, 140-43
Tepatitlan Poultry Farmers Association, 195
TFR (Total Fertility Rate), 123-24, 131, 170, 177, 188, 202
Thailand, 67, 202
Thermodynamics, Second Law of, 77
Tibet, 136
Tigers, 8-9, 45, 48, 54-55, 67-68
Time, 74-75
Tonight Show, The, 111
Topsoil and Civilization, 109
Toronto, 174
Traven, B, 81
Tribalism, 45, 135
Trujillo, Cardinal Alfonso Lopez, 127
Tsao, Jeff, 151
Tuchman, Barbara, 196
Tucson Citizen, 56
Tunisia, 127
Turkey, 67, 105, 127

Uganda, 67, 127
Ukraine, 136
United Kingdom (England), xx, 30, 34, 61-62, 121, 123, 175, 206, 208, 223, 225, 237
United Nations, 3, 8, 10, 15, 66, 93, 99, 120, 122, 126f, 228
UN Conference on the Human Environment (Stockholm) 1972, 77, 130
UN Millennium Development Goals, 128
UN Population Conference 1984 (Mexico City), 126
UN Population Conference 1994 (Cairo), 127-28
United States of America, xix, xx, 19, 26, 34, 44, 50-51, 53, 54f, 56-57, 60, 64, 66, 76, 95, 98, 101, 105-6, 110, 116, 120, 123-27, 131-33, 136, 145-48, 151, 154-55, 158-63, 167-201, 203-205, 214-16, 220, 223-28, 230-31, 233, 244, 248, 253-54
University of California San Francisco, 3, 10, 16, 202, 220, 226
University of Colorado, 10, 79
University of Maryland, 69
University of Michigan, xi, 113
University of Nevada, 166
University of New Mexico, 18, 111f, 203f
University of Wisconsin, xi, xx, 25, 54, 113
U.S. Census Bureau, 68, 162, 168-71
U.S. National Research Council, 77
USSR, 174

Vietnam, 68, 161
Vietnam War, 95, 122
Virginia Tech, xiii, 6, 22
Vogt, William, 107-9, 108f

Wallace, Alfred Russell, 30
Wall Street, 87, 118
Wall Street Journal, 73, 80, 133
Walt Disney's First Law, 81
Wamela, Cardinal Emmanuel, 127
War (see Resource War)
War on Drugs, The, 187, 193, 196-98
Washington, DC, 125
Washington Post, 195
Weeden, Don, xii, 133, 209
Weeden Foundation, xii, 133, 209
Weekly Reader, 52
Weighing Sprawl Factors in Large U.S. Cities, 147-49
Weiner, Anthony, 76
Wellcome Trust, 228
Werbach, Adam, 165
Whale, Blue, 8
Whales, 7, 52, 230
Whole Earth Catalog, 86
Wild Earth, 20, 20f, 22, 51, 51f, 122, 133, 203
Wilderness, v, xii, xix, xxii, 6, 22, 36, 42, 65, 72, 131, 167, 178, 203, 205, 211, 216, 218-19, 238-40, 243, 248
Wilderness Act, The, 132, 241
Wilderness and the American Mind, 209
Wilderness Areas, 24, 56, 132, 187, 192, 244, 248
Wilderness Destruction, 26, 34, 36, 42, 46, 53-56, 65, 132, 146, 159, 175f, 211, 247-48
Wilderness Society, The, 19, 165-66, 241
Wild Farm Alliance, 25f
Wildfire, 4, 7, 57
Wild Havens, 9, 45, 54, 187, 211, 213, 221, 248, 254-55
Wildlife, xi, xii, xviii, xviiif, xix, xx, 7, 18f, 22, 24-25, 28, 36, 42, 44-47, 49-50, 52-58, 65, 68, 72, 108, 131, 146, 159, 162-63, 173, 175, 178, 187, 192, 197, 210-13, 221, 239-41, 246-48, 252-55
Wild Neighborhoods (Ecosystems, Communities), xi, 3, 21, 22f, 26, 36, 43, 46, 48-49, 52-54, 56, 146, 150, 178, 185, 239, 245
Wilson, E. O., 41, 114, 166
Wisconsin, 133, 166, 209
Wolves, xxii, 7, 27, 34, 37, 48, 57, 67, 163
World According to Pimm, The, 4, 38-39
World Bank, 122, 174
World Food Program, 130
World War II, 13
World Watch Institute, 117, 166

Yard, Robert Sterling, 72
Yemen, 82

Xanadu, 83

Zero Population Growth, 121, 124, 171, 188, 213, 223
Zetas, 197
Zogby International, 180, 191
ZPG (Zero Population Growth), 129

About the Author

For 40 years, **Dave Foreman** has been one of North America's leading conservationists, working to shield and rebuild wilderness and wildlife. He is acknowledged for having a matchless depth and breadth of fighting for wild things, and for bringing together traditional conservation lore, the science of conservation biology, and wild-things-for-their-own-sake ethics into a mighty vision for the future—The North American Wildlands Network. With *Man Swarm,* he also shows his bold leadership on the knotty plight of overpopulation. He is the author of *Rewilding North America, Confessions of an Eco-Warrior, The Big Outside,* the novel *The Lobo Outback Funeral Home,* and other books. He was also the lead author and designer for the Sky Islands Wildlands Network Vision and the New Mexico Highlands Wildlands Network Vision. Among the wilderness clubs with which he has worked as a staffer or volunteer leader are Black Mesa Defense, River Defense, The Wilderness Society, New Mexico Wilderness Study Committee, *American Rivers, The Nature Conservancy, *Earth First!, **Wild Earth Journal,* *The Wildlands Project, the *New Mexico Wilderness Alliance, the Sierra Club, and now *The Rewilding Institute (*cofounder of these clubs). Foreman is a sought-after speaker on rewilding and other wilderness and wildlife issues. He has canoed and rafted some of the wildest rivers in North America, and is a hiker, backpacker, birder, and photographer. He lives in his hometown of Albuquerque, New Mexico, with his wife, Nancy Morton, who is a nurse, and two cats, named Gila and Blue.

About the Editors

John Davis is a fellow of The Rewilding Institute, co-founder of The Wildlands Project (now Wildlands Network), founder and former editor of WILD EARTH, and former program officer at the Foundation for Deep Ecology. He has been working and studying with his friend and mentor Dave Foreman for a quarter century. At the end of 2010, John stepped down from his position as conservation director of the Adirondack Council to begin a continental wildways trek, intended to help realize the goals Foreman set out in *Rewilding North America.* He will be on TrekEast throughout 2011 and will begin TrekWest in 2012. (See wildlandsnetwork.org for details.) John is also a conservation landowner, protecting a 55-acre wildlife sanctuary in the middle of Split Rock Wildway on the eastern edge of New York's Adirondack Park.

Susan Morgan, PhD, has worked for six years with the Whatcom County Library System in Maple Falls, Washington and is a free-lance copy editor. In 1968 she began her conservation career as outings coordinator for The Wilderness Society, then became Director of Education, and has subsequently worked on wilderness, wildlands, and public lands conservation for over forty years. Susan was a founding board member of Great Old Broads for Wilderness. She served as staff with LightHawk, the New Mexico Environmental Law Center, the Washington Wilderness Coalition, The Wildlands Project (now Network), and was communications director for Forest Guardians (now WildEarth Guardians) in New Mexico. Susan volunteers for the Alaska Coalition of Washington and the American Alps Legacy Project in the North Cascades and is a conservation fellow with The Rewilding Institute.

Conservationist's Overpopulation Pledge

I understand that the human population explosion is still happening and that it is the main driver of mass species extinction, wildland destruction and development, and global weirdness (greenhouse gas pollution).
I support stabilizing population worldwide and in the United States (or your country:_______________________),
and I ask conservation groups to once again make population stabilization a priority.

Name ___________________________

Address ___________________________

City _______________ State __________ Zip __________

Country ___________________________

Email ___________________________

Organization ___________________________

__ Check here if you want a wallet-sized card with the pledge for you to sign & keep.

Please send me __ copies of the pledge so I can get others to sign.

Return to:
The Rewilding Institute
PO Box 13768
Albuquerque, NM 87192

For more information:
www.rewilding.org and www.applythebrakes.org

Order Form

Wilderness and wildlife clubs and individuals may buy *Man Swarm* in bulk from The Rewilding Institute for resale or to give away. Bookstores and other commercial outlets should buy copies from Raven's Eye Press (www.ravenseyepress.com).

	QTY	TOTAL
One copy ($20 each)		
2 - 5 copies ($12 each)		
6 or more copies ($10 each)		
S&H ($5 first copy/$7 priority/$12 foreign)		
(additional copies, $2 each)		
	TOTAL	

Name ____________________

Organization ____________________

Address ____________________

City ____________ State ________ Zip ________

Country ____________________

Email ____________________

Phone number ____________________

Please make check payable to:
The Rewilding Institute

Send to:
The Rewilding Institute
PO Box 13768
Albuquerque, NM 87192

Designer

elle jay design

Lindsay J. Nyquist
www.ellejaydesign.com
lindsay@ellejaydesign.com

Press

Raven's Eye Press

Rediscovering the West
www.ravenseyepress.com

Try our other Raven's Eye Press titles:

Why I'm Against it All
Ken Wright

The Monkey Wrench Dad
Ken Wright

Livin' the Dream
B. Frank

Ghost Grizzlies, 3rd edition
David Petersen

Racks
David Petersen

CPSIA information can be obtained at www.ICGtesting.com
Printed in the USA
LVOW09s1346310515

440596LV00005B/389/P